DEVIANT
HOLLERS

DEVIANT
HOLLERS

QUEERING APPALACHIAN ECOLOGIES FOR A SUSTAINABLE FUTURE

EDITED BY
ZANE McNEILL AND REBECCA SCOTT

FOREWORD BY STEPHANIE FOOTE

UNIVERSITY PRESS OF KENTUCKY

Scholarly publisher for the Commonwealth, serving Bellarmine University, Berea College, Centre College of Kentucky, Eastern Kentucky University, The Filson Historical Society, Georgetown College, Kentucky Historical Society, Kentucky State University, Morehead State University, Murray State University, Northern Kentucky University, Spalding University, Transylvania University, University of Kentucky, University of Louisville, University of Pikeville, and Western Kentucky University.
All rights reserved.

Editorial and Sales Offices: The University Press of Kentucky
663 South Limestone Street, Lexington, Kentucky 40508-4008
www.kentuckypress.com

Cataloging-in-Publication data available from the Library of Congress

ISBN 978-0-8131-9930-6 (hardcover)
ISBN 978-0-8131-9933-7 (paperback)
ISBN 978-0-8131-9931-3 (pdf)
ISBN 978-0-8131-9932-0 (epub)

This book is printed on acid-free paper meeting
the requirements of the American National Standard
for Permanence in Paper for Printed Library Materials.

Manufactured in the United States of America.

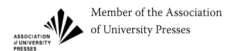
Member of the Association
of University Presses

CONTENTS

Foreword   *vii*
Stephanie Foote

Introduction   *1*
Rebecca Scott and Zane McNeill

Re-presenting the Narrative: Pursuing Stories amid
Addiction   *23*
Tijah Bumgarner

Intoxicated Subjects: Queer Bodies and Ecologies in
"Trumpalachia"   *35*
Rebecca-Eli M. Long and Zane McNeill

Queers Embracing Place in Appalachia: The Importance of
Masculinities for Queer Acceptance   *55*
Baker A. Rogers

Unsilencing Indigeneity: Appalachian Studies, Appalachian
Ecologies, and the Continuation of Settler Colonialism   *79*
Jessica Cory

It's Grandpa's Land: Settler Property, Heteropatriarchy, and
Environmental Disasters   *105*
Kandice Grossman, Aaron Padgett, and Rebecca Scott

Edible Kent: Collaboration, Decentralization, and Sustainable
Agriculture in Urban Food Systems   *129*
Lis Regula and MJ Eckhouse

Arboreal Blockaders: "Queer/Trans Moments of Critical
Appalachian Eco-action"   *151*
Chet Pancake

Masculinities in the Decline of Coal: Queer Futures in the
Appalachian Coalfields   *183*
Gabe Schwartzman

"I Fixed Up the Trees to Give Them Some New Life": Queer
Desire, Affect, and Ecology in the Work of LGBTQIA+
Appalachian Artists   *207*
Maxwell Cloe

List of Contributors   *227*

FOREWORD

Ordinary cruelties thread through virtually every conversation about how to define Appalachia. They structure policy decisions about what Appalachians should want or need, and they underwrite speculation about the self-defeating economic and political choices Appalachians seem to make. Appalachians, the common political wisdom holds, always work against their own interests. They mistake the way that power operates and misunderstand their relationship to the structures of capitalism. When, well-intentioned progressives lament, will Appalachia understand itself?

Representations of Appalachia as a strange and untraveled place inhabited by rubes, rustics, and hillbillies have existed since at least the nineteenth century, and as Rosemary Hathaway has recently argued, every historical moment seems to have generated the Appalachia it most needs.[1] But those versions of Appalachia are almost always the uncanny double of normative US culture—that is to say, they always present Appalachia and Appalachians as wilder, more ignorant, less cultured, and less civilized than any other region or its people: still American but somehow not quite modern. Appalachia has been stereotyped and degraded, often at the same time it has been celebrated as authentic.

Across the twentieth century, regional stereotypes about Appalachia have contributed to policy debates about rural life at the national level. In these instances, Appalachia is a test case: How can legislation connect people with strong regional identities to the nation? But such federal interventions—the drive to electrify and modernize households and towns in the 1930s, the once-heralded War on Poverty in the 1960s, the attempt to address the opioid crisis in the 2010s—are really addressing Appalachia's long history of exploitation by corporations that have profited at the region's expense. The history of Appalachia is not, as contemporary progressives believe, the history of Appalachia's inability to understand its own interests. The history of Appalachia is where the United States' contradictions, like its reverence for local cultures and its desire to exploit them, has been most efficiently worked out. Appalachia has been the site of some of the worst resource exploitation in the nation, and its impoverishment has made possible the everyday political stance that wonders, from positions on the left and the right, why Appalachia seems to consent to its own poverty.

But as you will see in this collection, a number of Appalachians are pushing back against conventional narratives about Appalachia. In particular, they are focused on the larger meaning of *extraction*. What does it mean, for example, that the region has provided raw material and human life to power the nation's grids? Even now, when the coal mines have been largely automated because of mountaintop removal, the deepest ones closed forever, Appalachia is still the site of resource exploitation for fracking wells that poison water, soil, air, and land. And finally, of course, Appalachia is now much in the news because it seems to have a ready supply of purchasers for opioids. The much reported on "deaths of despair" have hit Appalachia hard; unemployment, disability, chronic illness, high unemployment rates, and the lack of opportunity for educational and class advancement have made the region, for reporters from major newspapers, the perfect site for the devastation wrought by addiction.

No surprise that Appalachia has also been understood as one of the last holdouts for Donald Trump, for white supremacy, and for conservative politics. If Appalachia is America's political Other, just as it was once its favored regional wild child, its perceived politics of racial and class resentment seem hard to fathom. Why, liberal news outlets ask, does Appalachia vote against its own interests? Why does it support candidates who are clearly in the pocket of the very corporations that have decimated it? There is no shortage of think pieces in newspapers and political blogs about Appalachia's self-defeating poverty and politics, and all of them rely on a flat understanding of what Appalachia is and wants. Steven Stoll and Elizabeth Catte have each written powerful books about the complicated histories and politics of Appalachia, and yet for liberal and progressive critics, it is still all too easy to think of Appalachia as univocal, uniform, and in need of salvation from itself.[2]

But as the essays in this volume argue, Appalachia is significantly less in need of salvation than, say, exploitative corporations are in need of prosecution. Nor is it in need of restoration, a return to a primeval natural world that can be enjoyed by urban elites, as with the establishment of the new national park at New River Gorge, the site of the Hawks Nest Tunnel disaster of the 1930s. It is easy to see that Appalachia is implicated in larger structures of exploitation and immiseration. It is harder to see that virtually every part of the United States is implicated in Appalachia's exploitation. Its history is the history of the US empire writ small and large; its internal contradictions are those at the very heart of imperial ideology.

Yet the question of what to make of Appalachia—what constitutes it, what accounts for its apparently self-destructive political attachments, what binds the region together—is not answerable if we think about Appalachia merely as the sum of the wounds it has sustained, the total of what journalists imagine as its resentments or insularity. Neither is it answerable if we only consider the landscape and the intense connection Appalachians have to their region. All of these ways of getting to Appalachia as a place, as an identity, and as a political or economic zone of impoverishment and extraction are partial and incomplete. And they all attempt to impose unity on a region that is structured by as many internal differences as any other region. Appalachia is not just white, not just rural, not just Republican, not just poor, and not just straight.

But what does that mean in practice?

The essays in this collection together imagine what happens if we queer Appalachia. The project of queering Appalachia is politically useful: What happens if we think about its oddness, its difference from everyday national structures of power and belonging? What new forms of collectivity and identity might become apparent if we think about a relation to power that queers the utility of normativity? But it's also useful if we think about queerness demographically: What happens if we think about Appalachia as not simply made up of straight and cis people who stay and queers who migrate away? What happens if we see the world of Appalachia as enlivened by queer social actors? What Appalachia have queers built and sustained, changed and empowered? What histories have queer actors shown us? What futures do they direct us to imagine? Such considerations allow us to see that Appalachia is not simply white, not simply straight, not simply homogenous. And finally, what happens if we apply the lessons of queer theory to the geographical place itself, to look at the way that queer theory can help to illuminate the relations among the subjects who live in Appalachia—their love for the decimated natural world and their reliance on the extractive economies that have ruined them?

Queer theory has, over its intellectual history, offered ways to imagine the relationship between subjects and normativity, between structures of power and biopolitical management of life and individual choices. It has imagined, as Mel Chen and Dana Luciano have argued, a long history in which the very category of the human has been challenged and recuperated. But as they have also argued, it has fundamentally imagined thinking as relational, about the ways in which categories of personhood and structures of power have been coordinated under various political regimes.[3] When the category of the human itself emerges as a site of critique in queer theory, it challenges the primacy of a liberal order that dangles abstract principles like agency or freedom before embodied actors whose real relations to the world prevent them from fully accessing those abstractions. In other words, it allows us to see the biopolitical regime that manages every element of life under capitalism and puts us in a new relationship to ideology.

When we queer Appalachia, then, we embark on a project that does not promise a unified idea of what queerness is or what the shape of an emancipatory queer politics looks like. But queering Appalachia—challenging the key terms of how subjects, agency, and desire are related to one another—promises that the way we imagine relationships to power can be changed and remade because every iteration of "things as they are" is deeply historical and thus available for revision. As the essays in this collection argue, Appalachia, which has been the site of so much fantasy and so much exploitation, has always held within itself alternate ways of knowing its relation to power. We just have to listen.

Stephanie Foote
West Virginia University

NOTES

1. Rosemary V. Hathaway, *Mountaineers Are Always Free: Heritage, Dissent, and a West Virginia Icon* (Morgantown: WVU Press, 2020).
2. Steven Stoll, *Ramp Hollow: The Ordeal of Appalachia* (New York: Hill and Wang, 2017); Elizabeth Catte, *What You Are Getting Wrong about Appalachia* (Cleveland: Belt, 2018).
3. Dana Luciano and Mel Y. Chen, "Has The Queer Ever Been Human?," *GLQ* 21, no. 2–3 (June 2015): 182–207.

INTRODUCTION
Rebecca Scott and Zane McNeill

I n the wake of the election of Donald Trump in 2016 and the publication of Ohio senator J. D. Vance's *Hillbilly Elegy*, renewed efforts have emerged from the Left to challenge reductive representations of Appalachia as an idiosyncratic and culturally backward extractive zone within US geography. The region has been culturally marginalized in dominant US narratives, while also facing environmental exploitation as a sacrifice zone.[1] Appalachia, as introduced by Stephanie Foote in the Foreword, has historically been portrayed as a fantastical borderland between the North and the South, a place apart and yet integral to the United States. Portrayed at the same time as the worst and best of America, Appalachia as the "uncanny double" of US culture offers both a reaffirmation and a disruption to American settler-capitalist heteropatriarchy.

Generations of scholar-activists have challenged and subverted false representations of Appalachia, effectively demonstrating the complexity, diversity, and beauty of the region. In addition, the editors of this collection contend that this Leftist recovery of the Appalachian narrative should not stop with the "reclamation" of Appalachian identity, but that it should continue to metaphorically excavate the historical and geographic space that the region inhabits which shapes its contemporary conditions. A complex understanding of the place, its people, and its histories within US economics and culture requires an intersectional examination not just of its marginalization but also its participation in structures of domination.[2]

The region currently known as Appalachia stretches across the traditional territories of many Indigenous Peoples, including the Shawandasse Tula (Shawanwaki/Shawnee), Moneton, Haudenosaunee (Iroquois), Tsalaguwetiyi (Cherokee, East), and Lenape Peoples, whose land was expropriated by forced and broken treaties and settler violence.[3] We write from the position of white Appalachian settler scholars attempting to grapple with this violent legacy and work for a more just and sustainable future.[4] Appalachian studies has long worked to correct historical misrepresentations of the region's marginalization and exclusion from the progress narratives of the United States, as a supposedly strange place with peculiar people, ripe for exploitation. But stopping there can obscure the ways in which Appalachia is also integral to the formations of US settler culture, including whiteness, heteronormativity, and econormative imaginaries. A simple reversal of marginalizing discourses, whether by centering Appalachia or by celebrating its difference from the mainstream in the United States, risks reiterating some of the same logics as those dominant discourses.[5]

In *What You're Getting Wrong about Appalachia*, Appalachian historian Elizabeth Catte writes, "Appalachians are a group of people burdened with the task of perpetually re-earning our place in narratives of American progress." She explains, "This burden manifests in calls for migration and the de-population of our home, an exodus of sacrifice that must be performed in order to prove that we are not the people you think we are."[6] Catte underlines that in the United States, Appalachian identity is connected in extraordinary ways to the land. In fact, it is this place-based identity that makes Appalachian culture special within the US context and that Appalachians are forced to give up in the name of national belonging. This conception of Appalachian identity reflects the idea that US Appalachians have a unique connection to the more-than-human natures of Appalachia and highlights the marginal place of Appalachians in a placeless and mobile US culture. Appalachians must always "prove" their citizenship in the face of larger US society's othering.[7] In short, this is an argument for a basic Appalachian exclusion from the "narratives of American progress," and it suggests that Appalachians are like colonized people forced to "assimilate or die."

In her ethnography of a low-income community in southern West Virginia, *A Space on the Side of the Road*, Kathleen Stewart elaborates how elements of Appalachian culture represent not only an "Other" America but also a liberatory alternative to the linear modern disciplinary culture of middle-class neoliberalism. The "space on the side of the road" (i.e., the linguistic detours, switchbacks, and stillnesses opened up metaphorically in the Appalachian poetics she analyzes) makes room for alternative forms of humanity (re)doubled affects and possibilities for existence outside the cultural imperatives of linear development. The space she depicts offers an off-ramp from the treadmill of production that continually drives acquisitive action in US culture. This metaphorical space on the side of the road is a little bit queer, a place where people don't get straight to the point but can hang out, unproductively, thinking about how strange things are.

However, all uncanny, the region's marginalization others Appalachian people at the same time as the very logic of that othering reaffirms the basic hierarchical stories of America. As an idealized place and as a space for difference, Appalachia exists as an exploited exception while the contradictions it represents in the national imaginary also promote elements of US white supremacism, heteronormativity, and settler colonial culture. A marginalized space in colonial-like relations with wealthier places and people, it performs a simultaneous undermining and reiteration of dominant US cultural, economic, and political logics.

As in all things American, settler colonialism and racialization are key to these weird processes. The homogenous whiteness that is usually presented in popular depictions of Appalachia erases the region's Indigenous and Black history and constructs the region's people as somehow essentially "American" within the racialized terms of national belonging. This happens at the same time as they are marginalized as hillbillies.[8] The creation of a sacrifice zone is also deeply implicated in the logic of capital and settler colonialism, as human inhabitants, mountains, and other nonhumans are treated as objects to be used or destroyed in the pursuit of coal, gas, and profit.[9] This cultural, economic, and environmental reductionism that shrinks people and places down to objects to be used instrumentally for others' benefit relies on fixed categories: human/nonhuman and rationality/emotion, among others.[10] But while the ideological whiteness of Appalachia is used to reinforce these hierarchies, its differences signal the possibility of more: of categorical indeterminacy, of receptiveness to other possibilities.

In an effort to reckon with the importance of racialization in Appalachia, to denaturalize the land as property, and to explore the potential queerness of Appalachian space, we must attempt to interrogate whiteness, settler colonialism, and heteronormativity. Hierarchies and fixed categories such as human/nonhuman or mind/body can be challenged through the lens of queer theory. Queer theory interrogates the diverse range of behaviors and discourses subsumed under the umbrella of sexuality as an organizing category for modern capitalist disciplinary culture, founded on the normative, which is defined against the deviant.[11] In this disciplinary culture, adherence to sexual and gender regulation becomes a requirement for being recognized as fully human.[12]

This narrowing of the definition of *human* through the terms of heteronormativity is also related to racialization and colonization, which operate in part through dualisms of civilized/savage that rely on sexual regulation. Therefore, these fixed categories and violent hierarchies can be interrogated through the lens of critical Indigenous and settler colonial theory, which also offer a critique of the principles of modern discipline, including linear time, heteronormativity, and objectification. The western category of sexuality doesn't necessarily coincide with Indigenous ways of thinking about the world, which often have a more comprehensive view of individuality in the social context.[13] For example, the "grounded normativity" of sexual and gender diversity in Nishnaabeg communities doesn't reflect the category of sexuality or queerness but rather the fundamental principle of consent.[14] However, these distinct and divergent approaches may nevertheless be productive if placed into careful conversation.[15]

To this end, we bring the two categories into careful dialogue because the heteronormative settler colonial project denies both forms of diversity. As Opaskwayak Cree scholar Alex Wilson points out, categories like race and sexuality reflect the normative subjectivities of modern knowledge systems, not Indigenous world views. White supremacism, heteropatriarchy, and settler colonialism are interwoven with one another in American culture. How can a critical exploration of Appalachia as a queer space, a queer ecological space, avoid recognition of the land rights and sovereignty of Indigenous Peoples?[16] To avoid critiquing the settler colonial is to confine the critique within the terms of US hegemony. It's worth noting that the term Appalachia itself is derived from the French name for an Indigenous community (Apalache) most likely located in the place currently known as Florida, which highlights how American settler colonial appropriations of Indigeneity are interwoven into regional identity.[17] In this volume, we seek to analyze how these intersecting systems contribute to the mutual constitution of both Appalachian identity and the larger American cultural, economic, and political formations to which it belongs.

RACIAL CONSTRUCTIONS, SETTLER COLONIALISM, AND INDIGENIZATION IN IMAGINED APPALACHIA

The economic and cultural marginalization of poor white people in Appalachia operates as a form of social regulation through a set of dualistic controlling images—self-sacrificing hard workers or backward welfare dependents—that delimit the discursive space in which they are legible.[18] These controlling images help construct a normative middle-class whiteness that is the unmarked center of American national identity. White Appalachians are represented simultaneously as pure white citizens, the most truly American, the backbone of the country, but also as degenerate hillbillies, victim to either genetic or cultural deficits that are seen as the root cause of the region's poverty. With *Hillbilly Elegy*, J. D. Vance carried that tradition forward and translated it for a new era.[19]

As J. D. Vance has outlined them, among the problems plaguing the Appalachian hillbillies he describes is the relative instability of the heteronormative nuclear family and traditional marriage. The stability of the heteronormative nuclear family has been linked in the popular imagination and in normative social science to the ideal American life. On the one hand, the alleged collapse of this nuclear family is identified as one of the causes of the poverty and dysfunction that supposedly characterize Appalachia.[20] In US culture, marriage and the nuclear breadwinner/caretaker family have long represented adulthood, middle-class health and virtue, and progress toward a better future for everyone.[21] On the other hand, the image of the hardworking and self-sacrificing coal miner represents the pinnacle of the family man: the breadwinner who gives it all for home and country. These images (welfare-dependent broken families or upstanding coal-mining families) offer racialized and gendered visions of the proper or improper way to live as an American citizen, demonstrating once again the libidinal underpinning of political and economic structures.[22] Appalachians' successes or failures in these family matters thus represent a referendum on their degree of civilization and their place in the US meritocracy.

Recurrent representations of Appalachia as a space of difference within America may have contributed to a "self-indigenizing" practice in Appalachian culture.[23] Growing up, both of us knew families with stories of a Cherokee grandmother somewhere in their ancestry. These claims of Indigenous ancestry are of course not limited to Appalachian people. These often-Cherokee ancestors enable settlers to self-identify as the rightful heirs to Indigenous land and identity.[24] However, other references to indigeneity are less directly tied to actual Native people and often come from regional outsiders. Turn-of-the-last-century journalists and mid-twentieth-century sociologists simply referred to the white residents of Appalachia as "indigenous mountaineers," erasing the original Indigenous Peoples of the mountains while closely identifying white settlers with the resource-rich landscape as "mountaineers."[25] The word *indigenous* here does a lot of cultural work, enabling a conceptual shifting between "our contemporary ancestors" [so-called primitive Appalachians] and Native Americans, in an example of the appropriation and disavowal at the heart of settler colonial structures.[26] These references and more point to the region currently known as Appalachia as not only a center for the discursive construction of whiteness and settler claims to this continent but also a critical site in the ideological construction of "nature" in American culture.[27]

These homogenizing and dualistic constructions of Appalachia as a white, heteronormative, or "traditional" space—more native, more all-American, or more backward than others—erase the abundant complexity of the region currently known as Appalachia, as queer, of color, Black, Indigenous, activist, settler, global, and multivocal. This complexity represents a rich potential for future thriving in the region and beyond, and this anthology attempts to create a platform to engage with this complexity. The essays in this volume explore the connections between patriarchal and heteronormative constructions of human nature, nonhuman nature, and the settler colonial and other dominating discourses that structure the US relationship to this land. This volume also contributes to the goal of creating an archive of queer voices as a step toward LGBTQIA+ people in Appalachia being able not only to survive but to thrive.

In other words, while Appalachia has been seen as primitive, backward, or traditional by outsiders, and while Appalachian ecological knowledges are valuable and promote sustainability, being Appalachian is not analogous to being Indigenous. However heuristically useful, references to colonization in analyses of the region's exploitation function to minimize or deflect the role of settler colonialism in the region's problems.[28] The term *indigenous* properly refers to politically sovereign Peoples who have long-standing and dynamic biological and cultural relations with specific ecologies and landforms.[29] Critical Appalachian studies must deal with the ways in which Appalachia serves as a paradigmatic site for the construction of white American identity and settler culture as well as with the more easily recognizable cultural and economic marginalization that actually enables that role. The invocation of a special Appalachian relationship with the landscape or nonhuman nature, in the form of widespread activities like gathering forest products, subsistence hunting or fishing, or "putting up a garden," represents both the wisdom that the region offers about ecological sustainability and the tendency in some progressive work in Appalachian studies to claim for the region the status of an innocent victim.

As settler scholar Stephen Pearson explains: "The exclusionary devaluation of the 'hillbilly' in wider settler society—coupled with economic and environmental exploitation—has had disastrous effects on the lives of many who live in the region. Indigenization provides settlers with identities that imbue their lives with meaning, render their situations sensible, valorize their existence, and provide models that increase their status within settler society. In viewing themselves as Indigenous victims of colonialism, even class-privileged White Appalachians are able to cast themselves in the role of the Native . . . [which] allows Appalachian Whites to maintain their whiteness while obscuring the privileges that whiteness bestows."[30]

Proceeding with this critical perspective that holds both the cultural and economic marginalization of the region and its role in the construction of ideologies related to whiteness and settler colonialism in American culture in productive tension, this volume has two main aims. First, the book presents a collection of underrepresented voices, examples of political activism, and diverse experiences to illuminate the multiplicity of Appalachian lives and communities. Second, the book offers a provocation challenging the white-centric, middle-class, and heteronormative conceptions of nature that shape environmentalism and environmental activism in the United States. The same dualistic discourses that constitute Appalachia as a sacrifice zone also structure an econormativity that neglects to challenge the hierarchical dualisms that are at the root of the environmental crisis.

QUEER ECOLOGIES AND ECONORMATIVITY IN APPALACHIA

To understand how Appalachian queer ecologies are connected to Indigenous sovereignty, we can start by exploring the intersections of gender, sexuality, and environmentalism. As a historically powerful keyword in Western modernity, *nature* indexes not only nonhuman nature but human sexuality, morality, and progressive evolutionary ideology.[31]

Rachel Stein explains: "By analyzing how discourses of nature have been used to enforce heteronormativity, to police sexuality, and to punish and exclude those persons who have been deemed sexually transgressive, we can begin to understand the deep, underlying commonalities between struggles against sexual oppression and other struggles for environmental justice."[32]

Sometimes, *nature* is used to refer to a dictated natural order of things. For example, cis heterosexuality is seen as biologically and morally normative (as in references to so called unnatural acts or in claims that so-called biological sex is truer or more natural than a transgender identity), a view that others transness and homo-sexuality as deviant and immoral. However, within the dualism of humanity/nature, supposed proximity to nature has also been used to justify numerous forms of oppression. The religious belief in the moral superiority of patriarchal heteronormativity has been instrumental in colonizing projects that portray Indigenous sexual and gender diversity as immoral or primitive.[33] "Civilized" humanity is associated with rationality, masculinity, development, and moder-nity, while sexuality is associated with emotion, the feminine, and the primitive.[34] A history of intersecting hierarchical dualisms such as mind/body, culture/nature, male/female, and human/nonhuman makes up an ideological scaffolding in which white cis heterosex-ual males are identified with rationality and cultural order and are seen as superior to those who are nonwhite, nonbinary, trans, nonheterosexual, and nonmen, who are each identified with the natural and the erotic.[35] But while perceived closeness to nature is devalued next to the (Western) human, the so-called natural law of heteronormativity reinforces the religious with the supposedly biological.

Catriona Mortimer-Sandilands and Bruce Erickson use "queer ecologies" to explore the "ongoing relationship between sex and nature that exists institutionally, discursively, scientifically, spa-tially, politically, and ethically."[36] Constructions of econormativity inform conceptions of the natural and vice versa.[37] Stacy Alaimo explores how a couple of homosexual penguins upset the heter-onormative imagination of a natural order of things.[38] Although bodies and their sexuality are undeniably part of nature, some bodies are portrayed as either "more natural" or "closer to nature" than others. David Bell and Gill Valentine explain that through "*subversive spatial acts* we can see how even the kiss of two men on the night bus home can fracture and rupture a previously seamless (homogenous) space."[39] This relationship between the self and the more-than-human allows our own bodies to be "sites of resistance" that *queer* space, opening it to meaning beyond the linear, productive, and capitalistic.[40]

Jack Halberstam writes that queer acts of unbuilding invite a "bewilderment" that can destabilize hegemonic white supremacist and heteronormative worlds.[41] Stacy Alaimo uses the concept of transcorporality to emphasize the interpermeability of human bodies and the environments we inhabit, thus challenging both the human/nature dualism that imagines humans as separate from our ecologies and the idealized impenetrability of human individualism.[42] As part of a web of open-ended interdependence in the biosphere, our bodies are in a continuous dialogue with spatial-political topographies. Our environment both creates us and is created by us. That gives us an immense amount of power to imagine new possibilities and futures that allow queer life to thrive. It also allows us to see through the normative image of Appalachia as a backward place and a sacrifice zone, to envision a queer and unsettling space of possibility.

Mary Gray, Colin Johnson, and Brian Gilley understand sexuality in rural space as extending from "geographic space" into "ideological space." They understand sexuality as inherently tied to *place*; being queer in rural space is inherently different from being queer in the city.[43] Here, the urban is a site of the new, the exotic, and the decadent, and the rural stands in for "traditional morality," biblical fundamentalism, or heteronormative "human nature." In an effort to deconstruct this metronormative view that sees queerness as out of place in Appalachia, we ask how rural queerness can inform our understanding of Appalachia itself. How do LGBTQIA+ folks conceive of the "natural," what relationships do we/they build with the more-than-human environment, and why does this matter? What's more, how does the conceptual linkage between queerness and the urban, and rurality and the heteronormative, affect the deep structures of queerness, progressive politics, and environmentalism in US culture?[44]

QUEER APPALACHIAN NATURECULTURES AND SETTLER COLONIALISM

The connections among sexuality, gender, and relationships to land might be relatively new to white academia, but they are not new to Indigenous Peoples' scholarship. The set of knowledges explored here have been formed through connections between LGBTQIA+ settler scholars and movements for Indigenous sovereignty that highlight livable alternatives to settler culture.[45] Wilson explains that Indigenous interpersonal ethics are rooted in "the deep interdependency between humans and nature."[46] Indigenous relations to land and people are based not on a logic of ownership but on multiple interdependencies between human and nonhuman kin, in a "relational web [that] requires us to pay attention to our relations and obligations here and now."[47] This Indigenous "grounded normativity" emphasizes "consent, body sovereignty, freedom, and individual self-determination," in community with other humans and nonhumans.[48]

Heteronormative patriarchal nuclear families are a colonizing institution that dispossess Indigenous people via claims to individual private property in land, by individually assigned land allotments that focus on men as heads of households and property owners, and by stigmatization of other family forms and gender identities.[49] Queer Appalachian futurisms that attempt to conjure a future free of heteronormativity and gender oppression, economic distress, and continued environmental degradation must grapple with the role of settler colonialism in constructing the region because Appalachia is stolen land.

As Sisseton-Wahpeton Oyate scholar Kim TallBear explains, "It is not only material dispossession of land and 'resources' that builds the settler state, but that 'dispossession' undercuts co-constitutive relations between beings. Property literally undercuts Indigenous kinship and attempts to replace it. It objectifies the land and water and other-than-human beings as potentially owned resources."[50] Progressive movements must come to grips with the connections among the very real forms of oppression experienced by settlers and arrivants on this continent, the environmental catastrophe of this continent, and the terms of the violent structure known as settler colonialism.[51]

Econormativity encompasses the intersections of heteronormativity and contemporary ecological frameworks, ranging from (metronormative) ideas of rural spaces as somehow inherently straight to extractive masculinities that uphold patterns of environmental destruction. Deconstructing the imagined econormativity of the region requires more than centering white LGBTQIA+ folks in Appalachia. Forms of LGBTQIA+ liberation can operate within the terms of other forms of oppression, as expressed in the notion of homonormativity, which underlines the class and race privilege of same-sex couples who have been able to achieve (almost) full citizenship through normative middle-class marriage.[52] The adaptation of existing laws and structures for LGBTQIA+ representation remains within a hierarchical system of (so-called modern) culture over (so-called primitive) nature. Better queer representation within that system leaves unchallenged the historical basis for the structure, which is the systematic attempted dismantling of Indigenous lifeways and relations to land and nonhuman nature and their replacement with settler ones.[53] White LGBTQIA+ Appalachians are also settlers. In other words, to argue that LGBTQIA+ folks in Appalachia are oppressed by non-Appalachians, by capitalism, or by heteronormativity is not wrong but represents a limited critique of the problem.

The role of settler colonial structures in Appalachia must be addressed as we envision a more just future. Ignoring this would simply be continued Indigenous erasure and more of the same. We wish to recognize Indigenous resistance and Indigenous futurity as essential to the flourishing of the region without appropriating Two-Spirit politics for US queer politics, which would not be revolutionary but settler colonial.[54] However, by imagining a critically queer Appalachia that challenges settler colonialism and white econormativity, we have the potential to begin conjuring a future in which the region currently known as Appalachia can be a truly radical space. This type of queer ecological imagining supports land back, or the "land restoration and repatriation that Indigenous theories of justice and decolonization . . . require," in addition to embracing antiracism, LGBTQIA+ community initiatives, direct action, and mutual aid.[55]

PLAN OF THE BOOK

In chapter 1, "Re-presenting the Narrative: Pursuing Stories amid Addiction," Tijah Bumgarner explores the media representation and politics of shame surrounding Appalachia's opioid epidemic. Specifically, Bumgarner considers the dominant narrative and imagery of addiction and recovery in Appalachia and how re-presenting Appalachia as a queer space may disrupt the power structures that govern stories of addiction, treatment, and recovery in the region.

In chapter 2, "Intoxicated Subjects: Queer Bodies and Ecologies in 'Trumpalachia,'" Rebecca-Eli M. Long and Zane McNeill explore how toxicity and environmental degradation, naturecultures and extraction, and ecological actants and other nonhumans trouble and disrupt normative cisheteropatriarchal constructions of the Appalachian region. In doing so, they consider the histories of settler colonialism and self-indigenization in Appalachian studies, especially how they are often centered in queer theory and critical geographies. This chapter is particularly interested in the concept of the figure of the "toxin" and the "toxic" that exists in Appalachian naturecultures and permeates the cultural construction of Appalachia and its people.

In chapter 3, "Queers Embracing Place in Appalachia: The Importance of Masculinities for Queer Acceptance," Baker A. Rogers examines the process in which queer folk in Appalachia and the South embrace place-based identities, despite the centering of the metronormative in the gay imaginary. Rogers particularly explores the potential contradictions embedded in these identities and the contradictions based on stereotypes and misconceptions that inform what it means to be queer and from Appalachia, rural areas, and the South.

In chapter 4, "Unsilencing Indigeneity: Appalachian Studies, Appalachian Ecologies, and the Continuation of Settler Colonialism," Jessica Cory investigates and excavates the tangled terrain of colonization in Appalachian studies and argues for a rethinking of the place of Indigenous literature in its syllabi. Noting the use of colonization as a frame of reference for the region, she builds on a tradition of querying this usage and explores how these frames help erase Indigenous people and settler colonialism from accounts of the region.

In chapter 5, "It's Grandpa's Land: Settler Property, Heteropatriarchy, and Environmental Disasters," Kandice Grossman, Aaron Padgett, and Rebecca Scott work through the discourse of white inheritance and property that shapes some anti-pipeline politics in southern West Virginia. They root out how the property structure both enables the state to exercise eminent domain in the name of a so-called public infrastructure project like a natural gas pipeline and enables landowners to oppose it in the name of their property rights. This contradiction shapes the form that pipeline opposition from landowners can take and illuminates how settler colonialism limits the range of the possible for environmental politics.

Chapter 6 moves to the ground to examine the organization Edible Kent. In "Edible Kent: Collaboration, Decentralization, and

Sustainable Agriculture in Urban Food Systems," Lis Regula and MJ Eckhouse recount how an urban agriculture movement in Kent, Ohio, reworked land use patterns, offered new opportunities for accessing food, and at the same time developed new community relations. These no-barrier community gardens challenged dominant narratives of land use and economic structure by repurposing downtown spaces in a people-centered, no-barrier project that queers (in D. Halperin's use of the term) the neoliberal capitalist space of the city.

In chapter 7, "Arboreal Blockaders: 'Queer/Trans Moments of Critical Appalachian Eco-action,'" Chet Pancake leads a phenomenological investigation of how queer tree sitters transform landscapes of extraction through their activism. Noting the failures of normative social science and environmental activism to get beyond the legal forms that propel extraction, he documents how direct action makes the familiar strange and provides a space for que(e)rying the cisheteronormative patriarchal and capitalist logic of extraction.

In chapter 8, "Masculinities in the Decline of Coal: Queer Futures in the Appalachian Coalfields," Gabe Schwartzman investigates the evolution of "pro-coal" politics in public discourse, rural resentment, and heteronormative temporality. Specifically, Schwartzman considers how post-coal nostalgia embodies cisheteropatriarchal anxiety in response to a shift in the gendered order, labor, and power relations in the regional political economy.

The last chapter of the collection, "'I Fixed Up the Trees to Give Them Some New Life': Queer Desire, Affect, and Ecology in the Work of LGBTQIA+ Appalachian Artists," by Maxwell Cloe, explores the intersections of queer Appalachian art and human relationships to nonhuman naturecultures. In doing so, Cloe investigates how a reconsideration of humanity, nature, culture, and queerness can aid in imagining liberatory Appalachian futures and queer ecological liberation.

NOTES

1. Appalachia represents such a sacrifice zone in at least two ways: primarily environmentally, as an extractive site for the lumber, coal, oil, and gas that helped fuel the development of the very same thriving modern economy that has always seemed elusive in the region; and secondarily culturally, as a sacrifice zone for the discursive foundations of whiteness and white privilege in the United States. Rebecca Scott, "Appalachia and the Construction of Whiteness in the United States," *Sociology Compass* 3, no. 5 (2009): 803; Scott, *Removing Mountains: Extracting Nature and Identity in the Appalachian Coalfields* (Minneapolis: University of Minnesota Press 2010).

2. Patricia Hill Collins, *Black Feminist Thought: Knowledge, Consciousness, and the Politics of Empowerment* (New York: Routledge, 2000).

3. "NativeLand.Ca," Native Land Digital, accessed June 7, 2019, https://native -land.ca/; Leanne Betasamosake Simpson, *As We Have Always Done: Indigenous Freedom through Radical Resistance*, 3rd ed. (Minneapolis: University Of Minnesota Press, 2017).

4. In this introduction, we identify cited authors in the way they identify themselves publicly, as enrolled members of Indigenous Nations or as settlers. We don't identify authors when we have not found such information shared publicly. Although *settler* is a shorthand that encompasses too many situations under one label to be completely accurate or to reflect the dynamism of identity and affiliation, we use it to refer to the non-Indigenous descendants of voluntary migrants and those who benefit from the settler state. Jodi Byrd (Chickasaw) uses the term *arrivant* to refer to those brought by force to this land or those excluded from the protections of the settler state, while Patty Krawec (Anishinaabe) uses the term *deplanted*.

5. Val Plumwood, *Feminism and the Mastery of Nature* (London: Routledge, 1994); Greta Gaard, "Toward a Queer Ecofeminism," in *New Perspectives on Environmental Justice: Gender, Sexuality, and Activism*, ed. Rachel Stein (New Brunswick, NJ: Rutgers University Press, 2004), 21–44.

6. Elizabeth Catte, *What You Are Getting Wrong about Appalachia* (Cleveland: Belt, 2018), 127.

7. Scott, *Removing Mountains*.

8. Scott, "Appalachia and the Construction of Whiteness," 803; Joe W. Trotter Jr., *African American Workers and the Appalachian Coal Industry* (Morgantown: West Virginia University Press, 2022); Cicero M. Fain, *Black Huntington: An Appalachian Story* (Urbana: University of Illinois Press, 2019); Gabe

Schwartzman, "Anti-Blackness, Black Geographies, and Racialized Depopulation in Coalfield Appalachia from 1940 to 2000," *Journal of Appalachian Studies* 28, no. 2 (2022): 125–43.

9. Patty Krawec, *Becoming Kin: An Indigenous Call to Unforgetting the Past and Reimagining Our Future* (Minneapolis: Broadleaf Books, 2022).

10. Dian Million, "Felt Theory: An Indigenous Feminist Approach to Affect and History," *Wicazo Sa Review* 24, no. 2 (2009): 53–76, https://doi.org/10.1353/wic.0.0043.

11. Michel Foucault, *The History of Sexuality*, vol. 1, *An Introduction*, reissue ed. (New York: Vintage, 1990).

12. Dana Luciano and Mel Y. Chen, "Introduction: Has the Queer Ever Been Human?," *GLQ: A Journal of Lesbian and Gay Studies* 21, no. 2 (2015): iv–207, http://muse.jhu.edu/article/581599.

13. David Delgado Shorter, "Sexuality," in *The World of Indigenous North America*, ed. Robert Warrior (New York: Routledge, 2015), 487–505.

14. Simpson, *As We Have Always Done.*

15. Kim TallBear, "What's in Ecosexuality for an Indigenous Scholar of 'Nature'?," *Indigenous STS* (blog), June 29, 2012, http://indigenoussts.com/whats-in-ecosexuality-for-an-indigenous-scholar-of-nature/.

16. Alex Wilson, "How We Find Ourselves: Identity Development and Two-Spirit People," *Harvard Education Review* 66, no. 2 (1996): 303-317.

17. Stephen Pearson, "'The Last Bastion of Colonialism': Appalachian Settler Colonialism and Self-Indigenization," *American Indian Culture and Research Journal* 37, no. 2 (January 1, 2013): 165–84, https://doi.org/10.17953/aicr.37.2.g4522v766231r3xg; Kimberly C. Borchard, "From Apalache to Apalachee: The Making of Early Modern Appalachia" (Goldsmiths History Society, online event, February 23, 2022), https://www.eventbrite.com/e/from-apalache-to-apalachee-the-making-of-early-modern-appalachia-tickets-258292538937?keep_tld=1.

18. Collins, *Black Feminist Thought*; John Hartigan, *Odd Tribes: Toward a Cultural Analysis of White People* (Durham NC: Duke University Press, 2005).

19. J. D. Vance, *Hillbilly Elegy: A Memoir of a Family and Culture in Crisis* (New York: Harper, 2016).

20. Lyman Stone, "The Appalachian Go-Round: Family Instability in America's Highland," Institute for Family Studies, accessed August 5, 2019, https://ifstudies.org/blog/the-appalachian-go-round-family-instability-in-americas-highland.

21. Daniel Patrick Moynihan, *The Negro Family: The Case for National Action* (Washington, DC: Office of Policy Planning and Research, US Department of

Labor, 1965); Defense of Marriage Act (DOMA), 7 U.S.C., 28 U.S.C. § 1738C (1996), https://www.govtrack.us/congress/bills/104/hr3396.

22. Neferti Xina M. Tadiar, *Fantasy Production: Sexual Economies and Other Philippine Consequences for the New World Order* (Hong Kong: Hong Kong University Press, 2004).

23. Pearson, "Last Bastion of Colonialism."

24. Kim TallBear, "Caretaking Relations, Not American Dreaming," *Kalfou* 6, no. 1 (2019), https://tupjournals.temple.edu/index.php/kalfou/article/view/228; Circe Sturm, *Becoming Indian: The Struggle over Cherokee Identity in the Twenty-First Century* (Santa Fe: School for Advanced Research Press, 2011).

25. Harry Caudill, *Night Comes to the Cumberlands* (Boston: Little, Brown, 1962); William Goodell Frost, "Our Contemporary Ancestors in the Southern Mountains," in *Appalachian Images in Folk and Popular Culture*, ed. W. K. McNeil (Knoxville: University of Tennessee Press, 1899), 91–106.

26. J. Kēhaulani Kauanui, "'A Structure, Not an Event': Settler Colonialism and Enduring Indigeneity," *Lateral* 5, no. 1 (2016), https://doi.org/10.25158/L5.1.7; Patrick Wolfe, "Settler Colonialism and the Elimination of the Native," *Journal of Genocide Research* 8, no. 4 (December 2006): 387–409, https://doi.org/10.1080/14623520601056240.

27. Raymond Williams, *Keywords: A Vocabulary of Culture and Society* (Oxford: Oxford University Press, 1985).

28. Eve Tuck and K. Wayne Yang, "Decolonization Is Not a Metaphor," *Decolonization, Indigeneity Education and Society* 1, no. 1 (2012): 1–40.

29. Kimberly TallBear, *Native American DNA: Tribal Belonging and the False Promise of Genetic Science* (Minneapolis: University of Minnesota Press, 2013).

30. Pearson, "Last Bastion of Colonialism," 166–67.

31. Williams, *Keywords*; Bruno Latour and Catherine Porter, *We Have Never Been Modern* (Cambridge, MA: Harvard University Press, 1993).

32. Stein, *New Perspectives*, 7.

33. Silvia Federici, *Caliban and the Witch: Women, the Body and Primitive Accumulation* (New York: Autonomedia, 2004).

34. Million, "Felt Theory."

35. Gaard, "Toward a Queer Ecofeminism," 23. As evidenced in the spate of "Don't Say Gay" bills cropping up around the nation to allegedly protect children from the threat of exposure to nonnormative gender and sexual identities.

36. Catriona Mortimer-Sandilands and Bruce Erickson, eds., *Queer Ecologies: Sex, Nature, Politics, Desire* (Bloomington: University of Indiana Press, 2010).

37. Mortimer-Sandilands and Erickson, *Queer Ecologies*, 5.

38. Stacey Alaimo, "Eluding Capture: The Science, Culture, and Pleasure of 'Queer' Animals," in *Queer Ecologies: Sex, Nature, Politics, Desire*, ed. Catriona Mortimer-Sandilands and Bruce Erickson (Bloomington: Indiana University Press), 51–72.

39. David Bell and Gill Valentine, eds., *Mapping Desire: Geographies of Sexualities* (Abingdon: Routledge, 1995).

40. Mortimer-Sandilands and Erickson, *Queer Ecologies*, 22; Jack Halberstam, *Wild Things: The Disorder of Desire* (Durham, NC: Duke University Press, 2020).

41. Halberstam, *Wild Things*.

42. Stacy Alaimo, *Exposed: Environmental Politics and Pleasures in Posthuman Times* (Minneapolis: University of Minnesota Press, 2016).

43. Mary L. Gray, Colin R. Johnson, and Brian Joseph Gilley, eds., *Queering the Countryside: New Frontiers in Rural Queer Studies* (New York: New York University Press, 2016), 15.

44. Mark Rifkin, *Beyond Settler Time: Temporal Sovereignty and Indigenous Self-Determination* (Durham, NC: Duke University Press, 2017).

45. Kim TallBear, "Caretaking Relations"; Zoe Todd, "An Indigenous Feminist's Take on the Ontological Turn: 'Ontology' Is Just Another Word for Colonialism," *Journal of Historical Sociology* 29, no. 1 (2016): 4–22; Scott Lauria Morgensen, *Spaces between Us: Queer Settler Colonialism and Indigenous Decolonization* (Minneapolis: University of Minnesota Press, 2011).

46. Wilson, "How We Find Ourselves," 305.

47. Kim TallBear, "Feminist, Queer, and Indigenous Thinking as an Antidote to Masculinist Objectivity and Binary Thinking in Biological Anthropology," *American Anthropologist* 121, no. 2 (2019): 3, https://doi.org/10.1111/aman.13229.

48. Simpson, *As We Have Always Done*, 122.

49. TallBear, "Caretaking Relations"; Dorceta Taylor, *The Rise of the American Conservation Movement* (Durham, NC: Duke University Press, 2016).

50. TallBear, "Feminist, Queer, and Indigenous Thinking," 8.

51. Jodi Byrd, *The Transit of Empire: Indigenous Critiques of Colonialism* (Minneapolis: University of Minnesota Press, 2011); Patrick Wolfe, *Traces of History: Elementary Structures of Race* (London: Verso, 2016).

52. Lisa Duggan, *The Twilight of Equality? Neoliberalism, Cultural Politics, and the Attack on Democracy* (Boston: Beacon Press, 2012).

53. TallBear, "Feminist, Queer, and Indigenous Thinking."
54. Scott Lauria Morgensen, *Spaces Between Us: Queer Settler Colonialism and Indigenous Decolonization* (Minneapolis: University of Minnesota Press, 2011). 83.
55. Pearson, "Last Bastion of Colonialism," 178; Tuck and Yang, "Decolonization Is Not a Metaphor," 1–40; Krawec, *Becoming Kin.*

RE-PRESENTING THE NARRATIVE
Pursuing Stories amid Addiction

Tijah Bumgarner

I stood in front of a small group of about thirteen people at Smather's Funeral Home in Rainelle, West Virginia. Beside me was the casket that my sister and I had picked out for our dad. Not the most expensive one, but not the cheapest one either. The funeral assistant commented on the number of funerals in recent years—due to the opioid epidemic. This was in July 2020. We based our casket decision on the color—blue, our dad's favorite color. I spoke about the *lasts* with my dad: *the last text message, the last phone call, the last time he said and heard I love you.* We mark down a lot of firsts, but the lasts are what we may long for. When I received the death certificate a month later, I read the cause of death: "combined intoxication by methamphetamines, heroin, acetyl fentanyl, fentanyl diphenhydramine, and alcohol." He had just got out of a yearlong jail sentence in June 2020 but had been in active addiction, as far as I know, since the late 1990s. It is a long story of back pain and OxyContin and friends and money and doctors and methadone and, and, and. . . . This is a well-known story in rural America, especially in Appalachia. The lives entangled and upturned are numerous. Nothing makes my family's dealing with addiction unique, but the ripple effects of the epidemic resound in a multitude of ways. The wailing of my grandma, crying out for her baby boy that day, is an effect of the opioid epidemic. I have spent the last several years working to capture the stories of the effects of this epidemic in multiple film projects.

When I first started making films around 2005, I was in my early twenties, living in Los Angeles and attending community college. In 2006, I traveled home to West Virginia to create a short film about my family in response to my first assignment prompt, titled "personal statement." We were to make a short film that shows the world what makes you who you are. I chose to focus on my family because my time in Los Angeles had strengthened my awareness of being from West Virginia, and I was questioning what that meant for me in spite of always wanting to leave the state where I had grown up. When I got home to my small town, there was my dad in his rocking chair nodding off, barely gripping a piece of toast. I caught it on my camera. Though we never discussed my dad's addiction, I knew it had started with OxyContin that he got from a friend to help with his back pain. His body ached from years of construction and mechanic work. Gesturing toward my dad, who didn't even realize we were standing there, my mom chimed in: "See? See why I'm depressed?" I never used this footage. I wouldn't even know where it is right now. In 2018, after moving back to West Virginia and spending years researching Appalachia and the ways images have contributed to the exploitation of the region, I was glad I never made that film. This experience inspired me to counter the negative stories about people with substance use disorder, and in 2018, I set out with Jena Seiler to make films about the opioid epidemic. We have made two documentaries and one pilot episode of a series, each project with a different focus. However, our most involved project has been in the making for over four years: our feature documentary *Picture Proof*.

Picture Proof unfolds chronologically around the lives of Ashley, Debi, and Piper. The film chronicles profound moments of joy over the course of three years (Ashley regaining guardianship of Piper and giving birth to her second child, Asher) and intimate moments of grief (Ashley learning her fiancé has died from an overdose; Debi breaking down while looking for Ashley on the streets when she is in the "madness"). In the bad times, Debi would ask Ashley for "picture proof": photographic evidence, a token of hope. In the good times, selfies confirm Ashley's own being in the world as a woman, mom, daughter, partner, sponsor, and friend. *Picture Proof* is a testament to a life worth documenting, the love and labor of recovery, and the beauty and potential each life holds. During all of these intimate moments, I have been allowed in—allowed in as a filmmaker and as someone who has been affected by substance use disorder firsthand. How do we tell a story about someone else's life in recovery and addiction? What responsibility does a filmmaker / image maker bear when representing another, especially in the context of addiction?

The extractive economy left Appalachia vulnerable to the opioid epidemic. This approach shows up not only in the extraction of coal from the ground but in the extraction of images—and in turn the extraction of stories. The prefix *re-* in the word *representation* implies an absence, presenting anew that which is no longer present. And whenever we present something anew, transformation is implied.[1] So, in the absence of a broad knowledge of what Appalachia is and what it isn't, perhaps the post-coal shift provides an opportunity to transform what narratives/stories are understood and made material. By illuminating a broader understanding of Appalachia as a queer space and re-representing its entrenched patriarchal masculinity, perhaps we can make space for a widening of the limited view of Appalachia. In the re-shaping and re-structuring, re-presenting is the potential to point to Appalachia as queer by highlighting the ways in which environmental degradation has queered the non-human landscape of the region. Of course, this degradation of the land and people did not begin with representation.

Historically, as Evelyn Nakano Glenn explores in the article "Settler Colonialism as Structure: A Framework for Comparative

Studies of U.S. Race and Gender Formation," "what emerged out of the settler colonial project was a racialized and gendered national identity that normalized male whiteness. Since settlers initially were exogenous others seeking to claim rights to land and sovereignty over those who already occupied the land, they needed to develop conceptions of Indigenous people as lesser beings, unworthy of consideration. They harnessed race and gender to construct a hierarchy of humankind. Conceiving of Indigenous people as less than fully human justified dispossessing them and rendered them expendable and/or invisible."[2]

These gendered and racialized constructs of human/nonhuman—visible/invisible—are rooted within the conception of the United States and consistently show up in contemporary spaces such as Appalachia. The mythic borders that outline the space of Appalachia replicate the very construction of race, gender, and place as referenced above. Exploring the history and future of Appalachia through a queer reading of the landscape and lived experiences that shape a counternarrative to these solidified constructions and well-known tropes has the potential to produce real change within the region.

Visual representations of Appalachia are entangled with a sordid history of image making that has produced the region's meaning. Storied spaces from Central Appalachia have long been a cultural marker of the region. And since the late 1990s, Central Appalachia has been marked and scarred and storied and shaped by the flow of opioids released within its rural spaces. In his book, *Death in Mud Lick*, Eric Eyre opens with the startling fact that "in two years, out-of-state drug companies shipped nearly 9 million opioid pain pills to Kermit, West Virginia, a town with 382 people."[3] This is one example of how the epidemic took hold, erupted like a rhizomatic weed, and spread. Taking up Deleuze and Guattari's notion of rhizome through "principles of connection and heterogeneity: any point of a rhizome can be connected to anything other and must be. This is very different from the tree or root, which plots a point, fixes an order."[4] The opioid epidemic did not follow a fixed order as it spread throughout Appalachia. It went on to infiltrate life by ripping families apart, creating a new population of the unhoused, and lowering the life expectancy for an entire generation of those in Central Appalachia and beyond.

While storytelling and narrative can be used to reinforce or resist the fixing of a region, there is little desire for the former when it comes to the powers that control the media. Sensationalized imagery of needles, baggies of drugs, people sleeping on the street, and other obscene imagery has been utilized as a tool for naming a problem through perception. However, the people—and not the overarching contexts of power and politics—are seen as the problem. Similar to narratives of poverty in the region created through the imagery of dirty children during the War on Poverty, the opioid crisis and those caught up in it fulfill an imagined Appalachia, and the region is once again presented as one thing only. Historically a region scarred by coal companies abandoning the people they made dependent through company towns and stores, Appalachia is now scarred by pharmaceutical companies. These companies' actions replicate those of the company towns that used to line the hollers of Appalachia—extracting the minerals, the citizens, the pride, the self-reliance, and the intersection of the natural and human world. They targeted a vulnerable group of people in pain and despair and left them dependent on OxyContin for solace and relief. In the vanishing image of coal, Appalachia is being distilled into a single narrative of existence and often a single narrative of experience. The battles of substance use disorder are continually being fought and evolving in and out of focus on a regular basis. From prescriptions to fentanyl, heroin, and meth—from cultural deviance to a medical condition and stories of resilience—the substances, reactions, representations, and narratives have varied across decades of drug crises. The narrative shaping the opioid epidemic is, of course, informed by the racialization of the War on Drugs of the 1980s and 1990s.

In the article "The Social Construction of the Crack Epidemic in the Print Media," authors Hartman and Golub state, "It is the collective perception of a problem within the general population that often drives government actions, not necessarily the actual problem itself."[5] While the collective perception of the crack epidemic was framed by images of Black people and inner-city inhabitants, the opioid epidemic has been cast as white and rural.

How race has influenced the perceptions and responses of each epidemic tells us about the role of race in American society. Despite the meaningful difference between them, a thread connects these two epidemics: individual blame, which reinforces entrenched ideology rather than addressing the societal problems, intergenerational trauma, or mental distress at the root of these epidemics. Self-destruction by drug use was and is framed as a moral failure.[6] However, oppressive systems such as segregation and exploitation historically have created lack of opportunity and dependence.

While similarities of blame and misimpressions of drug use continue to infiltrate the mass media, Khiara M. Bridges notes, "During that apocalyptic moment in this nation's history, however, one was hard pressed to find narratives that described the black persons dependent on crack cocaine as turning to drugs to cope with trauma, or mental health issues, or personal tragedy, or poverty. Few commentators broached the possibility that users of crack cocaine might have been trying to silence the demons in their heads. Instead, those who used the drug were themselves demonized. They were portrayed as highly dangerous, hopelessly pathological, and intrinsically criminal."[7]

While there have been some small steps forward in the response to the opioid epidemic, including moving from jail time to drug courts or from criminals to victims, which has helped to destigmatize substance use disorder, in journalist Katharine Q. Seelye's article "In Heroin Crisis, White Families Seek Gentler War on Drugs," she states, "When the nation's long-running war against drugs was defined by the crack epidemic and based in poor, predominantly black urban areas, the public response was defined by zero tolerance and stiff prison sentences."[8] While there have been efforts to humanize those who use drugs through more nuanced stories, this racialized history is generally absent from the media's depiction and discussion of the opioid crisis. Instead, many Appalachian portrayals invest in stereotypes of backward, toothless hillbillies. These images have an effect similar to the demonization during the crack epidemic: they dehumanize people, externalize the problem, and keep people down. While there are variations across time and space, "it is a framework that is amenable to intersectional understanding because it is widely understood that colonial projects simultaneously structure race, gender, class, and sexual relations within and between colonists and the colonized."[9] These constructed narratives continue to take hold and shape politics and policy, weaving together a portrait of systemic problems while working to lift up or demean those who have suffered because of it.

Just as the War on Poverty representations revolved around mostly white, heteronormative, masculine ways of being, so too has the imagery of the opioid epidemic. The role of whiteness and queerness in the narrative of addiction and recovery must be acknowledged along with the nuances and differences shaping the multiplicity of drug crisis stories in order to create policy change within the region (and beyond). In her article "In Appalachia, the Face of Addiction Is White—and So Is the Story of Recovery," Crystal Good notes, "Drug dependency for Black Appalachians does not discriminate between alcohol, heroin, meth, opioids, cocaine—but treatment, experiences, and access to recovery sometimes does."[10] Overall, historical, political, and economic situations feed and strengthen narratives that create conditions for acknowledging who deserves recovery.

In *The Invention of Appalachia*, Allen Batteau states, "The making of Appalachia was a literary and a political invention rather than a geographical discovery."[11] This ghost or mythic border that Batteau makes visible delineates what is considered Appalachia and what is not, which in turn marks who is Appalachian and who is not. The dual quality of this border—as both a myth and a structural experience—presents a kind of in-between. Because it is a border, a fluid map of the region demonstrates the unstable ghost line that is often used to set Appalachia as a place apart, as a place in between America and not. This in-between of being a place and not being a place provides a space or gap. This is not necessarily a gap to fall through but a space to plant and grow and raise up. Appalachia did not begin with coal, nor will it end in a post-coal space. These "absolutes" of beginning and end erase multiple stories that make up the history and future of the region. As Douglas Powell notes, "When we talk about a region, we are talking not about a stable, boundaried, autonomous place but about a cultural history, the cumulative, generative effect of the interplay among the various, competing definitions of that region."[12] Appalachia's competing definitions are often constructed around coal, a nonhuman object that has been instrumental in shaping its history. Therefore, the landscape becomes an oppressed nonhuman for extraction. In *Strange Natures: Futurity, Empathy, and the Queer Ecological Imagination*, Nicole Seymour explores a discursive construction of oppressed humans and oppressed nonhumans through queerness and landscape.[13] Seymour considers "how any emotional investment in particular spaces or environments—be they gay bars or gardens— might be considered queer."[14] Re-presenting Appalachia as a queer space in the shift toward a post-coal landscape can widen that gap between place and not place to shape narratives that materialize LGBTQIA+ lives within this space—including those seeking treatment for substance use disorders.

Of course, narrative and story can only do so much work in untangling the power structures that govern the futurity of Appalachia. In *Narrating Space / Spatializing Narrative*, Marie-Laure

Ryan, Kenneth Foote, and Maoz Azaryahu explore how space serves not only as a location but also as a narrative. Using the concept of the spatial turn, they take up narratology and place by saying, "A map of spatial form is not a geographical map, but rather a diagram of formal relations between narrative elements."[15] These narrative elements are pieces of history, but they lack continuity as a whole, or an expanded, multistory. At stake is an exclusive acceptance of who deserves recovery on the basis of place, race, and representation. In the introduction to *Critical Perspectives on Addiction*, Julie Netherland begins by saying, "There has been no graceful arc from deviance to medicalization—from badness to sickness—in the case of addiction."[16] Netherland constructs an argument about the medical and moral implications of addiction. This too has implications for who deserves treatment. Is it the father of three who hurt his back while working in the coal mines? The single mom who had to take a job in the steel plant and crushed her hand after her husband was deployed and killed in Afghanistan? The younger guy down the street who used to mistreat animals and now has a heroin addiction? The queer kid who just started college, had trouble keeping up, and started off with speed? There are no factors or boxes to check when someone takes up substances as an escape; however, there are when that person seeks treatment.

While a restructuring of narratives cannot undo the historical damage to the environment and cultural damage to the people in the region, it can open a space for agency for those who claim an Appalachian identity and yet have historically been left out of the narratives that create this place. For example, the stereotypes of "backwardness" as a cultural form are closely tied through etymology to queering. Being backward or heading in a contrary direction, toward the past, or toward a worse state can be a link to time and place in relation to Appalachia.[17] Toward a definition of queer environmental affect, Nicole Seymore posits that "the alternative forms of attachment, emotion, and response that emerge within the context of queer or non-normative spaces" relate to the attachment to place for Appalachians.[18] In "Placing Nostalgia: The Process of Returning and Remaking Home," Allison Hui concludes that "places do not produce affective attachment—rather, people do, through their practices."[19] These practices can be seen as traditions in Appalachia, but these traditions are not only performed by the heterosexual cis citizens of the region. To theorize on the everyday activities in these spaces, it takes a curiosity and speculation rather than assumed truths. This notion provokes attention to the impact or habits of everyday as ordinary. Kathleen Stewart says of ordinary affects, "The question they beg is not what they might mean in an order of representations, or whether they are good or bad in an overarching scheme of things, but where they might go and what potential modes of knowing, relating, and attending to things are already somehow present in them in a state of potentiality and resonance."[20] The potentialities of a queer environmental affect support a more expansive reading of Appalachian history and futures, using representation as a way to converse on the limitations, possibilities, and everything in between and move toward a queering of place with attention to how "the logic, tenets, and identities engendered by settler colonialism persist and continue to shape race, gender, class, and sexual formations into the present."[21]

Deeply rooted rather than rhizomatic, these instances of "othering," these utterances of "backwardness," can be uprooted to create a productive space for a queer Appalachia through relationships with nature. However, while we work against the gendered and racial structures and systems toward a queering of Appalachia, it is important to recognize the deeper roots and understand that what these "frameworks share is an appreciation that racial hierarchy and inequality are not simply the products of individual beliefs and attitudes but are built into American social structure and that whites have historically benefited from racial inequality."[22] As an artist and educator who makes films and teaches students to make films, I work to conceptualize single narratives by articulating the unrepresented stories and their potential to offer a counternarrative. Stories that resist becoming extractive and consciously do not reinforce a single representation of the region can provide an alternative to the rhetoric of people "choosing drugs" or becoming "junkies" or "addicts" or "pillheads." This work of re-presenting can acknowledge the past while considering the futurity of Appalachia by connecting the environment, exploitation, and identity to provide narratives that can uproot and challenge historical concepts.

NOTES

1. Louise Spence and Vinicius Navarro, *Crafting Truth: Documentary Form and Meaning* (New Brunswick, NJ: Rutgers University Press, 2011), 14.
2. Evelyn Nakano Glenn, "Settler Colonialism as Structure: A Framework for Comparative Studies of U.S. Race and Gender Formation," *Sociology of Race and Ethnicity* 1, no. 1 (2015): 58.
3. Eric Eyre, *Death in Mud Lick: A Coal Country Fight against the Drug Companies That Delivered the Opioid Epidemic* (New York: Scribner, 2020), xi.
4. Gilles Deleuze and Felix Guattari, *A Thousand Plateaus: Capitalism and Schizophrenia* (Minneapolis: University of Minnesota Press, 1987), 7.
5. Donna M. Hartman and Andrew Golub, "The Social Construction of the Crack Epidemic in the Print Media," *Journal of Psychoactive Drugs* 31, no. 4 (1999): 423–33.
6. David Russell et al., "Where the Fault Lies: Representations of Addiction in Audience Reactions to Media Coverage of the Opioid Epidemic," *Contemporary Drug Problems* 47, no. 2 (2020): 83–102.
7. Khiara M. Bridges, "Race, Pregnancy, and the Opioid Epidemic: White Privilege and the Criminalization of Opioid Use during Pregnancy," *Harvard Law Review* 133, no. 3 (2020): 791.
8. Katharine Q. Seelye, "In Heroin Crisis, White Families Seek Gentler War on Drugs," *New York Times*, October 30, 2015, https://www.nytimes.com/2015/10/31/us/heroin-war-on-drugs-parents.html.
9. Glenn, "Settler Colonialism as Structure," 55.
10. Crystal Good, "In Appalachia, the Face of Addiction Is White—and so Is the Story of Recovery," *Scalawag*, February 26, 2021, https://scalawagmagazine.org/2021/02/black-appalachia-recovery-addiction/.

11. Allen Batteau, *The Invention of Appalachia* (Tucson: University of Arizona Press, 1990), 1.

12. Douglas Powell, *Critical Regionalism: Connecting Politics and Culture in the American Landscape* (Chapel Hill: University of North Carolina Press, 2007), 5.

13. Nicole Seymour, *Strange Natures: Futurity, Empathy, and the Queer Ecological Imagination* (Urbana: University of Illinois Press, 2013).

14. Nicole Seymour, "The Queerness of Environmental Affect," in *Affective Ecocriticism: Emotion, Embodiment, Environment*, ed. Kyle Bladow and Jennifer Ladino (Lincoln: University of Nebraska Press, 2018), 237.

15. Marie-Laure Ryan, Kenneth E. Foote, and Maoz Azaryahu, *Narrating Space/ Spatializing Narrative: Where Narrative Theory and Geography Meet* (Columbus: Ohio State University Press, 2016), 48.

16. Julie Netherland, *Critical Perspectives on Addiction: Advances in Medical Sociology* (Bingley: Emerald Group, 2012), xiii.

17. Definition taken from *Merriam-Webster*, s.v. "backward," August 13, 2023, https://www.merriam-webster.com/dictionary/backward.

18. Seymour, "Queerness of Environmental Affect," 235.

19. Allison Hui, "Placing Nostalgia: The Process of Returning and Remaking Home," in *Ecologies of Affect: Placing Nostalgia, Desire, and Hope*, ed. Tonya K. Davidson, Ondine Park, and Rob Shields (Waterloo, ON: Wilfrid Laurier University Press, 2013), 70.

20. Kathleen Stewart, *Ordinary Affects* (Durham, NC: Duke University Press, 2007), 3.

21. Glenn, "Settler Colonialism as Structure," 55.

22. Glenn, "Settler Colonialism as Structure," 67.

INTOXICATED SUBJECTS
Queer Bodies and Ecologies in *"Trumpalachia"*

Rebecca-Eli M. Long and
Zane McNeill

We live in a world of many Appalachias. These are places of extravagant natural wealth, and enduring poverty, places where the raw consequences of unsustainable economic practices predicated on human and environmental exploitation are unusually stark. . . . These places also represent some of the weakest links in the far-flung supply chains of global capitalism because they are home to indigenous movements contesting the apparent imperatives of gross economic inequality, environmental degradation, and the antidemocratic power of elites.
—Stephen Fisher and Barbara Smith, *Transforming Places:*
Lessons from Appalachia

Published in 2012, Stephen Fisher and Barbara Smith's coedited volume, *Transforming Places: Lessons from Appalachia*, remains a keystone work in the tradition of Appalachians fighting to raise their voices and challenge the normative stereotypes and perceptions of Appalachia and its people. This legacy has been continued by responses to J. D. Vance's *Hillbilly Elegy* and the recent growth of queer Appalachian studies.[1] Appalachian scholar-activism, including queer scholar-activism, disrupts standard perceptions of Appalachia as a devoid place, a "sacrifice zone," a place lost in its backward traditions, a site where people shoot themselves in the foot politically and culturally, and a region that produced the Trump presidency.[2]

Queerness in Appalachia has most frequently been examined through oral histories and personal testimonies, and yet the popular othering of Appalachia certainly points to an understanding of the entire region as queer in the national imagining. We contend that the place itself, Appalachian natures and more-than-human ecologies, can be thought of as *queered* through resource extraction and, therefore, that the bodies touched by environmental toxicity can also be considered *queer*.[3] In examining Appalachia as a queer place, we draw critical attention to a set of bad relations to the land, such as extractive industries, that are predicated on the dispossession of Indigenous territories. "White, capitalist-industrial entitlement to the land" has shaped both settler colonialism and continued development at the expense of settler Appalachians.[4] Thus, rather than simply focus on land as a setting for Appalachian queer narratives, we recognize the interplay and ultimate inseparability of nature and culture, itself a colonial binary. Naturecultures, as explored especially by feminist philosopher Donna Haraway, recognizes our interrelationships with different forms of being.[5]

Despite attempts to develop the region beyond extractive industries, toxicity lingers. Mel Chen argues that "figures of toxicity have moved well beyond their specific range of biological attribution, leaking out of nominal and literal bounds while retaining their affective ties to vulnerability and repulsion."[6] These ties connect the hillbilly with the coal miner with environmental damage with *Hillbilly Elegy*. While Appalachian history is replete with descriptions of the region as toxic, these depictions are no less prevalent today. Indeed, Appalachia has been seen as politically toxic, being symbolically the portion of the country that has threatened democracy by electing President Trump. Paradoxically, toxins, associated with death and morbidity, provide a potential framing to reinvigorate static understandings of the Appalachian landscape as a damaged ground for development efforts. Toxins become the material, yet also metaphorical, connection that animates the nature-culture divide. If the toxic body is *between* a living body and a dead body,[7] then Appalachia itself exists in a queer time and place.[8]

Queerness in Appalachia is experienced through individual bodies, as well as the broader landscape. As described by the editors of *Storytelling in Queer Appalachia*, "Queer identities and experiences are . . . crossed by and created within economics, destructive land practices, political turmoil, and stereotyping."[9] Our interest is not only in exploring LGBTQIA+ life in Appalachia as part of the larger turn to the rural queer from the metronormative focus on the urban as a queer utopia but in expanding on the argument that, "put simply, 'rural America' is strange. Some might even go so far as to say it is queer."[10] Not only do LGBTQIA+ folks live in Appalachia, a fact erased in works like *Hillbilly Elegy*, but the region itself can be examined as a *queer* entity.[11]

Queerness is inextricably related to these histories of violence, and it also offers ways of relating to place that counter colonial knowledges. Starting with the concept of Appalachia as an othered place, we ask how queer theory can complicate this narrative of cultural marginalization.[12] As a component of this, we raise the voices of LGBTQIA+ Appalachians archived in the oral history project Country Queers to explore the vibrancy left out of representations of Appalachia as a monolith of conservative values. We then explore how toxicity, both in our natural environment degraded by resource extraction and in toxic bodies poisoned by this degradation, can queer non-LGBTQIA+ Appalachian bodies. Lastly, we engage with queer ecologies and toxic animacies to imagine an Appalachian futurity that embraces its queerness and centers those historically excluded from being considered Appalachian.[13]

SETTLER COLONIALISM AND SELF-INDIGENIZATION

This project of (re)claiming Appalachia as queer takes place among larger histories of settler colonialism. We are attempting to queer a place that does not belong to us. As settlers writing from the lands of the Cherokee and Moneton peoples, our experiment in queering place is inherently intertwined with histories of violence but hopefully represents a disruption of the normative discourses that describe Appalachia as a conservative place stuck in a mythological past devoid of LGBTQIA+ lives, leftist activists, and people of color.

Appalachian activists frequently claim a position of indigeneity when extolling the virtues of resistance movements and Appalachian culture more broadly speaking. Stephen Fisher and Barbara Smith do just this in the paragraph we have selected as our epigraph, even as they elsewhere critique the concept of the internal colony.[14] While their intent was to highlight histories of resistance that we also find valuable and worth uplifting, their wording also erases actual Indigenous movements—including resistance to settler colonialism. As Ada Smith reminds us, "We have forgotten that the creation of Appalachia as a region stemmed from way before coal. We neglect daily the true colonization that happened in the mountains and in this country."[15] Building Appalachian resistance movements should not elide Indigenous history.

Too often, Appalachian studies scholars ignore this history and instead depict white Appalachian settlers as indigenous and even colonized, rather than colonizers, in their analyses of oppression. For example, the hillbilly, as prototypically white, also works to uphold systems of white supremacy in that the figure of the hillbilly has allowed Appalachian studies scholars to favor explanations of class and sidestep the examination of race. This creates the "inaccurate and highly misleading position that 'hillbillies' are, in effect, a racial minority."[16]

Helen Lewis's "internal colony" model refuted popular explanations of Appalachian marginalization based on the culture of poverty model.[17] While the internal colony model provides a way to understand the patterns of resource extraction from Appalachia and speaks against stereotypes, it does not engage with Native American histories in Appalachia and therefore erases the histories of settler colonialism and genocide. This leads to what Stephen Pearson refers to as "self-indigenization," an appropriation of the term *indigenous* "for settler Appalachians [that] precludes the settler from engaging in decolonization efforts in solidarity with Indigenous peoples."[18]

Thus, while analyzing popular representations of Appalachia as a marginalized region has yielded many promising queer perspectives, here, we seek to acknowledge the limitations of many of these perspectives and to engage in a queer critique that can contribute to a broader project of social justice and decolonization. By turning to naturecultures, we recognize the importance of engaging with land not simply as a resource but as part of a web of more-than-human relations.

QUEERING THE ARCHIVE

Queer Appalachian projects emerge in the space between the often-heteronormative Appalachian studies and the metronormative, urban bias of LGBTQIA+ narratives. The editors of *Storytelling in Queer Appalachia* explain that "Appalachian queerness remains underrepresented, misunderstood, sometimes muted, and sometimes invisible."[19] "Metronormativity," a term coined by J. Jack Halberstam to describe the privileging of urban sexual enlightenment, "reveals the rural to be the devalued term in the urban/rural binary governing the spatializations of modern U.S. sexual identities."[20] As Rae Garringer, founder of the Country Queers project, explains:

Mainstream LGBTQIA media and movements have long assumed a shared desire to escape from the country to more liberal "gay meccas" in urban and metropolitan areas. This assumption has been buoyed by stories of violent homophobic murders, such as those of Brandon Teena and Matthew Shepard—which, until very recently, have served as some of the only accessible evidence of rural queer existence. But for some of us this highly celebrated narrative of queer "success"—one in which you leave the farm and never look back, one in which you enter a fabulous landscape of glitter and queer dance parties—isn't all that appealing. For many of us raised in the country, following this normative queer migration narrative rips us from the landscapes, communities, and traditions that are as much a part of ourselves as our queerness.[21]

Creating a counternarrative to outsider stereotypes of Appalachia by curating queer oral histories is inherently a political project. Lydia McDermott explains that "projects and renamings such as these echo Appalachia but subvert dominant narratives of time and space and identity in Appalachia, causing a productive disorientation."[22] Our existence—not only the survival of queer people in Appalachia but the thriving of our communities—has been historically erased. Our stories have been eclipsed and written out of the archive. This reflects our marginalization in larger structural systems. As Adam Denney has written, "By the act of storytelling, these stories resist the active process of erasure and survive through the narration as they are retold . . . stories have magic; they illuminate our potential to manifest psychic bonds between person, space, and place."[23] Uplifting the voices of queer Appalachians is an activist act that challenges both metronormativity and Appalachian heteronormativity.

Queerness in Appalachia is often place based. Appalachian landscapes, communities, and traditions are deeply important to

Appalachian queer identity. This rural community flies in the face of "the narrative of rural to urban migration [that] graphed gay visibility as a political accomplishment onto the space of the city."[24] These queer identities, like Appalachian identities more broadly, are tied to place, even as the precise boundaries of Appalachia might be hard to pin down. Justin Ray Dutton explains that "telling one's story of being queer and Appalachian represents an important aspect of naming and claiming one's place."[25]

Ethan, a Kentuckian interviewed for Garringer's Country Queers project, speaks to the connection of Appalachian identity and place: "Appalachians have an extreme sense of family and sense of place, those are very extreme where I come from, I mean those are very obvious. Every, you know, family is not just your blood kin, it's everybody that you grew up with, everybody that you know. And then sense of place is you *know* where you're from and a sense of pride around that."[26]

To Ethan, his queerness is inherently connected to his identity as a "mountain boy"—he even created a new term for his identity by mixing the words *fabulous* and *Appalachian*: Fabulachian. This place-based queer identity disrupts the normative perception of Appalachia and the rural as an abrasive region for LGBTQIA+ people to exist in. This perception is so ingrained that even *Queering the Countryside* reproduces narratives of the rural as a hostile environment for queer folk. As Mary Gray, Colin Johnson, and Brian Gilley explain, "The naturalization of rural heteronormativity finds its footing in the equally negative experiences of violence, intolerance, and right-wing political discourse."[27] Though it is not arguable that existing as an LGBTQIA+ person can be difficult, many Appalachian queers don't feel any more marginalized than their counterparts elsewhere in the country. The politics of rural queer visibility are complicated by navigating relationships of familiarity and belonging, as well as notions of queer visibility that are premised on the urban.[28]

QUEER TOXICITIES: APPALACHIAN NONHUMAN ECOLOGIES AND THREATENED BODIES

The Appalachian region as an imagined space in American mythology paints the culture and its people as "queer" in the sense of "peculiar."[29] While the exact boundaries of Appalachia may shift, the idea of Appalachia has been perpetuated for the last century and a half. This construction of Appalachia as a separate region, seen as in need of development, has positioned it as "queer" in the national imaginary. We argue that this broad view of the region as queer opens the door for a more specific queer analysis of Appalachian naturecultures, drawing connections between the perceived peculiarity of Appalachia and its non/human inhabitants, including, but not limited to, LGBTQIA+ Appalachians. We understand this diffuse sense of queerness through the lens of toxicity, which connects with regional histories of development and environmental exploitations that have profoundly shaped Appalachian naturecultures.

In Garringer's master's thesis, one of her interviewees, Kenny Bilbrey, speaks directly to how nature and culture are intertwined, as well as how queerness moves beyond human queer identities: "I feel like a part of being Appalachian is inevitably queer—whether or not you identify as queer. I think the whole experience is. Because it's very self-sufficient in some ways: figuring out your own thing to do if you live in a rural part of Appalachia. Navigating the importance of family and all the other importance that can often be associated with this area—the closeness of family or being in love with this biodiverse place that has a bunch of weird bugs and plants. I just think the whole thing is really queer."[30]

According to Bilbrey, Appalachian queerness expands beyond their experience as a trans person, to include other elements that are thought of as fundamentally Appalachian—including close kinship ties and the richness of nonhuman life.[31] Bilbrey's perception of Appalachia as not only a culturally but also an ecologically queer place speaks to Mortimer-Sandilands and Erickson's call for "offering new modes of theorizing human/more-than-human relationships" as a form of queer spatial/ecological politics.[32] Beyond that, however, Bilbrey contends that *being* Appalachian itself is a queer experience.

Bilbrey understands this queerness as explicitly existing in a relationship with nature. This destabilizes the nature/culture divide, which would posit that culture, which exists in the realm of the human, exists separately from nature and nonhuman life-forms. Instead of reproducing this divide by solely examining the important work of documenting LGBTQIA+ life in Appalachia, we engage with the concept of naturecultures, examining the ways in which human and nonhuman life exists in the context of an Appalachian region that is already queer.[33]

This expansive view of queerness maps onto the larger discussion of "queer inhumanisms," a term selected by Dana Luciano and Mel Y. Chen because "[they] wanted to emphasize the processual aspects of queer inhumanness, the way it invoked becoming, rather than dividing the world into two static and antagonistic camps; [they] meant to highlight the dynamic and diffuse encounters through which those two categories were continually re/constituted."[34]

Queer inhumanism works to decenter the norm of the human and examines more-than-human relationships.[35] This move in scholarship may be novel in Appalachian studies, but as Métis scholar Zoe Todd points out, to Indigenous ways of knowing, there is nothing novel about this recognition of the inhuman and environmental entanglements.[36]

We understand Appalachian naturecultures through the lens of toxicity, as a recurring theme that has marked the bodies and landscapes as Other. Rather than simply reading the Appalachian environment as toxic because of the presence of material toxins, we seek to go further to discuss how the figure of the "toxin" has permeated Appalachian naturecultures. According to Stacy Alaimo, "The environment has been drained of its blood, its lively creatures, its interactions and relations—in short, all that is recognizable as 'nature'—in order that it become a mere empty space, an 'uncontested ground,' for human 'development.'"[37] Countering this static understanding of the environment, we examine the naturecultural interactions that are exemplified through toxins and toxicity.

Toxins become the inhuman element that animates queerness in Appalachian landscapes. *Toxic* serves as a descriptor of both the damaged landscapes and Appalachian culture. Through a relational approach, these two toxic elements are not separate; they reinforce each other to create a queered Appalachia. Mel Chen defines *toxin* as something threatening that "enlivens morbidity and a fear of death."[38]

Appalachia's recent history has been marked by decades of resource extraction. As Mamone of Queer Appalachia[39] and Sarah Meng write, "Minorities in Appalachia are in the trenches of the culture war. The entire region is addicted to fossil fuel and, as of November 2016, the coal industry has affected every person."[40] Histories of timber and coal, and more recently pipelines, such as the Mountain Valley Pipeline, have been a cornerstone of Appalachian economies. Even tourism, offered as an alternative form of economic development, can be conceptualized as a different form of extraction, often capitalizing on the images of Appalachia's bucolic past.

These marginalizations, both economic and cultural, have positioned Appalachia as Other, simultaneously more proximate and prone to harm and also romanticized and revered as closer to nature. These dual images, a staple in depictions of Appalachia, show two different yet related ways of approaching Appalachian naturecultures, each with their ties to queer toxicity. The positive image of Appalachia as closer to nature evokes ties to the landscape damaged by coal mining, as well as a temporal positioning removed from modernity. The negative image of Appalachia relies on depictions of the region as violent and drug addicted. Yet these depictions, while inherently queer in an inhuman sense, also position Appalachia as anti-queer, as a racist, backward, insular region that is intolerant of differences.

These depictions can be countered by the queer counterarchive. As discussed earlier in this chapter, Appalachian queers argue against metronormative depictions of the region as hostile to queer life. Appalachian queers also relate their queerness to decolonial praxis by blockading pipelines and using histories of nuclear war to ask how we can build accountability in the ways we encounter difference.[41] Extractive industries and violence are part of Appalachian toxicity and queer experiences.

The trope of toxicity provides another connection to queering on an inhuman scale. The work of the toxin as enlivening certain discourses and connections provides a form of queering. According to Mel Chen, this amounts to a form of animacy. "Animacy is built on the recognition that abstract concepts, inanimate objects, and things in between can be queered and racialized without human bodies present, quite beyond questions of personification."[42] Queerness is, as Jasbir Puar argues, not an identity but an assemblage that is temporally and spatially contingent.[43] Queerness is also materially contingent, we argue, shaped by the ongoing transcorporeal interactions with toxicity that is both material and metaphoric.

As Adam Denney writes, "[Appalachia is] a region where poverty is rampant [and] ecological resources are privatized . . . [this] takes a toll on the body of Appalachia."[44] Not only has Appalachia been considered culturally toxic but it is also perceived as environmentally toxic as a result of decades of resource extraction.[45] Appalachians can be perceived as "intoxicated subjects" of the nation for falling prey to environmental pollution caused by fracking, coal slurry, and factory farm runoff.[46] Toxins do not just exist as part of the landscape but seep into bodies, becoming incorporated, providing evidence for the imbrication of nature and culture. According to Chen, "Images of the cultural practices of others, if sought from a vulnerable position, can easily slide into fodder that strengthens defensive or protective nationalist sentiment and build a sovereign project."[47] The toxicity of Appalachia becomes a threat to nationalist projects of development that seek to absorb the region into the rest of the nation.

Toxins work to queer the Appalachian body and also position it as more proximate to harm, as well as making Appalachia seem more likely to be harmful to the rest of the country. As a place labeled as deviant and dangerous, Appalachia becomes a site for nationalist interventions or serves as a counterexample to illustrate national progress. Toxicity becomes a justification for further damage to Appalachia, through continued practices of extraction, as well as an explanation for Appalachia's seeming political backwardness, making it an easy political scapegoat. Toxicity then becomes both a cause and consequence of Appalachia's long-standing queerness. Such as queerness extends well beyond human identities or the anthropomorphization of the landscape to focus squarely on the inhuman elements that queer the region.

Seeing Appalachia as queer goes beyond the important work of uplifting LGBTQIA+ voices in the region. Queering Appalachia allows us to not only examine the past, through cultural representations and archiving projects, but also ask what queer futures might be possible in Appalachia.

CONCLUSION

Today when I hear queer activists say the word *redneck* like a cuss word, I think of those men, backs of their necks turning red in the summertime from long days of work outside, felling trees, pulling fishnets, bailing hay. I think of my butchness, grounded there, overlaid by a queer, urban sensibility. A body of white, rural, working-class values. I still feel an allegiance to this body, even as I reject the virulent racism, the unexamined destruction of forest and river.[48]

—Eli Clare, *Exile and Pride: Disability,*
Queerness, and Liberation

Futurity has been a key concept in queer studies and a pressing topic in mainstream conversations about Appalachia, especially in relation to questions of sustainability and the transition away from a coal-based economy. Understanding Appalachia as a queer region with more-than-human ecologies suggests that we might require a queer type of sustainability. A queer sustainability builds on these more-than-human queer ecologies. Queer ecologies contend that we cannot separate nature and culture in our efforts, and thus a view of sustainability focused solely on the natural world is inherently insufficient. Indeed, we must recognize the past exclusions of sustainability, including the settler colonial legacies of viewing the wilderness as something to be controlled—a gendered and racialized pursuit.[49] Sustainability today is likewise limited. A "greenwashed" capitalism fails to grapple with the excesses and environmental damage enacted by large corporations and shifts the focus to a neoliberal attention on individual responsibility. This misdirection replicates existing inequities, such as ableist scapegoating of disabled people's use of resources necessary to survive, complaints about poor and working-class folks' lack of "good choices," and perhaps even depictions of people in Appalachia as too stupid to know what is good for them.[50]

We argue for a post-coal future in Appalachia that seriously engages with the history of not only extractive industry but its legacies of toxicity and queerness. In the national imaginary of Appalachia, the dominance of coal has been equated with a dominance of conservative tradition that erases queer lives. However, we argue that extractive industries have worked to queer the entire region. Environmental toxins engage with human and more-than-human histories, creating a dynamic cast of queer agents. Seeing Appalachia as a queer region avoids static, single-issue approaches to regional development that separate the Appalachian landscape from the complexities of naturecultures.

However, as Eli Clare and Aurora Levins Morales contended in 1999, our bodies and lands can be reclaimed.[51] Our bodies and the Appalachian environment—queered through extraction and represented as the Other in the national imagining—are political. Clare pushes us to explore our bodies as "liberation, joy, fury, hope, a will to refigure the word."[52] If our Appalachian bodies and our Appalachian natures are queer, what does an Appalachia futurity based on queer liberation look like?

Queering the region also involves acknowledging the history of colonialism, genocide, and self-indigenization that contributes to the erasure of Indigenous lives. This past is crucial to reckon with, as post-coal sustainability must not be equated with a postcolonial sustainability that glosses over the settler-colonialism and relegates racist and anti-Native sentiment as something of the Appalachian past. While we argue against Appalachia being stuck in the past, these histories are still with us, as are movements that reckon with them.

stef schuster cautions against a queer (or quare) intersectional methodology that is simply additive.[53] While projects documenting LGBTQIA+ life in Appalachia and elsewhere are important in challenging dominant representations, in this chapter, we try to push beyond a formula in which queer people in Appalachia equal a queer Appalachia. Instead, we destabilize these categories, recognizing the multiple groups, especially nonwhite folks, who have been excluded both from representations of Appalachia and from mainstream queerness, as well as from representations of specifically Appalachian queerness.[54] We also attempt to move discussions of queerness beyond the human, to encompass queer toxicities and ecologies.[55] Through this, we argue that Appalachia is already queer—a point of view that is best exemplified through the examination of the queer inhumanisms and ecologies.

Queer ecologies bring together the contradictory and surprising histories of Appalachian places to help us imagine new potential futures. These futures are possible not in spite of histories of environmental extraction and damage but *because* of them. Queer ecologies suggest the need to live with damaged environments.[56] When Luciano and Chen ask if the queer has ever been human, they respond both yes and no—yes because the interrogation of how queer people have been dehumanized inherently positions the human as the ideal and no "because queer theory has long been suspicious of the politics of rehabilitation and inclusion to which liberal-humanist values lead, and because 'full humanity' has never been the only horizon for queer becoming."[57]

This *no* answer is especially instrumental in our reading of how Appalachia is queer. Seeing queer Appalachia as an assemblage consisting of a diversity of actors—both human and nonhuman—contests development policies that engage with only economic or human aspects of sustainability or that position a rehabilitation to a normative state as the only possible future. Queer existence suggests that other worlds might be possible and even more desirable. Perhaps one important aspect of LGBTQIA+ archiving projects is that they show us histories of queer resistance and queer world making—providing a history to help guide us into the future.

NOTES

1. J. D. Vance, *Hillbilly Elegy: A Memoir of a Family and Culture in Crisis* (New York: Harper Collins, 2016); Elizabeth Catte, *What You Are Getting Wrong about Appalachia* (Cleveland: Belt, 2018); Anthony Harkins and Meredith McCarroll, eds., *Appalachian Reckoning: A Region Responds to Hillbilly Elegy* (Morgantown: West Virginia University Press, 2019); as well as Steven Stoll, *Ramp Hollow: The Ordeal of Appalachia* (New York: Hill and Wang, 2017); Jessica Wilkerson, *To Live Here You Have to Fight: How Women Led Appalachian Movements for Social Justice* (Urbana: University of Illinois Press, 2019); Jessica Cory, *Mountains Piled upon Mountains: Appalachian Nature Writing in the Anthropocene* (Morgantown: West Virginia University Press, 2019).

2. *Place* is a loaded term meant to describe, as explained by Stephen Fisher and Barbara Ellen Smith, "at once a symbolic landscape of cultural tradition and human connection (the place of home) and the tangible ground that is a source of livelihood and focus of contestation (forests, watersheds, farms)." S. L. Fisher and B. E. Smith, *Transforming Places: Lessons from Appalachia* (Urbana: University of Illinois Press, 2012), 1; Julia Fox, "Mountaintop Removal in West Virginia: An Environmental Sacrifice Zone," *Organization & Environment* 12, no. 2 (1999): 163–83; Catte, *What You Are Getting Wrong*, 8.

3. Beth Berila explains that "in hegemonic discourses of the nation, references to the 'public' usually refer to the 'general population' from which queers, people of color, the poor, women, and people living with AIDS have presumably already been purged." Beth Berila, "Toxic Bodies? ACT UP's Disruption of the Heteronormative Landscape of the Nation," in *New Perspectives on Environmental Justice: Gender, Sexuality, and Activism*, ed. Rachel Stein (New Brunswick, NJ: Rutgers University, 2004), 127–36. The America/Appalachia dualism then not only erased LGBTQIA+ folk living in Appalachia but depicted Appalachia itself as *outside* the nation.

4. Hannah Conway, "Crafting Queer Histories of Technology," in *Y'all Means All: The Emerging Voices Queering Appalachia*, ed. Z. Zane McNeill (Oakland, CA: PM, 2022), 174–75.

5. Donna J. Haraway, *The Companion Species Manifesto: Dogs, People, and Significant Otherness*, vol. 1 (Chicago: Prickly Paradigm Press, 2003).

6. Mel Y. Chen, "Toxic Animacies: Inanimate Affections," *GLQ* 17, no. 2–3 (2011): 265–86, 266.

7. Chen, "Toxic Animacies," 279.

8. Queer theory was partially born from the AIDS epidemic and, therefore, is very interested in the *queer* as the dying. Keystone works are Lee Edelman's *No Future: Queer Theory and the Death Drive* (Durham, NC: Duke University Press, 2004); Jasbir Puar's *Terrorist Assemblages: Homonationalism in Queer Times* (Durham, NC: Duke University Press, 2007); and Jose Esteban's *Cruising Utopia: The Then and There of Queer Futurity* (New York: NYU Press, 2009). For queer time, see Jack Halberstam, *In a Queer Time and Place: Transgender Bodies, Subcultural Lives* (New York: NYU Press, 2005), 36–37.

9. Hillery Glasby, Sherrie Gradin, and Rachael Ryerson, introduction to *Storytelling in Queer Appalachia: Imagining and Writing the Unspeakable Other* (Morgantown: West Virginia University Press, 2020), 1–15, 1.

10. Mary L. Gray, Colin R. Johnson, and Brian J. Gilley, eds., *Queering the Countryside: New Frontiers in Rural Queer Studies* (New York: New York University Press, 2016), 4.

11. Despite the breadth of examples of trans and queer life in Appalachia; leftist thought, histories of labor resistance, and radical politics and organizing; feminist and pro-life community groups; environmental activists fighting for ecojustice and mobilizing direct action efforts; Affrilachian existence; and a history of thriving immigrant populations, Appalachia is still most often perceived as "why we have a Trump Presidency." This illustrates Catte's explanation that "defining Appalachian culture is often a top-down process, in which individuals with power or capital tell us who or what we are." Catte, *What You Are Getting Wrong*, 11. Vance is certainly one of those voices, despite him being perceived as an "'authentic' and 'credible' voice of the region and the white working class." *Hillbilly Elegy* supposedly explains the region's embrace of Trump and conservative politics in the wake of the 2016 election. Because of this book, Vance has received not only symbolic accolades, such as prestige and popularity, but also financial gifts, as he has sold over a million copies, gone on speaking tours around the country, and had his book turned into a movie.

12. Fisher and Smith, introduction, 2. This includes both the historic conceptualization of Appalachia as backward and also contemporary understandings of Appalachia as a "lost" place riddled by poverty and opioid addiction.

13. LGBTQIA+ people, people of color, immigrants, leftists, feminists, and ecojustice activists.

14. Stephen Fisher and Barbara Ellen Smith, "Internal Colony—Are You Sure? Defining, Theorizing, Organizing Appalachia," *Journal of Appalachian Studies* 22, no. 1 (2016): 45–50.

15. Ada Smith, "Appalachian Futurism," *Journal of Appalachian Studies* 22, no. 1 (2016): 73–75.

16. Barbara Ellen Smith, "De-gradations of Whiteness: Appalachia and the Complexities of Race," *Journal of Appalachian Studies* 10, no. 1/2 (2004): 38–39.

17. *Journal of Appalachian Studies* 22, no. 1 (2016) has robust debate on this subject. For a response to these articles, see also Jacob Stump, "What Is the Use of the Colonial Model (or, Better Yet, the Concept of Coloniality) for Studying Appalachia?," *Journal of Appalachian Studies* 24, no. 2 (2018): 151–67.

18. Stephen Pearson, "'The Last Bastion of Colonialism': Appalachian Settler Colonialism and Self-Indigenization," *American Indian Culture and Research Journal* 37, no. 2 (2013): 166.

19. Glasby, Gradin, and Ryerson, introduction, 1.

20. Halberstam, *In a Queer Time and Place*, 36–37.

21. Rae Garringer, "'Well, We're Fabulous and We're Appalachians, so We're Fabulachians': Country Queers in Central Appalachia," *Southern Cultures* 23, no. 1 (March 22, 2017): 79–92, 80.

22. Lydia McDermott, "The Crik Is Crooked: Appalachia as Movable Queer Space," in *Storytelling in Queer Appalachia: Imagining and Writing the Unspeakable Other*, ed. Hillery Glasby, Sherrie Gradin, and Rachael Ryerson (Morgantown: West Virginia University Press, 2020), 113–27, 121.

23. Adam Denney, "A Drowning in the Foothills," in *Storytelling in Queer Appalachia: Imagining and Writing the Unspeakable Other*, ed. Hillery Glasby, Sherrie Gradin, and Rachael Ryerson (Morgantown: West Virginia University Press, 2020), 61–72, 63.

24. Mary L. Gray, *Out in the Country: Youth, Media, and Queer Visibility in Rural America* (New York: New York University Press, 2009), 9.

25. Justin Ray Dutton, "Challenging Dominant Christianity's Queerphobic Rhetoric," in *Storytelling in Queer Appalachia: Imagining and Writing the Unspeakable Other*, ed. Hillery Glasby, Sherrie Gradin, and Rachael Ryerson (Morgantown: West Virginia University Press, 2020), 37–57, 51.

26. This quote is from an interview that was published on the Country Queers website in 2013. It is no longer posted.

27. Gray, Johnson, and Gilley, *Queering the Countryside*, 13.

28. Gray, *Out in the Country*.

29. McDermott, "Crik Is Crooked," 114.

30. Garringer, "'Well, We're Fabulous and We're Appalachians.'"

31. Garringer, "'Well, We're Fabulous and We're Appalachians,'" 1.

32. Catriona Mortimer-Sandilands and Bruce Erickson, eds., *Queer Ecologies: Sex, Nature, Politics, Desire* (Bloomington: University of Indiana Press, 2010), 23.

33. Donna J. Haraway, *The Companion Species Manifesto: Dogs, People, and Significant Otherness*, vol. 1 (Chicago: Prickly Paradigm Press, 2003).

34. Dana Luciano and Mel Y. Chen, "Queer Inhumanisms," *GLQ: A Journal of Lesbian and Gay Studies* 25, no. 1 (2019): 113–17, 13.

35. See Dana Luciano and Mel Y. Chen, eds., "Queer Inhumanisms," *GLQ* 21, no. 2–3 (2015): 284.

36. Zoe Todd, "An Indigenous Feminist's Take on the Ontological Turn: 'Ontology' Is Just Another Word for Colonialism," *Journal of Historical Sociology* 29, no. 1 (2016): 4–22.

37. Stacy Alaimo, *Bodily Natures: Science, Environment, and the Material Self* (Bloomington: Indiana University Press, 2010), 2–3.

38. Chen, "Toxic Animacies," 265.

39. On August 3, 2020, investigative reporter Emma Copley Eisenberg published "The Tale of Queer Appalachia" in the *Washington Post* that alleged that Queer Appalachia, the collective Mamone formed, mismanaged donations, censored criticisms from Black and Indigenous People, and used artwork from Black creatives without their permission. To learn more about this incident, we recommend reading Maxwell Cloe, "Our Own Images and Truths? The Futures and Failures of the Queer Appalachia Project," *Journal of Appalachian Studies* 28, no. 1 (2022): 30–48, https://doi.org/10.5406/23288612.28.1.03.

40. Gina Mamone and Sarah E. Meng, "Queer Appalachia: A Homespun Praxis of Rural Resistance in Appalachian Media," in *Storytelling in Queer Appalachia: Imagining and Writing the Unspeakable Other*, ed. Hillery Glasby, Sherrie Gradin, and Rachael Ryerson (Morgantown: West Virginia University Press, 2020), 197–218, 205.

41. Z. Zane McNeill, *Y'all Means All: The Emerging Voices Queering Appalachia* (Oakland, CA: PM Press, 2022).

42. Chen, "Toxic Animacies," 265.

43. Puar, *Terrorist Assemblages*.

44. Adam Denney, "A Drowning in the Foothills," in *Storytelling in Queer Appalachia: Imagining and Writing the Unspeakable Other*, ed. Hillery Glasby, Sherrie Gradin, and Rachael Ryerson (Morgantown: West Virginia University Press, 2020), 63.

45. Illustrated through Vance's emphasis on the genetic disposition of the Scots-Irish to be violent or the conception of incest as "poisoning" the national body. Beth Berila, "Toxic Bodies? ACT UP's Disruption of the Heteronormative Landscape of the Nation," in *New Perspectives on Environmental Justice: Gender, Sexuality, and Activism*, ed. Rachel Stein (New Brunswick, NJ: Rutgers University, 2004), 127–36. This perception engages with a further set of dualisms, such as "stained/unstained and impure/pure [which are] integral to the interlocking projects of nation building and heteronormativity." Berila, 127–36.

46. Chen, "Toxic Animacies," 276.

47. Mel Y. Chen, "Racialized Toxins and Sovereign Fantasies," *Discourse* 29, no. 2 (2007): 367–83, 371.

48. Eli Clare, *Exile and Pride: Disability, Queerness and Liberation* (Durham, NC: Duke University Press, 2009), 11.

49. Karl Jacoby, *Crimes against Nature: Squatters, Poachers, Thieves and the Hidden History of American Conservation* (Berkeley: University of California Press, 2001); Jake Kosek, "Purity and Pollution: Racial Degradation and Environmental Anxieties," in *Liberation Ecologies: Environment, Development, Social Movements*, ed. M. Peet and R. Watts (New York: Routledge, 2004), 125–65; Bruce Braun, "On the Raggedy Edge of Risk: Articulations of Race and Nature after Biology," in *Race, Nature, and the Politics of Difference*, ed. D. Moore, J. Kosek, and A. Pandian (Durham, NC: Duke University Press, 2003), 175–203.

50. Imani Barbarin, "Climate Darwinism Makes Disabled People Expendable," *Forbes*, November 2, 2019, https://www.forbes.com/sites/imanibarbarin/2019/11/02/climate-darwinism-makes-disabled-people-expendable/; Alice Wong, "The Rise and Fall of the Plastic Straw," *Catalyst: Feminism, Theory, Technoscience* 5, no. 1 (April 1, 2019): 1–12.

51. Clare, *Exile and Pride*, xix.

52. Clare, *Exile and Pride*, 13.

53. stef m. schuster, "Quaring the Queer in Appalachia," *Appalachian Journal* 46, no. 1–2 (2018): 72–84, 80.

54. Cloe, "Our Own Images and Truths?," 30–48.

55. We recognize that categories are shifting and unstable. schuster turns to Jasbir Puar's *Terrorist Assemblages: Homonationalism in Queer Time* (Durham, NC: Duke University Press, 2007) concept of assemblages to challenge notions of inclusion that are based on the idea that categories are discrete and knowable. schuster, "Quaring the Queer in Appalachia"; Puar, *Terrorist Assemblages*.

56. As Anna Tsing in *The Mushroom at the End of the World* (Princeton, NJ: Princeton University Press, 2015) shows by tracking the growth and transnational production of a mushroom, surprising ways of coming together can arise out of the end of the world. These formations, much like Appalachia, are queer.

57. Dana Luciano and Mel Y. Chen, "Has The Queer Ever Been Human?," *GLQ* 21, no. 2–3 (June 2015): 182–207, 188.

QUEERS EMBRACING PLACE IN APPALACHIA

The Importance of Masculinities for Queer Acceptance

Baker A. Rogers

I'm the guy who drinks whiskey and moonshine on the tailgate of his truck with his bird dog, that's the category I fit into.
—Mason, a thirty-four-year-old Indigenous, Two-Spirit, trans man of color

I feel like a part of being Appalachian is inevitably queer—whether or not you identify as queer. I think the whole experience is. . . . Navigating the importance of family and all the other importance that can often be associated with this area—the closeness of family or being in love with this biodiverse place that has a bunch of weird bugs and plants.
—Kenny Bilbrey

Land Acknowledgment of some *of the Indigenous Nations who have historical claim to the territory now known as Appalachia*: Massawomeck, Moneton, Tutelo, Abenaki/ Abenaquis, Lenni-Lenape, Susquehannock, Pocumtuc, Munsee Lenape, Cherokee, Mochican, Piscataway, Monacan, Nanrantsouak, Paugussett, Manahoac, Penobscot,

Wappinger, Arosaguntacook, Wabanaki Confederacy, Pequawket, S'atsoyaha (Yuchi), and Nipmuc.

These are the nations acknowledged by the Appalachian Trail Conservancy whose land touches this trail; there are many other nations who have a claim to the larger region of Appalachia.

In the foothills of the Blue Ridge Mountains sits the little town of Toccoa, Georgia. Toccoa is in Stephens, Georgia, one of thirty-seven counties in the state considered part of the Appalachian region. Toccoa is the location of the 2001 documentary *Southern Comfort*,[2] "the first non-fiction film to intimately tell a trans-to-trans love story."[3] The documentary tells the story of Robert Eads, a fifty-two-year-old "female-to-male transsexual," and his battle to find health care to treat his ovarian cancer as a trans man in the rural South. However, the story is about much more than his individual struggle; it is a story of hope, perseverance, and love among queer people, which has always existed in Appalachia, the southern United States, and rural areas.

Southern Comfort provides an early, and honest, glimpse into the real lives of trans people in this region of the country. Through the voices of Robert and his chosen family, audiences, many for the first time, were able to hear from those "rarely heard . . . [and] commonly thought to be non-existent." Despite the discrimination Robert faced and his resulting untimely death, his story also demonstrates a degree of the acceptance that accompanies conventional masculinities, even when they are queer, in Appalachia and in the South more broadly. Robert presents as "a striking figure: sharp-tongued, bearded, tobacco pipe in hand," and proudly claims his hillbilly identity.[4] At the beginning of the film, Robert even discusses how the local Ku Klux Klan attempted to recruit him. As one film reviewer put it, "As he speaks in a slow cadence, taking a pull on his pipe and drawing his long, lined face into a grin . . . *Southern*

Comfort almost feels like a film about a Southern fella spinning a tall tale about things he couldn't possibly have seen." Like Robert, many queer people claim their homes in locations where queers are expected to flee, such as Appalachia, rural areas, and the southeastern United States.

Applying queer, Indigenous, and Appalachian studies methodologies, I explore stories of queers embracing their Appalachian, southern, Indigenous, and rural identities. By embracing place identities—individuals' use of place and physical environments to define their personal identity, as in identification as Appalachian, southern, or country—some queer Appalachian people can overcome the pull of the "gay imaginary."[5] *Gay imaginary* refers to the metronormative story that says queer people must move to the city to find safety and happiness because queer life and urban life are assumed to be synonymous.

Here, with Robert's story, my own story, and the stories of two trans men from Appalachia whom I interviewed for my research on trans men in the southeastern United States, I seek to challenge the limited view of queer life. Our stories demonstrate a broader trend for queer people in Appalachia, rural areas, and the South—that is, happiness is often found where one feels at home, as opposed to where one is "supposed to be." I seek to examine the ways that many queer people are embracing place identities—particularly, place identities that cultural knowledge would tell us are contradictory to our gender and sexuality.

MY STORY AND CONNECTION TO APPALACHIA

My family members are "rednecks," not "hillbillies." To outsiders, this may seem like splitting hairs, but to rednecks and hillbillies, it isn't. Sure, they look similar—white working class or lower-middle class—and they usually get along okay, but the two identities have different origins and meanings. Historian and educator Anthony

Harkins explains what these concepts have in common today: since the 1970s, they have been "reappropriated by some working-class and lower-middle-class whites as badges of class and racial identity and pride." He goes on: "In this context, they mark opposition to (or at least distinction from) hegemonic middle-class social aspirations and norms and, less explicitly, to the relative gain in status of African Americans and other minority social groups."[6] Where they differ is that hillbillies are almost always tied to the mountains. No one I knew lived in the mountains or made moonshine, but my family had a guy up in the hills of North Carolina who did. Hillbillies also seem more benign in popular imagination, whereas rednecks are more politicized. *Redneck* signifies "a cultural identifier positioned in dual opposition to both the power and cultural values of the upper-middle class and what it perceived to be a welfare-dependent and minority underclass."[7]

Coming from a "redneck" family, steeped in racism and anti-intellectualism, my accent and background weren't "right" for academia, and still aren't, for that matter. I didn't know what I was "supposed" to know when I got to college, nor did I know how to act or perform outside of my home setting. I was expected to leave home if I wanted to "make it," but I had no idea what *making it* meant or how to go about that. I didn't even know which fork to pick up first or that you weren't supposed to eat fried chicken with your fingers.

My family suffers from many of the same problems that have been used to define a limited version of Appalachia, including being racist, having drug and alcohol problems, and dealing with crippling poverty, obesity, and poor health more generally. We did not have it easy, but we are white, *very* white according to my 23andMe DNA results. I was not taught about racism or colonization in school. To be fair, I wasn't taught much of anything in my rural South Carolina school, but I definitely did not learn about injustices experienced around the world. My family members owned slaves at some point, they worked with corrupt people, and I am sure that my direct connections to the KKK are no further than three generations behind me.

Although I didn't know Appalachia was a distinct region at the time, as I was growing up my idea of Appalachia was the North Carolina mountains. This included Maggie Valley, Cherokee, Blowing Rock, and Grandfather Mountain (in Linville, but we just called it Grandfather Mountain); Popcorn Sutton, the infamous moonshiner and bootlegger from Maggie Valley, whom my dad claims to have known; the Cherokee Qualla Boundary, where we bought bows and arrows, as well as "Indian" clothes and moccasins; and Tweetsie Railroad, where, as kids, we were dressed as prostitutes (since we were girls; boys were dressed as cowboys) and put onstage to dance for the guests. Riding the "Tweetsie Railroad" as children, my sister and I watched fights performed live between the "cowboys and Indians," then went to the bar to get fake beers and watch a gunfight in the streets. All in all, my sister and I loved Appalachia and all the misinformed and racist entertainment we could get. Just to be clear, I applaud the Native American people who made a lot of money off us *yonega*s engaging in racist tourism, but I know that most of that money went to colonizers, not Native people.

When I was twenty-six years old, I moved to Starkville, Mississippi, for graduate school at Mississippi State University. Starkville is in Oktibbeha County, which is one of the 420 counties across thirteen states that make up Appalachia according to the Appalachian Regional Commission (ARC). Of course, the ARC is a federal-state government partnership that arose out of the Johnson administration's War on Poverty in 1965 and is mainly concerned with the economic development of the region,[8] so these boundaries can be contested by actual Appalachian people. As Elizabeth Catte expounds, because the primary lens of ARC is economic, "one of its first tasks was to grade each county thought to be Appalachian on a scale of economic distress to administer federal aid efficiently. By its design, the region came to be defined by poverty, and subsequently poverty came to be defined by the region."[9]

Nonetheless, for four years I lived in a county at least coded as Appalachia during my late twenties. However, being in graduate school often insulates people from the actual communities in which they live, so my own personal experience of Appalachia is limited at best. On the contrary, my southern and rural experiences are rich, and my feelings that the South, for better or for worse, is my home helped me understand the importance of embracing place identities where one feels comfortable, not where one is "supposed to be" happy. After a brief two-year stint in the Midwest, I am now back home in the South and so happy to be here. My "exile" outside the South was "laced with pain, instability, and longing," a similar experience for many queer southerners and Appalachians.[10]

People often ask why I would choose to live in this region of the country as a genderqueer, trans masculine lesbian who is married to a woman and has a child who is one-fourth Hispanic. My answer is that I love the South, and even though there are problems here, at least I understand them. I know how to navigate my home. I know where to go and where to avoid. I know who to befriend and who to dodge. I do not know these things in other areas of the country, where bigotry often runs just as deep although it is less obvious and is often concealed. Through my research on queer people in the South, I find that my feelings of home and connection with this region of the country and rural areas are not unique. Like scholar Mary L. Gray explains in *Out in the Country*, "Far from feeling estranged out in the country . . . I felt at home."[11] Many queer people are embracing Appalachia, the South, and rural areas across the country.

WHAT/WHERE IS APPALACHIA?

Defining Appalachia, as with any region, is always political. By Appalachia, I am referring to the region writer and historian Elizabeth

Catte succinctly defines in *What You Are Getting Wrong about Appalachia*: "Appalachia is, often simultaneously, a political construction, a vast geographic region, and a spot that occupies an unparalleled place in our cultural imagination. . . . Appalachia is an approximately 700,000-square-mile region of the eastern United States . . . loosely defined by the arc of the Appalachian Mountains that begins in Alabama and ends in New York. . . . There are thirteen states with Appalachian counties . . . and West Virginia is the only state entirely within Appalachia. Appalachia's population is approximately twenty-five million individuals . . . [the region's] biggest export . . . people."[12]

Much of Appalachia is rural, "geographically and geopolitically," which "complicates queer identity, queer community, and queer experiences" because many queer people in rural areas must "combat stereotypes that associate their ruralness with backwardness, ignorance, and dirt(iness) and their queerness with urbanity."[13]

One important and well-known feature of the Appalachian region of the United States is the Appalachian National Scenic Trail, commonly called the Appalachian Trail or AT. The AT "is the longest hiking-only footpath in the world, measuring roughly 2,190 miles in length." The Appalachian Trail Conservancy explains that the AT "travels through fourteen states along the crests and valleys of the Appalachian Mountain Range, from its southern terminus at Springer Mountain, Georgia, to the northern terminus at Katahdin, Maine."[14]

I bring up the AT as a reference point for also understanding the rich Native lands that make up Appalachia. The AT "runs through 22 Native Nations' traditional territories and holds an abundant amount of Indigenous American history." Therefore, it is impossible to answer the question of what and where Appalachia is without acknowledging the Native Peoples whom these lands belong to. While there are more than twenty-two Native Nations within Appalachia at large, researchers and activists have worked to clearly name and map the nations along the AT. These include Massawomeck, Moneton, Tutelo, Abenaki/Abenaquis, Lenni-Lenape, Susquehannock, Pocumtuc, Munsee Lenape, Cherokee, Mochican, Piscataway, Monacan, Nanrantsouak, Paugussett, Manahoac, Penobscot, Wappinger, Arosaguntacook, Wabanaki Confederacy, Pequawket, S'atsoyaha (Yuchi), and Nipmuc.[15]

APPALACHIA IS ALREADY QUEER

To be clear, this chapter is not my attempt to queer Appalachia; rather, my goal is to demonstrate that Appalachia is, and has always been, already queer. From the Radical Faeries and queer-safe Short Mountain Sanctuary in rural Tennessee to the over ten thousand queer people who gather yearly in Asheville, North Carolina, for the Blue Ridge Pride Festival.[16]

As Karina Walters and colleagues explain, many Native societies incorporated gender diversity beyond the binary far before European colonization.[17] It was colonization of Native lands that led to the condemnation of those who lived outside the binary gender and sexual expectations of the European norms. Walters et al. discuss current Native efforts to "transcend the Eurocentric binary categorization of homosexual vs. heterosexual or male vs. female; to signal the fluidity and non-linearity of identity processes; and to counteract heterosexism in Native communities and racism in LGBT communities."[18] The study of Appalachia, or any Native lands, cannot proceed without acknowledging the impacts of colonization. Scott Lauria Morgensen explains that "Heteronormative national whiteness established its rule by sexualizing the racial, economic, and political subjugation of peoples of color in the name of protecting white settler society from queer endangerment."[19] Overall, Appalachia needs no queer saviors to make it a queerer place. However, I argue, what is needed is more storytelling and spotlight on the wonderful ways this region is queer and the reasons this matters so deeply for queer equity in the United States.

An intersectional, feminist, queer lens that considers how the various aspects of identity (including gender, sexuality, sex, race, ethnicity, class, location, etc.) intersect with one another to create unique views of the world for everyone is essential. As I discuss stories of queers in Appalachia, I explore how identities intersect with rural environments and regional locations. I also demonstrate the importance of masculinities and their effects on queer people's experiences in rural areas.

While theories provide a way to better understand our world, as with any type of microscope or lens, they also have the consequence of limiting our scope. Therefore, to be truly intersectional, we must broaden our theoretical knowledge. I have been privileged to see the world anew through the lens of queer Indigenous studies, Appalachian studies, and queer ecologies. Each of these lenses values the importance of stories and storytelling to understanding truth. I particularly appreciate how author and educator Robert Gipe explained the importance of stories in his essay "How Appalachian I Am":

> I was raised to make meaning by telling stories and listening to stories. I was taught that meaning is complex and shifting and difficult to state . . . that one won't be able to make any sense of a thing until one hears not one but many stories about it. . . . I was raised to believe this ability to make our own meaning out of the world is what freedom is, and what joy is, and meaning making is a right we all have. . . . And we are all obliged to work to make sure each of us has the right to hear and tell all the stories and each make our own meaning out of them and the world.[20]

My new lens and the stories I have been privileged to live and hear have made the social world seem bright and exciting to me again.

When thinking about queer life and experiences, which are what all my work is about, I feel like a kid with a new kaleidoscope. I am looking at the same materials, in this case the lives and experiences of queer people, but the new lens and mirrors allow me to see that everything is "reflected in an endless variety of patterns."[21] Another important aspect of kaleidoscopes is that the materials in the instrument must also be "held loosely."[22] This reminds me of sociologist Dorothy Smith's call for an institutional ethnography and standpoint theory where concepts and ideas are never taken as if they represent a static reality. Smith argues that all lived experiences are ongoing and interactive processes. Therefore, any concepts or ideas that we reach through the social sciences must be held lightly so that they are allowed to move about and transform into an endless variety of beautiful patterns. This is the only way we can ever approach any semblance of understanding of the social world.[23]

With my new kaleidoscope of theories and perspectives in hand and my own intersectional standpoint at the forefront of my mind, I realized my original proposal for this chapter was flawed and missed much of the color of queer lives in Appalachia. I originally proposed a chapter about how place identities can outweigh queer identities in Appalachia, but now this makes little sense to me. While the premise that queers, particularly trans men, masculine lesbian women, and cisgender gay men, seem to be embracing place identities more than in the past holds some truth, it misses the point and the fullness of queer lives and experiences. Therefore, I shift my focus away from my flawed starting point of creating any type of hierarchy of the importance of personal identities, because no identity can outweigh any other at any time and each identity is always intersecting with all other identities, as well as place, to shape our experiences. The seeming contradictions between queer identities and place-based identities are founded on stereotypes and misconceptions about what it means to be queer and what it means to be from a specific place, in this case, Appalachia, rural areas, and the South more generally.

Here, I centralize the voices of those of us actively navigating the intersections of queerness, Appalachia, ruralness, and the South. As editor and scholar Zane McNeill reveals, the "act of self-definition is extremely important in queer Appalachian communities." Self-definition through storytelling allows queer Appalachians to "create their own narratives to explain what queerness in Appalachia looks like" and to "create a communal history of queerness in the rural . . . [and] in Appalachia." Therefore, McNeill argues, "For many of us, self-definition of Appalachia is in and of itself activism: by reclaiming what it means to be 'Appalachian,' we imagine a place of resilience in which *y'all* really means *all*."[24] For McNeill, and myself, a vital component of self-definition is "to hear your voice and experience it reflected as authentic."[25] More broadly, scholar Reta Ugena Whitlock explains, "Writing the South is political. Writing queerness is political."[26] Telling our stories aloud, or in writing, is always an act of resistance to the dominant structure.

Highlighting queers in Appalachia and the South contributes to the ongoing project of avoiding the erasure of queer people outside of urban centers on the coasts.[27] As Mary L. Gray explains, "Keeping cities as the unquestioned center of our inquiries belies the reality that we have barely scratched the surface of the social terrains that warrant our intellectual and political attention."[28] Speaking of the importance of place identities, trans journalist and author Samantha Allen demonstrates that although queer peoples' identities are "not contingent on geography," queer people often do identify with various geographies in the same ways that cis heterosexual people do.[29] Meaning that queer people also identify as southern, rural, or urban, for example, just as cis and straight people do. This becomes problematic when the geographies we identify with are portrayed to be anti-queer, as is the case with most rural areas. Professors Mortimer-Sandilands and Erickson explain:

> The pervasive assumption that gay and lesbian communities are essentially urban has had the lasting effect of erasing the ongoing presence of rural gay men and lesbians whose lives might not look much like white, metronormative, male-dominated Christopher Street. . . . The concomitant erasure of rural gay and lesbian possibilities has *contributed* to . . . the widespread assumption that country spaces are inherently hostile to anything other than monogamous heterosexuality.[30]

Likewise, Mary L. Gray explains, "The rhetoric of the countryside's 'isolation' from gay identity, implicit in this progress narrative . . . helped stabilize gayness as an inherent trait just waiting for the right (urban) conditions to come together so it could come out and proudly shine."[31] By focusing only on queer people in cities, both in academic work and in media, the narrative that rural spaces are not where queer people do or should live is perpetuated. The erasure of queer rural folks allows rural spaces to appear as *fully* cisheteronormative. On the other hand, as Reta Ugena Whitlock demonstrates in *Queer South Rising*, "Notions of a queered South rend the veil of nostalgia and chip away at a 'solid South' through the stories of folks whose very lives counter traditionally held assumptions of what it means to be Southern."[32]

Regarding the experience of erasure of and hostility toward queer people in nonurban areas, Rae Garringer, an Appalachian scholar and storyteller, describes their own experience:

> I had bought into the dominant narrative . . . that because I am queer I could never live back home. I was told . . . I could not have my queerness and my mountains, too, that I would not be safe there, that I would not be able to survive, much less thrive.[33]

Repeatedly, queer people are told they must choose between home and happiness. We are told we cannot stay home, be queer, and succeed; we must choose *only* two of the three. Unlike cisgender, heterosexual people (especially if they are white), we are told we can't have it all.

While leaving Appalachia, rural areas, and the South may lead to more acceptance of queer identities for some, there is also the likelihood that other parts of our identities will not be accepted or that we will feel out of place in geographies we do not call home.

Hillery Glasby, Sherrie Gradin, and Rachael Ryerson discuss these experiences and feelings of queer people leaving home as a "unique form of displacement": "Appalachian queers who leave Appalachia, especially those who leave because of their queerness, experience a unique form of displacement, a certain kind of exile, forming a queer (Appalachian) diaspora, often finding themselves in places that, although accepting of their queer identity, are not always accepting of their Appalachian identity."[34]

Whether it's our accents, our colloquialisms, or something else in our mannerisms, leaving the rural, the South, or Appalachia doesn't usually mean it leaves us. As the saying goes, "You can take the girl out of the country, but you can't take the country out of the girl." Therefore, being exiled from our homes often means being exiled from our cultures and ways of being that we are familiar with and possibly most comfortable with. Again, forcing queer erasure and exile leaves rural, southern, and Appalachian queers in lose-lose situations.

THE POWER OF MASCULINITIES

It is not an accident that the four stories I discuss in this chapter about claiming place identities in Appalachia and the South all revolve around trans masculine presentations. That is, I find that masculinities are often key to mitigating anti-queerness and finding acceptance in rural spaces. The way masculinities intersect with ruralness allows queer masculinities to gain greater acceptance in these spaces and places than queer femininities. The metronormative narrative of the feminine gay guy moving to the city to find acceptance and happiness may still hold some truth if we consider how femininities are devalued in rural areas. Even cisgender women are expected to display more masculine traits in rural areas to fit in and gain acceptance.[35]

Through these stories, I address the two main aims of this anthology. First, I contribute to the project of updating the stereotypical and marginalizing view of the Appalachian region by providing underrepresented voices and experiences. I join the chorus of queer and other diverse voices attempting to challenge and update the limited view of the Appalachian region, a view that has once again circulated back into the mainstream media with the *Hillbilly Elegy* capitalistic franchise. Second, by exploring the connections between rural environments and masculinities, I address the aim of understanding whether all queers are being allowed the same access to Appalachian place identities. I argue that masculinities are still an important resource for fully embracing queer Appalachian place identities. The necessity for masculinities leaves many queer people (femmes, trans women, feminine gay men, etc.) feeling like outsiders within the region they call home and experiencing pressure to flee Appalachia for urban spaces with the hope of more acceptance. It is important to note that this critique of the exclusion of queer people from Appalachian place identities may not expand to Native communities and lands that have persisted beyond the colonization process. For instance, Walters et al. find that many Native Two-Spirit women feel "a deep sense of belonging that could only be found for them in Native communities."[36]

While I critique the limited and problematic narrative of Appalachia and rural life, I concurrently critique the persistent connections between rural environments and masculinities, to the exclusion of other ways of doing gender. The ability to fully embrace Appalachian place identities, as well as southern and rural identities, while being queer continues to largely hinge on the performance of masculinities. Heteronormative, cissexist, and white Eurocentric expectations of masculinities remain tied to the outdoors, rurality, and the Appalachian landscape. The rural outdoors, along with humanity's "personal domination" over nature "in the guise of hunting, fishing, climbing, and other outdoor activities," is a site "for the enactment of a specific heteromasculinity."[37] These uses of rurality are particularly tied to white, cis men's superiority in the region.

Labeling the rural and nature as masculine leaves many queer people (femmes, trans women, feminine gay men, etc.), as well as some cis women, feeling like outsiders within the region of the United States they call home. Queers who embrace femininities (and other ways of doing gender) continue to be marked as Others. Simultaneously, because of the conflation of masculinities with land and rurality, some masculine queer people (including, but not limited to, trans men, masculine lesbian women, and cis gay men) feel a greater degree of acceptance in Appalachia. The acceptance of masculinities makes it easier for some queer people to *stay home*, while others continue to be encouraged to leave.[38]

EMBRACING PLACE

Many queer people in the South whom I have spoken with for my research have discussed embracing place-based identities. The most illustrative of these stories is that of Mason, a thirty-four-year-old, Indigenous, Two-Spirit, trans masculine, trans man of color. Everything Mason shared with me during our hour and forty-five-minute interview tied back to his identity as Indigenous, Southern, and rural. Due to past violence, Mason did not feel comfortable telling me exactly where he lived in Tennessee, but based on his description, he lived in the rural Tennessee mountains, in or very near

Appalachia. He described where he lived as north of Nashville and "30 miles from the nearest anything."

As a trans man, Mason had legally changed his name to align with his gender identity [Mason is a pseudonym]. When choosing his name, Mason was intentional in allowing his mother to take part in the process and in ensuring he honored his Indigenous roots. Mason declined to share his deadname with me because it was an Indigenous name, and he said, "It tends to get butchered quite a bit and that just adds insult to the injury." Mason's choice of a new name was tied to his deep connections to family and ancestry, which prevail within the Indigenous culture and southern culture.

In describing his gender identity, Mason used both Two-Spirit and trans masculine interchangeably, depending on the space. He explained, "In TPOC, which is trans people of color, spaces, I use Two-Spirit. . . . Mainly in white spaces that are usually pretty hostile to Indigenous bodies, I use trans masculine." Opaskwayak Cree scholar Alex Wilson explains that the term Two-Spirit is increasingly accepted among LGBT Indigenous people in the US because it connects to the past and highlights the "the interrelatedness of all aspects of identity, including sexuality, gender, culture, community and spirituality."[39]

Though Mason strongly identified as trans and Two-Spirit, he explained that his gender presentation was binary: "Folks see me as a heteronormative binary trans man. I don't know if heteronormative, heterosexual, binary trans man fits. I do certainly present that way. You know, I live in rural areas, so I'm the Indigenous Paul Bunyan out here."

Although he presents this way, he clarified that his identities don't fit into any binary boxes: "Overall, with gender and sexuality, minus physical appearances, I'm a queer person. I don't fit in any of those binary boxes . . . as trans people and Two-Spirit people, and especially going back to my Indigenous culture, gender and sexuality weren't binary. They are constructs of the white colonial, western European world, not the Indigenous world, where every-thing is fluid, and where we can be sensitive and masculine, and that sensitivity doesn't have to be female in body. I would say in gender and sexuality I identify more as queer and fluid, with a very binary presentation."

While taking on the label *trans masculine* was "pretty easy" for Mason, he said that "identifying as Two-Spirit has been more complicated."

Mason's choice of which gender identity label to use depending on the setting and his masculine and binary presentation of gender allowed him to be accepted in Appalachia, rural areas, and the South in ways that other queer people are often denied. Wilson explains that Two-Spirit is a way of "proclaiming sovereignty [for Indigenous] bodies, gender expressions and sexualities . . . to resume our place as a valued part of our families, cultures, communities, and lands, in connection with all our relations."[40] Yet, while Mason's identities as Two-Spirit and queer have the ability to challenge the gender status quo, his trans masculine identity along with his presentation as a rugged, country man also allow him the ability to blend into the binary and slide under the radar enough to be accepted in Appalachia despite his queerness, not because of it.

Mason understood this privilege of fitting in and being accepted. For him, making his home in the South and in rural areas was the only thing that made sense. Mason said, "I think that we tend to make our homes in places where we blend more with the culture than not."

He continued: "So, like me with my cowboy boots, jeans, and cowboy hat, I don't fit in an urban area. Stick out like a sore thumb. Or as somebody from an urban area who takes the metro and is used to walking down to whatever they need, and wears whatever popular style is in that place, they're not gonna fit out here, right? Somebody wearin' stilettos going out on the farm is gonna stick out like a sore thumb, too."

Overall, Mason explained, "I find that I fit and belong more in these rural areas than I do in a city setting. . . . Different cultures have different values." Mason's stories indicate that a big part of his fitting in was related to his presentations of masculinity and the ways they relate to expectations of what it means to be Appalachian, rural, and Southern.

One of the stories Mason shared with me about fitting in was a kind of coming-out narrative. One of Mason's friends, a Black cisgender woman, was in an interracial, lesbian relationship. Mason's friend was invited to Thanksgiving dinner at her partner's house in a rural area in the mountains. He described the location as "out in the hollers . . . out in the mountains . . . like fifty miles, sixty miles from town, and town is different than city, right? Town is just a town that might have a Walmart and a gas station." His friend was afraid to go alone and asked Mason to join them. Though he was a little anxious, Mason agreed to join them for Thanksgiving dinner.

After dinner, Mason and some of the men were out back drinking. After "a couple of mason jars of moonshine," Mason told the men he was drinking with that he was trans. This was how he described their response: "The guys kinda looked at me for a second and said, 'Have you told anybody else?'" Mason responded, "Nah, I never felt comfortable." After a pause, during which Mason said he had no idea what was about to happen, one of the men said, "Get out the Wild Turkey 101 (bourbon); we're gonna celebrate." Mason described it as a very "interesting" experience, after which the men spent the "rest of the night . . . welcoming [him] into this man's world, this brother kind of world."

While Mason felt comfortable in rural areas, in Appalachia, and in the South more generally, he acknowledged that this was a privilege not extended to all queer people. He had many stories of being "welcomed into a man's world" but also understood that some people were not welcomed into the worlds they wished to inhabit. Mason said his acceptance was clearly a benefit of his "passing privilege" as a trans man. He said that other people did not have that privilege and specifically discussed issues of concern for trans women of color, who are "not safe unless they do have a degree of passing privilege. Or are able to blend."

"A TOMBOY THING"

Another trans man I spoke with for my research discussed how masculinities can make it easier for some queer people to be accepted in rural areas, Appalachia, and the South. Sage, a twenty-three-year-old white trans man from an Appalachian county in Georgia, explained that he wanted to better understand the relationship between being queer or trans and belonging to what he called the "tomboy niche . . . that is very much a social location within the South." Sage said he is curious when he hears trans men talking about how they knew they were trans, using examples of not wanting to wear dresses or playing sports with the boys. In response to this, Sage explained:

> I know at least ten other women who still identify as women who are exactly like that. That was a tomboy thing, that was something you could still do and still be a woman; it wasn't necessarily as deviant as it could be. There's definitely more of that pressure to be woman and feminine and all that, like that was still very much there, but it was like this weird little niche. And it's something that never really tripped any alarm bells for my parents because my mom also grew up as a tomboy, as someone who was just very sporty, very athletic, never very feminine.

Sage's experiences were similar to many of my experiences.

Growing up in a rural area, girls were allowed to be more masculine, more "rough-and-tumble." Yes, dresses were encouraged occasionally, but you didn't play in the woods in dresses. My masculinity as a child did not trigger any concern from my parents or anyone around me. However, there was no space for boys to be feminine to any degree where I grew up. Any bit of femininity displayed by boys was met with a firm, and often violent, response.

Other research shows this carries over in many ways into adulthood in rural areas. For instance, sociologist Emily Kazyak demonstrates that rural areas may in fact offer more ways of being for those who do masculinities, such as lesbian women or trans men. Kazyak notes that women can benefit from rural masculine ideals, much like cis men. Heterosexual women's adoption of rural masculinities as part of farm and country life more generally allows some queer people the ability to also exercise "country masculinities" without being questioned. As Kazyak puts it, "Masculinity underpins both the categories 'rural' and 'lesbian' . . . [on the contrary] femininity aligns with gay sexuality but not rurality."[41] Therefore, anyone doing masculinities, whether it be heterosexual women, lesbian women, gay men, trans men, or other nonbinary people, are able to gain more acceptance in rural areas, while in the same areas doing femininities is only acceptable for cis women.

CONCLUDING THOUGHTS

Mason and I have claimed our places in the South, as did Robert. Mason's place is in rural Appalachia, in the mountains of Tennessee; mine, at least for now, is in the midlands of South Carolina, an hour from where I grew up; and Robert's was in rural Appalachian Georgia. Sage moved to New York for graduate school, but, he said, when he is done with school, "I think that at some point, I will return (to the South). I could see myself very happily going back." We are only four queers who claim(ed) this region of the United States as home. Through my life in the South, in rural areas, and in Appalachia, as well as my research on queer life in the South, I can say with 100 percent certainty that queers are everywhere, and we make our homes in places that may seem contradictory to some. Nevertheless, we're here, we're queer, and we don't care what others think about where we choose to call home.

Queers in Appalachia, rural areas, and the southeastern United States challenge the idea that we must move away from our homes to find happiness. The push to move away comes not only from conservatives who would rather not be faced with the fact that we exist but also, as Catte discusses, from "progressives" who believe that the only way to "demonstrate our ambition" is to leave the so-called backward areas, like Appalachia, that we call home: "People are often blindly classist while remaining self-congratulatory about their other progressive credentials. One of the most insidious manifestations of this attitude is the belief that people could escape the problems of the region if they would just move. This attitude rarely acknowledges the personal factors that may impact someone's desire to move. Rather, it flatly equates migration with opportunity in ways that are disappointing."[42]

This doesn't only apply to queer people, but we also must deal with the pull of the gay imaginary, in addition to the push from conservatives and progressives alike to get out!

To continue the fight for queer equality, it is vital that we see queer people in all the places that we live and in all the varieties that we come in. The erasure of queer people in rural areas, the South, and Appalachia makes life more difficult than it must be for queer people in these locations. Once we allow queer people to stay home, be queer, *and* succeed, we can create a whole new world where queer equality is a closer reality. Additionally, queer equality depends on the continued push for other types of equality, particularly socioeconomic equality. A society that does not judge southerners and Appalachians as less intelligent and more in need of "culture" is a society that is more accepting of queer people also.

Overall, despite having "the enemy in our face every day,"[43] many queer people choose to stay in our homes. I personally prefer to have the enemy in my face because at least I can see them coming. While most of my life I have spent in the Deep South, with four years of that in Appalachia, I lived briefly in the Midwest, and it did not go well. I did not fully understand the culture, "Iowa nice," or "Midwest nice," which led me to run into the enemy far more than I do in the Southeast or Appalachia. So, to slightly modify a quote from Allen, "Not only am I not afraid to be queer in [Appalachia, rural areas, and the Southeast], this is where I prefer to be queer."[44]

NOTES

1. Rae Garringer, "'Well, We're Fabulous and We're Appalachians, so We're Fabulachians': Country Queers in Central Appalachia," *Southern Cultures* 23, no. 1 (March 22, 2017): 79–92, 1.
2. Kate Davis, *Southern Comfort,* New Video Group, 2003.
3. Next Wave Films, "*Southern Comfort,*" accessed February 23, 2021, https://www.nextwavefilms.com/southern/. Kate Davis, *Southern Comfort,* New Video Group, 2003.
4. Elvis Mitchell, "Film Review: Genders That Shift, but Friends Firm as Bedrock," *The New York Times,* February 21, 2001.
5. Kath Weston, "Get Thee to a Big City: Sexual Imaginary and the Great Gay Migration," *GLQ: A Journal of Lesbian and Gay Studies* 2 (1995): 253–77.
6. Anthony Harkins, "Hillbillies, Rednecks, Crackers, and White Trash," in *The New Encyclopedia of Southern Culture,* vol. 20, *Social Class,* ed. Larry J. Griffin and Peggy G. Hargis (Chapel Hill: University of North Carolina Press, 2012), 370.
7. Harkins, "Hillbillies, Rednecks, Crackers, and White Trash," 369.
8. Elizabeth Catte, *What You Are Getting Wrong about Appalachia* (Cleveland: Belt, 2018), 11.
9. Catte, *What You Are Getting Wrong about Appalachia,* 11.
10. Hillery Glasby, Sherrie Gradin, and Rachael Ryerson, introduction to *Storytelling in Queer Appalachia: Imagining and Writing the Unspeakable Other,* ed. Hillery Glasby, Sherrie Gradin, and Rachael Ryerson (Morgantown: West Virginia University Press, 2020), 1–15, 2.

11. Mary L. Gray, *Out in the Country: Youth, Media, and Queer Visibility in Rural America* (New York: New York University Press, 2009), xi.

12. Catte, *What You Are Getting Wrong about Appalachia*, 10–11.

13. Glasby, Gradin, and Ryerson, introduction, 4.

14. Appalachian Trail Conservancy, "About Us," accessed January 20, 2021, https://appalachiantrail.org/our-work/about-us/.

15. Trey Adcock, "Native Lands," *A.T. Footpath Blog*, Appalachian Trail Conservancy, February 23, 2021, https://appalachiantrail.org/official-blog/native-lands/.

16. Blue Ridge Pride Festival, accessed February 2, 2021, https://blueridgepride.org.

17. Karina Walters et al., "'My Spirit in My Heart': Identity Experiences and Challenges among American Indian Two-Spirit Women," *Journal of Lesbian Studies* 10, no. 1–2, (2006): 125–49.

18. Walters et al., "'My Spirit in My Heart,'" 127.

19. Scott Lauria Morgensen, *Spaces Between Us: Queer Settler Colonialism and Indigenous Decolonization* (Minneapolis: University of Minnesota Press, 2011), 43.

20. Robert Gipe, "How Appalachian I Am," in *Appalachian Reckoning: A Region Responds to Hillbilly Elegy*, ed. Anthony Harkins and Meredith McCarroll (Morgantown: West Virginia University Press, 2019), 318.

21. *Merriam-Webster*, s.v. "kaleidoscope," accessed January 15, 2021, https://www.merriam-webster.com/dictionary/kaleidoscope.

22. Dictionary.com, s.v. "kaleidoscope," accessed January 15, 2021, https://www.dictionary.com/browse/kaleidoscope.

23. Dorothy E. Smith, *The Everyday World as Problematic: A Feminist Sociology* (Boston: Northeastern University Press, 1987).

24. Z. Zane McNeill, ed., *Y'all Means All: The Emerging Voices Queering Appalachia* (Oakland, CA: PM Press, 2021).

25. McNeill, *Y'all Means All*, 2021.

26. Reta Ugena Whitlock, ed., *Queer South Rising: Voices of a Contested Place* (Charlotte, NC: Information Age, 2013), xxvii.

27. For examples, see Miriam Abelson, *Men in Place: Trans Masculinity, Race, and Sexuality in America* (Minneapolis: University of Minnesota Press, 2019); Samantha Allen, *Real Queer America: LGBT Stories from Red States* (New York: Back Bay Books, 2019); E. Patrick Johnson, *Sweet Tea: Black Gay Men of the South; An Oral History* (Chapel Hill: University of North Carolina Press, 2008); Baker Rogers, *Trans Men in the South: Becoming Men* (Lanham, MD: Lexington Books, 2020).

28. Gray, *Out in the Country*, xiv.

29. Allen, *Real Queer America*, 11.

30. Catriona Mortimer-Sandilands and Bruce Erickson, eds., *Queer Ecologies: Sex, Nature, Politics, Desire* (Bloomington: Indiana University Press, 2010), 16–17.

31. Gray, *Out in the Country*, 9.

32. Whitlock, *Queer South Rising*, xxvii.

33. Rae Garringer, "'Well, We're Fabulous and We're Appalachians, So We're Fabulachians': Country Queers in Central Appalachia," *Southern Voices* 23, no. 1 (March 22, 2017): 79–92, 80.

34. Glasby, Gradin, and Ryerson, introduction, 2.

35. Emily Kazyak, "Midwest or Lesbian? Gender, Rurality, and Sexuality," *Gender & Society* 26, no. 6 (2012): 825–48.

36. Walters et al., "'My Spirit in My Heart,'" 140.

37. Mortimer-Sandilands and Erickson, *Queer Ecologies*, 3; Nicolas W. Proctor, *Bathed in Blood: Hunting and Mastery in the Old South* (Charlottesville: University of Virginia Press, 2002).

38. See Abelson, *Men in Place*; Rogers, *Trans Men in the South*.

39. Alex Wilson, "How We Find Ourselves: Identity Development and Two-Spirit People," *Harvard Education Review* 66, no. 2 (1996): 303–17, 304–5.

40. Alex Wilson, "Our Coming In Stories: Cree Identity, Body Sovereignty and Gender Self-Determination," *Journal of Global Indigeneity* 1, no. 1 (2015): 1–5, 3.

41. Kazyak, "Midwest or Lesbian?," 825.

42. Catte, *What You Are Getting Wrong about Appalachia*, 127.

43. Monica Roberts, quoted in Allen, *Real Queer America*, 10.

44. Allen, *Real Queer America*, 14.

UNSILENCING INDIGENEITY
Appalachian Studies, Appalachian Ecologies, and the Continuation of Settler Colonialism

JESSICA CORY

INTRODUCTION

Living in western North Carolina, I am surrounded by mountains, rivers, streams, and the trails and roads that wind between them. I am privy to the colorful evolution of autumn leaves and clouds that appear to form mountains in the air. With so much natural beauty eclipsing my fragile humanness, it can be easy for me to overlook the total ecology of the area in which I live, not noticing the people and other-than-human living beings that inhabit this space. When we talk about Appalachia and explore the region through its literature, one of the primary elements is landscape and environment. As queer ecology scholars Catriona Mortimer-Sandilands and Bruce Erickson argue, however, discussing the environment doesn't end at "nature": "understandings of nature inform discourses of sexuality, and also . . . understandings of sex inform discourses of nature," as the actions of organisms (including humans) are very much influenced by their environments and the power structures that dominate those environments.[1] Thus, examining notions of the environment and nature through a queer theory lens allows us to confront the ways in which heteronormativity and other portrayals of colonial "normalcy" both pervade our ideas of what is considered natural in Appalachia and prevent settler Appalachians from engaging with Native voices and viewing the region as Native space.[2] This essay begins with a base of queer theory (i.e., destabilizing constructs of "normalcy" in society, particularly in Appalachia) and then more specifically engages with a decolonial framework to explore the ways that normative understandings of Appalachian ecology are queered through the teaching of Native literature as part of an Appalachian studies curriculum. Through including and accurately representing the region's Indigenous connections and the experiences of Indigenous Peoples in what is now known as Appalachia, we are queering the settler Appalachian ecology and challenging white settler Appalachian complicity in the perpetuation of Native erasure and settler colonialism.

There is some overlap between anticolonial, ecocritical, and queer theories, though they are often used toward different ends. Ecofeminists argue that Indigenous Peoples have been forced to inhabit the "nature" side of the nature-culture binary, along with female-identifying and feminized people, children, and other-than-human animals, while there has been some debate about the existence of such a divide.[3] Native Peoples have also long been associated with the land, often described in texts by white settlers as the ultimate stewards of this continent or as part of the "natural world" itself. Such alignments of Indigenous peoples with "nature" reduces them, in settler eyes, to a subhuman level, allowing for the continuation and defense of genocide. Evidence of these problematic associations can be found in the many portrayals of "wilderness" areas or the desert Southwest being wild and unpeopled territories, along with depictions of this continent's original inhabitants as animalistic. By queering our perspectives of the region's ecology, especially in considering which human presences are normalized in Appalachia, we are able to challenge not only these stereotypes of

Native Peoples and the problematic binaries that delimit the terms we can think with but also the settler colonial power structure that produces such inequalities.

QUEERING APPALACHIAN ECOLOGIES

Ecologies are the relationships between organisms and the environments they inhabit through spatial and temporal means, and as mentioned previously, they include humans and other-than-human entities. Because of the dominant powers of settler colonialism (and I'm focusing on the United States here but realize this extends to many other nations), Appalachian people are forced to live under an anthropocentric patriarchy that privileges whiteness and cis heterosexual (cishet) identities. Thus, through queering these dominant ideologies, we're able to explore ecological relationships that exist outside of and beyond such power structures. Using a lens of queerness—that is, a way of looking at our ecological relationships that questions what we've been told is "natural" or "normal"—is particularly helpful in interrogating ecology.

As Nicole Seymour notes, "Some curious things have happened to 'nature' in these discussions. For one, the concept of nature itself, rather than the de-historicizing and discriminatory processes of naturalization, has come under fire. 'Nature' thus starts to look like something that can function only oppressively—or, at best, naively; it is rendered monolithic even as it is decried for being farcical."[4]

Queer ecological theory disrupts the nature-culture binary and Seymour's suggestions of an "oppressive" nature by "demand[ing] intimacies with other beings," as Timothy Morton explains, notions that are shared by Donna Haraway and other queer ecologists as well as Indigenous scholars.[5]

Exploring these "kinships," a term used by Haraway and many Indigenous scholars and creative writers, including Kim TallBear and Glen Coulthard, disrupts the settler colonial hierarchies and creates space to engage in relationships based on consent, respect, and reciprocity.[6] Viewing ecology through a kinship lens creates a web, rather than a hierarchy, and has the potential to reframe the hierarchical ecologies of settler colonialism, such as human-animal and nature-culture binaries. Without such rankings in place, we can then reconsider how we spatially and temporally inhabit what we know as Appalachia.

These hierarchical disruptions are particularly important in Appalachia, which has often been considered spatially rural and thus unfriendly to queer people and subject to LGBTQIA+ flight from the region because of the pervasiveness of the myth of metronormativity. The region temporally has also been considered backward or historical, especially if we explore depictions of time through canonized Appalachian literature.[7] Adding to these complexities of space and time is what Mishauna Goeman (Tonawanda Band of Seneca) writes of as "the fixity of Native people in time and space," the ways in which settler colonialism has perpetuated the idea that Native Peoples only live in the past (or must appear that way to be considered authentic or traditional) or solely inhabit reservations.[8] While the temporal and spatial perceptions of Native and non-Native communities are "provided by settler discourses, structures, and perceptions," as Mark Rifkin argues, the distinction should also be made that settler colonialism affects Indigenous Peoples and non-Native Appalachians differently.[9] It is important to consider how scholarly omissions of Native literature and the focus on historical literature in the teaching of Appalachian studies continue the settler colonial violence of Goeman's "fixity" and perpetuate the idea of Appalachia as a lily-white place stuck in the past. While the myth of Appalachia as a backward or historical place certainly damages societal notions of white Appalachians, it does not erase their very existence, as they are still represented in the Appalachian literary canon. Through queering the notions of which humans belong on the web of Appalachian ecology by teaching Native writers, we can begin to undo some of the damage wrought by settler colonialism within the region.

EXCLUSION OF NATIVE AMERICAN TEXTS AND WRITERS

In their 2015 essay "Writing Appalachia: Intersections, Missed Connections, and Future Work," Appalachian studies scholars Chris Green and Erica Abrams Locklear explore the absence of Native American literature in Appalachian studies curricula.[10] However, because their essay engages with a multitude of gaps in the field and does not focus solely on the exclusion of Native writers, they do not have ample space in which to discuss the potential repercussions of omitting Native literature and scholarship from Appalachian studies nor to surmise how such exclusion benefits Appalachia's non-Native (and particularly white) inhabitants. Some of the benefits include power structures built on white supremacy and heteronormativity. Together, these structures decide which bodies are considered normative or deviant in portrayals and perceptions of the region and, more broadly, which bodies are considered part of Appalachian ecology.

Green and Locklear clearly find that Native bodies and writers are largely excluded from the region's literature: "Looking back at the work of Appalachian literary studies with contemporary Native American authors and communities, one finds surprisingly sporadic discussion. When such work occurs, it is almost always about the Eastern Band of Cherokee or Marilou Awiakta, with no mention of the Shawnee, Muscogee, and Lenape, all of whom continue to inhabit the Appalachian region but without official recognition."[11]

I, too, found this erasure to be the case in reviewing Appalachian studies syllabi posted online to the Appalachian Studies Association's website. Very few syllabi included Native writers or

Native experiences, and of the documents that did, nearly all (in a variety of fields, from geography to anthropology and literature) appeared to focus solely on the Cherokee as the original inhabitants of Appalachia or on Eastern Band of Cherokee Indians (EBCI) individuals.[12] While the former is certainly true of some areas of Appalachia, particularly the southern part, it is not accurate for the entire central and northern parts of the region, as Green and Locklear note. Green and Locklear expand a bit to discuss how "remarkable" it is that the EBCI is so widely represented (at least in those cases in which Native American literature and scholarship is included in Appalachian studies) because, according to Wilburn Hayden Jr. and the US Department of the Interior, "only about one of every ten Native Americans in the region defined by the Appalachian Regional Commission is from this band, which has 13,562 members."[13]

One of Green and Locklear's potential reasons for Native exclusion in Appalachian studies is that "it would seem that many Native American authors see themselves and their work in terms of being Native American rather than in relationship to Appalachia."[14] One reason for this method of identifying might be the moniker Appalachia itself.

As Donald E. Davis explains in his chapter "Apalatchi: Naming the Mountains," "The word itself comes from a Native American tribe, the Apalachees, who did not actually live in the southern mountains. By all historical accounts, the Apalachee Indians lived within a forty-square-mile area of the central Florida panhandle, from the western bank of the Aucilla River to the lands just west of the Ochlockonee River."[15]

David S. Walls reveals that French artist Jacques le Moyne, who had been painting in Florida, is responsible for naming the mountains Appalachia in the mid-sixteenth century.[16] This term does not originate among the Indigenous Peoples of what we now call Appalachia, and the term itself was not used in a Native language to refer to the mountains, both reasons that it may not be a desirable identifier for Native Peoples. A potentially larger reason, though, is that Appalachia, like the rest of the United States, is a settler construct, and thus identifying as their own Native Nations instead of part of "Appalachia" supports Native sovereignty. Clearly there are many reasons that Native writers may not identify as Appalachian; however, this idea of "self-exclusion" noted by Locklear and Green might also function to absolve Appalachian studies scholars of their roles in perpetuating this erasure, what Eve Tuck and K. Wayne Yang call a "settler move to innocence."[17] Essentially, if scholars do not view the region as Native space still inhabited by Native Peoples, they continue to uphold that Native people are deviant bodies in settler space but do not see themselves as contributing to the problem.

It is important to note that there are Native authors who do work within Native and Appalachian paradigms. Marilou Awiakta engages with both Cherokee and Appalachian identities in both *Abiding Appalachia* and *Selu*, and Susan Deer Cloud (Mohawk/Seneca/Blackfeet/European), who resides in northern Appalachia (New York), engages a great deal with Appalachian culture in her many works of poetry, particularly her book *Hunger Moon*. Undoubtedly, it is true that some (indeed, probably many) Native writers primarily focus on their tribal/national identity/ies.[18] Does this mean, however, that they should not be included in an Appalachian studies curriculum? Does one need to self-identify as Appalachian to, in fact, *be* Appalachian? And what exactly does "being Appalachian" mean in the first place, and how did whiteness become an assumed part of this identity? In a very broad sense, an "Appalachian" would be someone with a connection to the region, its ecology, and its territory. With that definition, then, whether someone chooses to identify as a citizen of their nation or tribe rather than an "Appalachian" seems irrelevant, as long as the connection to the region is present. Additionally, connection to one's current or ancestral lands is also *part of* one's tribal/national identity, and therefore a separate regional identifier is, frankly, unnecessary.

DEVIANT BODIES AND SETTLER SELF-INDIGENIZATION IN APPALACHIA

"Deviant" bodies in Appalachia have been the focus of recent research, particularly in reference to queer or disabled bodies that inhabit the human ecology of the region.[19] However, queering settler colonial notions of bodies through anticolonial theory is less common in the regionally focused research, though no less important. As Audra Simpson (Kahnawake Mohawk) notes, Indigenous bodies that continue to exist are seen as deviant, in direct opposition to the genocidal project of settler colonialism.[20] Through expanding our notion of queering societal or regional norms to extend to anticolonial interrogation of settler colonial normalcies, we are able to reconfigure our idea of how Native bodies inhabit the region and the ways in which we, as Appalachian studies scholars, engage with Native Peoples and their experiences.

The first issue to overcome in implementing vast changes to Appalachian studies curricula and thus to a broader understanding of the region is to recognize that Native Peoples are still living in Appalachia. This may seem like an obvious aspect to address, but in areas where the streets and rivers are derived from Native languages or directly named after the Peoples themselves, there is often a disconnect (perhaps subconscious) between Native imaginaries and actual, living Native Peoples. In my hometown, there is a heavily commodified celebration of Native culture that has devolved into little more than a street fair; we have sacred mound sites that tell the stories of the Indigenous Peoples of the area, but these sites are routinely disrespected (e.g., they are climbed on, and pray-ins are held there) by white Appalachian settlers. This disrespect for Native land (which is, frankly, all of Appalachia) and Native Peoples is due in part to different frames of reference held by Native and non-Native Appalachians, which result in vastly different lived experiences. The way the ecology is viewed (hierarchical versus webbed, as I addressed earlier) is just one such key difference.

Human bodies are clearly part of ecologies, and the human aspect of Appalachian ecology faces a particular issue in settler self-indigenization. It is paramount to realize that ecologies are not just composed of the present; they also engage with what one might consider the past and future temporalities.[21] We must first recognize *how* we come to inhabit our place(s) in the ecological balance in order to consider how past ecologies affect the present webs we inhabit. Such a task necessarily interrogates the structures in place that have labeled some bodies "deviant" (Native bodies, LGBTQIA+ bodies) and privileged other bodies (cishet white bodies, for instance), though there may, of course, exist intersections that privilege some aspects of one's identity and disadvantage other aspects.

Identifying as coming from a "colonized" place (even if such a model is applied to the area erroneously, as we will see shortly) may lead to denying white privilege and furthering settler colonial violence. This identification is likely due (at least in part) to white settler desire in Appalachia to separate oneself from one's "colonizers," or those deemed responsible for the region's ills and exploitations. This identification, then, "for settler Appalachians precludes the settler from engaging in decolonization efforts in solidarity with Indigenous peoples," argues Stephen Pearson.[22] Pearson adds that this self-indigenization appears to be largely based in land ownership (or the lack thereof) in the region, with the large amount of absentee-owned land in Appalachia causing white settler Appalachians to feel displaced. This feeling is then countered by the misplaced pride of "possessing" the land by living and surviving on it for (often) more than one generation and thus feeling it is in one's "possession."[23]

Pearson posits that this is not a new phenomenon and points to the work of Harry Caudill, a well-known figure in Appalachian studies whose work was popularized by Helen Lewis. Caudill's anti-Native sentiments are extremely visible in his work, and in *Night Comes to the Cumberlands,* he portrays his ancestors as having been in Kentucky "since the beginning."[24] Lewis and Edward Knipe echo this sentiment, often referring to white settlers in the region as "indigenous."[25] As Pearson notes, this starting of the clock at European invasion is both clearly an erasure of Native Peoples and spaces and an indication of the desire of white settlers to replace the original stewards of the land and become "indigenous" to the region themselves.

Such self-indigenization might be obvious, as when white settlers refer to themselves as "native Appalachians," but it is also visible in the region's literature in another, more complex way. In ample amounts of Appalachian literature, particularly early works, white settlers are often portrayed as learning from Native Peoples in the region and then taking on the imagined aspects of the erased Indigenous populations, essentially presenting themselves as indigenous instead. While there are countless examples of this method of self-indigenization, for the sake of space, we will just briefly examine *Cold Mountain,* the 1997 historical novel by Charles Frazier, which became a *New York Times* bestseller and won several prestigious awards. The white protagonist, Inman, is trying to return home after sustaining injuries in battle during the Civil War. The only identifiably Native character in the tale is Swimmer, a Cherokee boy with whom Inman is friends during their childhood. Throughout the novel, Inman recalls his friend's stories, particularly tales about the spiritual realms present in the Appalachian Mountains. The characterization of Swimmer is overly romanticized, and his character in the novel only serves to provide Inman with spiritual guidance and hope on his travels, essentially allowing Inman to use Swimmer's knowledge to then learn to "become indigenous" to the land. Other settler characters in the novel also are imbued with this "indigenous connection to the land," particularly Ruby, the illiterate though extremely knowledgeable counterpart to Ada Monroe, and The Goat-Woman who cares for Inman and nurses him back to health. Both characters are well versed in planting by the signs, using herbal medicines, and other (again, overly romanticized) techniques that, the novel suggests, originated with Native Peoples who lived (yes, past tense, since the novel only shows us Swimmer) in the region. The issue of these "indigenous" characters being forced to inhabit a romantic settler imaginary in the regional ecology aside, this book is also a prime example of white settler Appalachian self-indigenization and the commodification and erasure of Native Peoples. Despite these traits though, it remains wildly popular and taught in many Appalachian studies courses.

To clarify, I am not suggesting that white Appalachians do not or cannot have knowledge of the land or that they are unable to, essentially, know a place. My own relatives have lived in the Ohio River Valley since the late 1700s, working the same land from their arrival to this very day. They certainly have knowledge of that land and what it needs in order to thrive and to help them survive. Their knowledge, however, differs from Indigenous traditional ecological knowledge (TEK) in some important ways. The most obvious and important difference is that TEK is based on information gathered and handed down through millennia. Living in an area for three hundred years, especially after the effects of industrialization, environmental degradation, and colonial-based pollution have already begun to take hold, is not the same as having knowledge of a place for thousands of years, including precontact. I am also not suggesting that white Appalachians cannot learn to be stewards of the land from Indigenous Peoples. Indeed, some environmental ideologies may have intersections with TEK or can be helpful in interrogating one's relationship with the environment.

As Kim TallBear notes of ecosexuality and its icons Annie Sprinkle and Beth Stephens, "As an indigenous and feminist scholar of science studies, I continue to search for voices that can provide more inclusive alternatives to the less democratic knowledge practices espoused by nature's self-appointed spokespersons, the overwhelmingly white, male, heteronormative scientific establishment that mistakenly equates its own historically-specific norms and knowledges with neutrality and universal truth."[26]

Thus, there is certainly room for diverse views, particularly from historically marginalized voices, in larger environmental conversations, especially as those conversations focus on queering the environment, as ecosexuality does. I would argue, though, and Tall-Bear also addresses this issue in an addendum to her blog post, that the relationship white Appalachians have with the land may differ from Indigenous relationships with land and landedness and that, in some cases, white Appalachians do appropriate Indigenous land-based knowledges and engage in cultural exploitation, sometimes by falsely claiming certain Indigenous identities or knowledges as their own, which is another form of self-indigenization.

Self-indigenization by white settler Appalachians allows this demographic to inhabit a place in the region's ecology through Native erasure. By queering settler notions of who belongs to the region, then, we can acknowledge this erasure and self-indigenization and take steps to rectify these issues, one of which is including works of Native people in an Appalachian studies curriculum.

SPATIALITY AND AN "INTERNAL COLONY"

Thinking more broadly about structures and ecology, we must consider the region as a whole and its ties to the larger settler state known as the United States. Related to settler self-indigenization is the notion of Appalachia as "an internal colony," essentially an area that has been "colonized" and exploited for its natural resources by powers sharing the same state or nation. While this model may seem plausible and, perhaps, even helpful in explaining the economic, environmental, and political problems facing the region, it is accompanied by a false equivalence to other forms of colonization, such as settler colonialism.

This notion of Appalachia as an "internal colony" gained prominence through the work of well-known Appalachian scholars Helen Matthews Lewis, Linda Johnson, and Donald Askins. The trio writes in the preface to their 1978 edited collection *Colonialism in Modern America: The Appalachian Case*: "Since we have chosen articles which predominantly represent only one point of view, the book can be labeled a biased interpretation. This is true and intentional. It is our purpose to demonstrate the usefulness of one particular perspective for understanding the region. The model has been variously called the Colonialism Model, Internal Colonialism, Exploitation or External Oppression Model."[27]

The goal of Lewis, Johnson, and Askins was to provide an alternative to the explanations given by the culture of poverty model and the underdevelopment model in order to find strategies that would *actually* address the above-mentioned issues faced by the region and its inhabitants. They do question the imbalance of Appalachian ecology by focusing on "that part of Appalachia . . . the portion of the Allegheny-Cumberland mountains in which bituminous coal mining developed. Portions of southwest Virginia, eastern Kentucky, and southern West Virginia form this area and are referred to by the Appalachian Regional Commission as Central Appalachia."[28] As far as exploring a viable alternative explanation for the focus area's ills, Lewis, Johnson, and Askins do, indeed, accomplish their goal, showing how "dominant outside industrial interests establish control, exploit the region, and maintain their domination and subjugation of the region."[29] However, their work also opens the door for settler Appalachians to self-indigenize, which upsets the regional ecology in myriad ways, not only through land ownership or land claims but also through Indigenous erasure and the viewing of Native bodies as "deviant."

The model of colonialism proposed by Lewis, Johnson, and Askins, of course, differs in important ways from settler colonialism; however, there are, unsurprisingly, certain similarities, such as the penchant for the "exploiters to label their work 'progress' and to blame any of the obvious problems it causes on the ignorance or deficiencies of the . . . people."[30] Blaming the colonized, while part of internal colonialism, also plays a large role in other models of colonialism, including settler colonialism. Internal colonialism and settler colonialism are also similar in that, in both cases, the colonizers are positioned within the nation-state of the colonized, though their motives are obviously different. In settler colonialism, the goal is to replace the original inhabitants, often through genocide, while in internal colonialism, the goal is the economic exploitation of the colonized (though this can also be seen in settler colonialism before or in addition to genocide). Despite these comparisons and the knowledge that settler colonialism and internal colonialism are different models, those living under the latter may latch on to the identity of someone "colonized" rather than their role of "colonizer," essentially allowing the individual (or demographic) to deny their role in the continuation of settler colonialism and the systems that privilege white cishet identities (again, the settler moves to innocence).

In a repositioning of settler Appalachians in the historical and present ecological web, Barbara Ellen Smith, in response to the 2004 Appalachian Studies Association Plenary (held in Cherokee, North Carolina, that year) argues: "Thinking of our common status—North and South American—as the 'New World' and the colonial domination that was the genesis of that construct, the genocide of indigenous people that was its prerequisite, the racialized labor exploitation of chattel slavery that built this new world, and the exclusionary criteria for citizenship that defined it only for certain people as a land of freedom and promise. Appalachia emerges in this context, not as a particularistic 'internal colony,' but as one manifestation of a larger history of colonialism whose legacies persist to this day."[31]

David S. Walls adds, in his consideration of Appalachia as an internal colony, that he finds Robert Blauner's "parallel to 'forced, involuntary entry' by the colonizer" far-fetched in relation to Appalachia and argues that Pierre van den Berghe's suggestion that internal colonies often have "an internal government within a government especially created to rule the subject peoples" is demonstrably false regarding the region.[32,33] Walls concludes that a "model of peripheral regions within an advanced capitalist society" suits Appalachia better than the model of an internal colony.[34]

While Walls and Smith are not overtly utilizing queer and anti-colonial theories to critique Appalachia and the settlers within it, both Walls and Smith are questioning the validity of the colonial construct and the norms that it upholds, creating room for Appalachian potentialities and futurisms beyond the cishet settler state. Smith, in particular, refuses to bend to the erasure of Appalachia as Native space, even though she does seem to leave Indigenous Peoples in the past, continuing the "fixity" of which Goeman speaks. Such oversights are just one reason why it is imperative that we teach Native literature in Appalachian studies courses.

WHY INDIGENEITY MATTERS

Teaching the works of Native writers and listening to the voices and stories of Native Peoples through an Appalachian studies curriculum is a queer act, in that it is recognizing the "deviant" bodies as belonging to the region, in direct opposition to the settler state that attempts to physically, psychically, and spiritually erase Native Peoples. While it is not an obviously sexual deployment of queer theory, Jack Halberstam reminds us that "queerness" can be "an outcome of strange temporalities" and "alternative methods of alliance," which clearly speaks to subverting the notion of Native fixity and engaging in reciprocal kinships through ecological webs rather than hierarchies.[35]

Including Native writers and scholars in Appalachian studies curricula also affects Appalachian ecology in a very tangible way: people who are literally indigenous to a place often have acute understandings of that place's historical, present, and future ecologies (e.g., the earlier-mentioned TEK). Examples of Native place-based knowledge in Appalachia abound.

Annette Saunooke Clapsaddle, a writer and citizen of the EBCI, shares insights from a conversation with Tribal Elder Marie Junaluska (EBCI). Clapsaddle writes that Junaluska "Continues to piece together her memory of the place [Qualla Boundary], we realize that what was once a part of her childhood life is now underground, blacktopped over—a concealed Cherokee we never think about. Tunnels, perhaps—like the ones on shows like *Unearthed*. We enjoy the mystery of it, but I can't help but lament knowing I will never see it and wondering if we can ever access it again."[36]

Lamentations of place-based change are common in depictions of the region, unfairly positioning Appalachia as stuck in the past. However, this conversation between Junaluska and Clapsaddle does not simply lament the changes in ecology from the addition of railroad tracks or the advent of logging, as portrayed in many works of non-Native Appalachian literature; instead, their insights stem from "a concealed Cherokee," a narrative of displacement that occurs even while on their ancestral lands—a displacement that is the result of settler colonialism.

Their experiences are indicative of what writer Lauret Savoy has observed: "The American landscape is palimpsest. Layers upon layers of names and meanings lie beneath the official surface. What came *before* colonial maps and names was vast and long. On the eve of contact the breath-taking diversity of Native languages exceeded that of Europe. . . . Imagine the names. Imagine their origins."[37]

Telling these stories of the Appalachian landscape that existed "before colonial maps" and the changes in the region is crucial to our understanding of Appalachian ecology, including the understanding of the experiences of the Native Peoples who live here.

As Daniel Heath Justice (Cherokee Nation) discusses in his book *Why Indigenous Literatures Matter*, through the study of Indigenous literatures, including as part of an Appalachian studies curriculum, we can learn to be human, to behave as good relatives, to become good ancestors, and to live together.[38] To expand on Justice's notion of "good relatives," this term includes living in right relation not simply with our human relatives but with *all* relatives, the total ecology, which Justice defines in an essay that focuses on the importance of "anomaly": "Humans share this dynamic cosmos with a diverse community of other-than-human beings, all of whom have their own subjectivities and powers, and each of whom has a particular set of relationships with all other entities, some more intimate than others."[39]

Justice borrows this "Mississippian category of *anomaly*—a specific articulation of difference drawn from Mississippian cosmology and iconography"—to understand queerness in an Indigenous context, though he notes that through this concept, he is exploring "belonging," which necessitates kinships.[40] It is Justice's use of *anomaly*, commonly defined as a valid entity that exists in contrast to given norms, through which we can see how Indigenous and queer notions (and queer Indigenous notions) of kinship come together to reenvision Appalachian ecology, as these relationships cannot exist within the region's hierarchical settler framework.

WHERE TO GO FROM HERE

Teaching Native American literature as part of Appalachian studies courses allows us, students and scholars, to reenvision Appalachian ecology as a web of kinship rather than a hierarchical mode rooted in extraction. However, there are barriers to be addressed in enacting such curricular changes, particularly in broadening our definition of Appalachian literature (often through the inclusion of "deviant bodies," as discussed earlier) and in reducing gatekeeping (of both texts and authors). Working through these barriers will allow a more accurate portrayal of the region and of the multitude of humans who play a role in its networks of relation.

Broadening Understandings of Appalachian Literature

We have discussed the importance of including Native writers and scholars in Appalachian literature courses, though the earlier focus was primarily on people who, for the most part, live or write from the region, such as Marie Junaluska, Annette Clapsaddle, and Susan Deer Cloud. Certainly, it is important to include Native writers who currently reside within the Appalachian Regional Commission (ARC) boundaries. My argument is based on anticolonial and queer theory, though, and as such requires a brief critique of these boundaries.

First, it is important to realize that what we now know as Appalachia has always been Native land. Before colonization, Native Peoples moved throughout and beyond the region freely, without regard to state lines or arbitrary colonial mappings. From an anticolonial standpoint, the ARC designations are yet another of these colonial mappings meant to create separation and division, this time marking Appalachia as somehow different from the remainder of the United States. However, Elizabeth Catte, among other writers and scholars, notes that there is not a single issue in Appalachia that is not also found in other US regions.[41] Further, the ARC boundaries were chosen during the War on Poverty to specifically include impoverished counties, effectively making the ARC's mapping no more than a meaningless political designation needed to enact specific policies upon the region's inhabitants and their other-than-human kin.

In regard to government policy, it is because of US policies of removal, relocation, dispossession, and termination that many Native Peoples whose ancestral lands fall within the arbitrary ARC boundaries of the region live and write from elsewhere in the country, though their writing may deal with the region. One such example is Laura Da', a member of the Eastern Shawnee Tribe who lives near Seattle, Washington. Despite writing from the Pacific Northwest, she clearly engages with areas in Appalachia, as her poem "The Tecumseh Motel," set in Chillicothe, Ohio (my hometown), evidences:

The first cultural event in Chillicothe
is a matinee performance
of an outdoor play
highlighting Tecumseh's life.
We are honored guests,
ushered backstage before the show.
How to approximate a scalping at the Tecumseh Outdoor
    Drama:
Hollow an egg with care.
Fill with Karo syrup and red tempera paint.
Soak a toupee with cherry Kool-Aid and mineral oil.
Crack the egg onto the actor's head.
Red matter will slide down the crown
and eggshell will mimic shards of skull
At the end of the performance
the crowd turns a standing ovation
to the representatives of our tribe
sitting in the middle rows.
Are we mocked or honored with such a display?[42]

The above excerpt clearly demonstrates an intimate knowledge of a particular area in Appalachia and provides insight into how historical ecological engagement through the web of relations very much affects the present perceptions and understanding. However, by maintaining that Appalachian writers need to be "from" a specifically mapped area, scholars are effectively continuing to gatekeep by engaging in the sorts of hierarchical settler notions of kinship and ecology rather than the queer alternative that is the focus of this essay.

Addressing Gatekeeping

In addition to including Native writers living outside the region who examine Appalachia, Appalachian studies scholars need to consider what counts as creative writing, literature, and scholarship in the academy, and particularly in Appalachian studies. Frankly, if we have white Appalachian settlers (yes, even if they have the best of inclusive intentions) as the sole gatekeepers of what counts, a lot of work is going to be overlooked, left out, or misinterpreted. Green and Locklear begin to venture into this contention by way of what is considered Cherokee literature by suggesting that "if one opens up Cherokee literature to storytelling, one might include the many books that Barbara Duncan edited and published with the University of North Carolina Press, but such work now seems to fall outside of the focus of those working with and in Appalachian literature and, all too often, Appalachian studies."[43] I do want to point out that some scholars of Appalachian studies are, in fact, opening up those boundaries and that the rest of us would do well to follow their lead.

Silas House, for example, shared on Twitter, "I tell my students that Judaculla Rock is the first piece of written Appalachian Literature."[44] *Written* is an important term here. In *Selu*, Marilou

Awiakta compares the organization of her book, and the art of storytelling more generally, to the weaving of a basket. If we expand our understanding to include artifacts beyond written texts, we broaden our knowledge not only of culture but of Appalachia. Think of the wisdom contained in pottery, baskets, weavings, drawings, oral traditions, storytelling, and other genres and modes that exist beyond the limitations of the book form! As with my earlier critique of maps and boundaries, we must recognize our own boundaries in regard to definitions. How do we define *text* or *literature*? What (and whom) do these definitions omit? Through introspection, we can identify our areas of weakness and make conscious choices to include "deviant bodies," other-than-human entities, and queer kinships into the ecological webs that help us (and our students) understand our worlds.

Returning for a moment to written texts, including Judaculla Rock, as potential gatekeepers, we also need to consider the role of language as a tool of settler hierarchy. All of the canonized Appalachian literature that I have personally been exposed to has been in English. And yet we know that a plethora of languages are spoken and written within the region. Marie Junaluska shared a wonderful story in the Fall 2009 edition of *Appalachian Review*, which publishes many talented wordsmiths, making Junaluska's inclusion no surprise. Yet "The Wolf's Ear" was published in Cherokee syllabary, phonetic Cherokee, and English, respectively.[45] While this essay focuses on the exclusion of Native writers, it is also important to be aware of the many other languages spoken within the region and to realize that not all Appalachians are speakers of English as a first language. To continue to acknowledge only the texts written in English is to continue to maintain the settler hierarchies of language. Maintaining such hierarchies not only carries on the tradition of excluding "deviant bodies," as discussed earlier, but prevents us from creating the relationships, in this case human relationships, that allow us to reenvision the region's ecology.

CONCLUSION

Barbara Ellen Smith's words at the Appalachian Studies Association Plenary seem to encapsulate my own thoughts, so I offer them to you here:

> We need to hold in one hand the experiences of African American Appalachians, Cherokee Appalachians, and other people of color in the region, whose historical memories— and contemporary experiences—bear witness to the trauma wreaked by white supremacy. In very different ways, in lost opportunities for alliances and unearned privileges masked by the injustices of class, so do the experiences of whites.[46] With our other hand, we can lay claim to the more hopeful memories with which Appalachian history is also replete. They lie in part in the rich legacy of our class and community-based struggles, which have sometimes transcended though too rarely challenged the unjust hierarchies of race.[47]

Queering Appalachian ecology, particularly through understanding of the human, challenges the ways in which white settler Appalachians are complicit in the perpetuation of Native erasure and settler colonialism and paves the way to ensure that the histories, experiences, and ecologies of all our relations within and with ties to the region are accurately represented and included in Appalachian studies curricula. Such representation and inclusion, I hope, will serve as a roadmap that can lead the future generations we encounter to further inquiry and to an understanding of the necessity of change to the systemic ravages of settler colonialism and white supremacy.

NOTES

1. Catriona Mortimer-Sandilands and Bruce Erickson, "Introduction: A Genealogy of Queer Ecologies," in *Queer Ecologies: Sex, Nature, Politics, Desire* (Bloomington: Indiana University Press, 2010), 1–47.

2. For a thorough and fascinating depiction of the ways in which settler colonialism perpetuated heterosexuality in the United States, particularly among Native Peoples, please read Mark Rifkin's *When Did Indians Become Straight? Kinship, the History of Sexuality, and Native Sovereignty* (New York: Oxford University Press, 2011).

3. This contestation is typically based on how "culture" often decides what counts as "nature" and "nature" can be understood to help cocreate "culture." For a thorough exploration of the idea of what Donna J. Haraway calls "natureculture," see her books *The Companion Species Manifesto: Dogs, People, and Significant Otherness* (Chicago: Prickly Paradigm, 2003); *Staying with the Trouble: Making Kin in the Chthulucene* (Durham, NC: Duke University Press, 2016). For one Indigenous perspective on the nature-culture binary, Kim TallBear has written extensively about how her Dakota teachings reject such a binary. I highly recommend her short article "An Indigenous Reflection on Working Beyond the Human/Not Human," *GLQ* 21, no. 2–3 (2015): 230–35.

4. Nicole Seymour, *Strange Natures: Futurity, Empathy, and the Queer Ecological Imagination* (Urbana: University of Illinois Press, 2013), 3.

5. Timothy Morton, "Queer Ecology," *PMLA* 125, no. 2 (March 2010): 273.

6. Leanne Betasamosake Simpson, Lisa Brooks, Glen Coulthard, and Kim Tall-Bear are just a few of the Native scholars who have examined kinship. Many Native writers, such as LeAnne Howe, Linda Hogan, and N. Scott Momaday, have also explored these ideas in creative texts.

7. Zackary Vernon explores the historicity and trajectory of Appalachian literature in his essay "Toward a Post-Appalachian Sense of Place," *Journal of American Studies* 50, no. 3 (August 2016): 639–58.

8. Mishauna Goeman, *Mark My Words: Native Women Mapping Our Nations* (Minneapolis: University of Minnesota Press, 2013), 88.

9. Mark Rifkin, *Beyond Settler Time: Temporal Sovereignty and Indigenous Self-Determination* (Durham, NC: Duke University Press, 2017), 1.

10. Chris Green and Erica Abrams Locklear, "Writing Appalachia: Intersections, Missed Connections, and Future Work," in *Studying Appalachian Studies: Making the Path by Walking*, ed. Chad Berry, Philip J. Obermiller, and Shaunna L. Scott (Champaign: University of Illinois Press, 2015), 62–87.

11. Green and Locklear, "Writing Appalachia," 75.

12. "Appalachian Studies Course Syllabi," Appalachian Studies Association, 2020, http://appalachianstudies.org/resources/syllabi.php.

13. Green and Locklear, "Writing Appalachia," 75.

14. Green and Locklear, "Writing Appalachia," 75.

15. Donald E. Davis, *Where There Are Mountains: An Environmental History of the Southern Appalachians* (Athens: University of Georgia Press, 2003), 3.

16. David S. Walls, "On the Naming of Appalachia," in *An Appalachian Symposium: Essays Written in Honor of Cratis D. Williams*, ed. J. W. Williamson (Boone, NC: Appalachian State University, 1977), 56–76, 58.

17. Eve Tuck and K. Wayne Yang, "Decolonization Is Not a Metaphor," *Decolonization: Indigeneity, Education & Society* 1, no. 1 (2012): 1–40, 19.

18. With *national*, I'm referring to Native Nations, not US citizenship.

19. Rebecca Eli Long, "Claiming Disability in Appalachia" (MA thesis, Appalachian State University, 2020); and Katy Ross, "At the Intersection of Queer and Appalachia(n): Negotiating Identity and Social Support" (PhD diss., Ohio University, 2019) are more recent examples of this type of scholarship, though there are certainly many other examples.

20. Audra Simpson, "The State Is a Man: Theresa Spence, Loretta Saunders and the Gender of Settler Sovereignty," *Theory and Event* 19, no. 4 (2016).

21. Arguably, the notions of past, present, and future are also colonial constructs. For an excellent discussion of this topic, see Rifkin's *Beyond Settler Time*. There are also many excellent texts that discuss queer(ing) temporalities, including a significant amount of work by Jack Halberstam.

22. Stephen Pearson, "'The Last Bastion of Colonialism': Appalachian Settler Colonialism and Self-Indigenization," *American Indian Culture and Research Journal* 37, no. 2 (2013): 166.

23. Pearson, "Last Bastion of Colonialism," 128.

24. Harry M. Caudill, *Night Comes to the Cumberlands: A Biography of a Depressed Region* (Boston: Little, Brown, 1963), xi.

25. Helen Lewis and Edward Knipe, "The Colonialism Model: The Appalachian Case," in *Colonialism in Modern America: The Appalachian Case*, ed. Helen Lewis, Linda Johnson, and Donald Askins (Boone, NC: Appalachian Consortium, 1978), 17.

26. Kim TallBear, "What's in Ecosexuality for an Indigenous Scholar of 'Nature'?," *Indigenous STS*, June 29, 2012. She addresses white environmental criticisms in the July 19, 2012, addendum to this post, which appears below the initial post on the same web page.

27. Helen Matthews Lewis, Linda Johnson, and Donald Askins, *Colonialism in Modern America: The Appalachian Case* (Boone, NC: Appalachian Consortium, 1978), 1.

28. Lewis, Johnson, and Askins, *Colonialism in Modern America*, 10.

29. Lewis, Johnson, and Askins, *Colonialism in Modern America*, 2.

30. Lewis, Johnson, and Askins, *Colonialism in Modern America*, 2.

31. Eduardo Duran et al., "From Historical Trauma to Hope and Healing: 2004 Appalachian Studies Association Conference [with Responses]," *Appalachian Journal* 32, no. 2 (2005): 177–78, https://www.jstor.org/stable/40934391.

32. David S. Walls, "Internal Colony or Internal Periphery? A Critique of Current Models and an Alternative Formulation," in Lewis, Johnson, and Askins, *Colonialism in Modern America*, 326. Walls is also the only contributor to the volume who references the plights of Native Peoples in Appalachia.

33. Walls, "Internal Colony or Internal Periphery?," 327.

34. Walls, "Internal Colony or Internal Periphery?," 339.

35. Arguably, this deployment of queer theory could be read as sexual, as that's how Native bodies, like most bodies, perpetuate. Also, the sexualization of Native women is a problematic stereotype that encourages settler violence (see the movement to locate missing and murdered Indigenous women, often known as MMIW). Jack Halberstam, *In a Queer Time and Place: Transgender Bodies, Subcultural Lives* (New York: NYU Press, 2005), 12–13.

36. Annette Saunooke Clapsaddle, "Marie Junaluska," in *Step into the Circle: Writers in Modern Appalachia*, ed. Amy Greene and Trent Thompson (Durham, NC: Carolina Wren, 2019), 79–80.

37. Lauret Savoy, *Trace: Memory, History, Race, and the American Landscape* (Berkeley, CA: Counterpoint, 2015), 80–81 (italics in original).

38. Daniel Heath Justice, *Why Indigenous Literatures Matter* (Waterloo, ON: Wilfred Laurier University Press, 2018), 28.

39. Daniel Heath Justice, "Notes toward a Theory of Anomaly," *GLQ: A Journal of Lesbian and Gay Studies* 16, no. 1–2 (2010): 218.

40. Justice, "Notes toward a Theory of Anomaly," 209 (italics in original).

41. Elizabeth Catte, *What You Are Getting Wrong about Appalachia* (Cleveland: Belt, 2018).

42. Laura Da', *Tributaries* (Tucson: University of Arizona Press, 2015), 13–14.

43. Green and Locklear, "Writing Appalachia," 75.

44. Silas House (@silasdhouse), Twitter, May 27, 2020, 11:24 a.m., https://twitter .com/silasdhouse/status/1265665070257897473. Another issue here might be using the term Appalachia as a placeholder for any text produced within or about the region, as I discussed earlier when writing about the origin of the term. By using it as a catchall to include works by Native Peoples, are we as Appalachian studies scholars perpetuating the white supremacy behind the word's origins?

45. Marie Junaluska, "The Wolf's Ear," *Appalachian Review* (previously *Appalachian Heritage*) 37, no. 4 (2009): 103–108.

46. Per the discussion earlier in this chapter, this designation may prove problematic in that it erases indigeneity.

47. Duran et al., "From Historical Trauma to Hope and Healing," 178.

IT'S GRANDPA'S LAND

*Settler Property, Heteropatriarchy, and
Environmental Disasters*

Kandice Grossman, Aaron Padgett, and Rebecca Scott

INTRODUCTION

Those guys that work on the pipeline, they're just transient.
I mean . . . do they have any roots at all? . . . If you have no
roots, do you even care whether you're tearing up somebody's
homeland? Because, really, I think in West Virginia we are such
a people of place that, no matter what, our land is sacred to
us, and when someone comes in, and they're tearing up our
land, they're tearing up our hearts, and . . . and I know way
down the road our ancestors did it. . . . We are a product of
white privilege. I think here [in West Virginia] we don't think
we are, but we are. . . . I remember driving and it wasn't even
my county, it wasn't anyone I knew . . . and . . . I saw them
blow up the side of a hill [for a surface mine] and I just sat
there and cried because that's someone's ancestors lived there,
that's where their life was. And I know I have to go [back to
my] home sometimes. It says, "no trespassing." Well, I'm sorry,
if I feel like I need to go home, I don't know the people who
own it, but they can arrest me because sometimes I have to
go back there, where that pile of rocks, made by people I did

not know, but they were my people, is, and I have to be there for a little bit.

—Rose, resident of a West Virginia county crossed by a
planned natural gas pipeline

In West Virginia, a natural gas boom has produced a large amount of gas without a clearly defined destination or preexisting market. To solve this problem, in conjunction with the planned Appalachian Storage Hub,[1] along the Ohio River, gas transportation companies have begun building a network of pipelines to bring the gas to power plants and export stations located in all directions from the heart of the West Virginia gas fields in Wetzel County.[2] Two such pipelines, Mountain Valley Pipeline (MVP) and the (now canceled) Atlantic Coast Pipeline (ACP), have been projected to travel from the gas wells of the north to the south and east, across some of the most bucolic and wild landscapes in West Virginia, crossing both the Greenbrier River and the Appalachian Trail.

Fracking and pipeline construction, along with the threat of a new petrochemical storage and processing hub on the Ohio River, actively shuts down alternative futures for the communities in their paths. Frack pads, the size of a city block, send their "legs" out in every direction to extract natural gas in what some have called a Ponzi scheme with few foreseeable winners.[3] Huge pipe yards, filled with meters-deep limestone gravel and enormous piles of forty-two-inch steel pipe, sit waiting for tree sitters to be taken down, for public hearings to conclude, and for lawsuits to be settled. Trees are cleared, and the right-of-way is sprayed with herbicide to prepare the way for the pipeline. This destruction and damage to surrounding farms and forests is permanent, even if, as happened with the ACP, the plans fall through. For the MVP, the fight for America's "future energy security" continues.

Unlike smaller, local pipelines that rely on landowners voluntarily leasing their property to the pipeline company, the MVP and

ACP use the eminent domain legal framework provided by the Federal Energy Regulatory Commission (FERC), which regulates US interstate energy infrastructure projects. When a project is designated as serving the public interest, eminent domain can be invoked to access land even without the permission of the landowner, although they still must receive "fair market value" for the lease. Locating this extractive industry in the context of settler colonial culture and land relations, this chapter focuses on the contradictions raised by this development for the residents living in several West Virginia counties in the path of the MVP and ACP.

In the quote above, Rose, a resident of a West Virginia county interviewed by Rebecca Scott in 2018, clearly lays out the obvious contradiction between extractive industry and the human inhabitation of a place, describing how the destruction of the land through fracking, mining, or pipeline construction "tears up our hearts." However, her comments signal a deeper contradiction. The tearing up of land and hearts didn't start with the coal and natural gas industries; rather, it goes back to the destruction by white settlers of Indigenous habitations, lifeways, and relations to place. She emphasizes how private property structures in general contradict the human-place relations that some West Virginians identify with and many Indigenous Peoples hold sacred—in other words, when someone else owns your home, your ability to spend time there or visit is curtailed.[4] However, Rose specifically focuses on harm to a homeplace rendered sacred by an individual family connection; this is a privatized connection based on private property, biological kinship, and patriarchal inheritance that can unfortunately be broken by a transfer of ownership. While there is a perception that rural Appalachians are "people of place," their relationships to humans, nonhumans, and nature are limited by the legal and cultural structures of whiteness as property, heteropatriarchy, land inheritance, and settler state sovereignty.[5]

Settler colonialism is a structure, not an event.[6] And this structure, which aims to replace Indigenous Peoples, inhabitations, and lifeways with settler ones, depends on the institution of private property. How does the ongoing structure of settler colonialism underpin settler sovereignty, biological kinship, racialized conceptions of property, and relationship to place? US sovereignty, wrested through the Revolutionary War from the sovereignty of the British Crown, underpins the institution of private property.[7] Huge land grants made before the revolution to men like George Washington enabled them to divide and sell their parcels to other white settlers.[8] Indigenous attachments to land, based on collective relationships to particular landforms, were the target of violent expropriation by settlers in the name of individual property ownership. When Indigenous land was not directly expropriated, their collective holdings were the target of a strategy of allotment that transferred Indigenous-held land to individual male heads of households in an effort to enforce settler land-ownership patterns.[9] In the minds and memories of many white landowners today, "grandpa's land" signifies the eternalization of this heteropatriarchal racialized inheritance of private property from a landowner to his descendants.

However, this relationship to "grandpa's land" is threatened by the implementation of eminent domain in the name of infrastructure projects like the MVP or ACP. Eminent domain is a feature of state sovereignty that evolved out of European parliamentary monarchies from the seventeenth century. Transplanted to the settler colonies of North America, in the United States it frequently appears to be in conflict with the sacrosanct rights of individual property ownership that define American national identity. Historically, eminent domain has been used to destroy Black, brown, and poor communities through urban renewal and for the construction of the major highways that characterize American cities. When used for building roads and housing developments that at least show some benefit, in theory, to the users of these forms of infrastructure, eminent domain can be seen as offering a public benefit (to the generalized economy) with the cost paid by minoritized communities. Similarly, the landowners in the way of the natural gas pipelines see eminent domain as forcing the inexplicable destruction of their property and the environment in the direct service of the private gain of the gas and pipeline companies.

The creation of pipelines to develop a market for fracked natural gas reflects the political and economic philosophy of neoliberalism. Since the 1980s in the United States, the economic philosophy of neoliberalism has prioritized privatization, trade liberalization, deregulation, and the integration of national industries into the global "free market."[10] "Neoliberalism is in the first instance a theory of political economic practices that proposes that human well-being can best be advanced by liberating individual entrepreneurial freedoms and skills within an institutional framework characterized by strong private property rights, free markets, and free trade."[11] Natural gas has become a key commodity in energy sectors, challenging the domination of the coal industry in the Appalachian region. However, the market for natural gas has to be facilitated by public investment in infrastructure. The natural gas industry also relies on laborers who are willing to work temporarily or who move from job site to job site (those rootless workers described by Rose, above). Hydraulic fracking, the primary form of natural gas extraction in the region, creates destruction, pollution, and health risks for humans and nonhumans throughout the stages of extraction, processing, and transportation.

When contradictions emerge within entangled settler colonial logics and institutions of private property, eminent domain, and neoliberalism, they disturb and unsettle the settled expectations of the residents of stolen lands in this study.[12] Erickson explains how a settled future promotes capitalist development: "The establishment of the regime of utility that permeates late capitalism requires a predictable view of the future . . . a future anterior; the space where things 'will have been.' I participate in activities, purchase goods, and engage in civic politics in order to have been a good citizen."[13] Similarly, what Mark Rifkin calls "settler time," like Erickson's future anterior, imposes a straightforward imagination of the (re)productive heteronormative patriarchal family that reflects the eternalization of the settler state and the free market.[14] With the implementation of eminent domain in the name of the pipeline, the eternalized settler state and its free market come into conflict with the individual settler's anticipated future of enjoying their property. Despite these contradictions, the privatized nature of settler attachments to the land in the path of the pipeline impedes radical, collective action.

In this chapter, we apply a critical settler perspective—a form of inquiry intended to expose how settler colonial structures, knowledges, and meanings are constructed to support asymmetrical systems of power in order to explore how settler colonial structures come into conflict with the sustainability of human inhabitations. The following section briefly explains the historical genealogy of the US colonial and racialized notions of sovereignty, private property law, and eminent domain that underpin the first contradiction raised by Rose, above. We offer an overview of the ways contemporary neoliberal economic structures and reasoning emerged from settler structures and evolved into a market imperative for development (or improvement) that often "tears people's hearts" as it destroys the places they inhabit. As Rose suggests, the destruction caused by the contemporary natural gas and pipeline boom is not comprehensible without an awareness of the historical structures of settler colonialism that put this relation to people, place, and land into effect.

The subsequent section examines data from qualitative interviews undertaken in 2018 with West Virginia residents who were fighting the pipeline. These interviews offer expressions of the contradictions between the free market in natural gas and the private property of settlers. These contradictions are articulated by the notion of "grandpa's land," a phrase that expresses the privatized white heteropatriarchal property of a landowner and his dependents, projected backward to previous generations and forward to future descendants, in an echo of the eternalization of the settler state. The ideal of holding on to grandpa's land comes into conflict with the neoliberal private property regime that sees the market as the arbiter of the best and highest use of resources. In other words, the sentence "It's grandpa's land" reflects the expectation that this property "will have been" in the white family forever.[15] This expectation that underlies settler time demonstrates the biopolitics of normative national citizenship. In other words, the settler ideal is represented by the white patriarchal family as a unit of inheritance and identity that upholds settler property relations (i.e., individual ownership of land).[16] However, individual private property as a structure diminishes the capacity for people to resist. The final section points to how the normative structures of the patriarchal property-owning nuclear family (i.e., respectability) function as discipline in the context of settler colonialism. These individualistic structures of settler property can function to preempt or shut down the imagined alternative futures presented by radical action groups that oppose the extractive industry.

HISTORICAL GENEALOGY

Kauanui argues that the heteropatriarchal expectations, norms, and legal structures of "the family" that were imposed upon Indigenous Peoples through settler colonialism are integral to the historical restructuring and subjugation of Indigenous sexualities and kinship relations. These expectations also undermined Indigenous sovereignty through land privatization in conjunction with institutions like heterosexual marriage.[17] Individual property rights became the bedrock of social structure under British (and subsequently, American) sovereignty, and individualized titles to land for both Natives and settlers depended on the authorization of the state.[18]

Historically, the ideology of "improvement" has underlain the expropriation of land from Indigenous Peoples and, later, from arrivants and settlers.[19] Projects for improvement generally included homesteading, developing infrastructure, or clearing acreage.[20] If "improvement" was not made a priority by Indigenous Peoples, arrivants, or settlers, colonial officials maintained the authority to retract titles to undeveloped land and hand them over to the state, which typically used these lands "to build roads and generally promote economic growth."[21] In the United States, the federal right of eminent domain was both institutionalized and limited when James Madison wrote the "just compensation clause" in the Fifth Amendment, which states, "Nor shall private property be taken for a public use without just compensation."[22] The meanings of *public use* and *public benefit* are much debated and especially fraught in the age of neoliberal capitalism, in which collective action and benefit is derogated.

Critical geographer David Harvey writes, "The founding figures of neoliberal thought took political ideals of human dignity and individual freedom as fundamental, as 'the central values of civilization.' In so doing they chose wisely, for these are indeed compelling and seductive ideals. These values, they held, were threatened not only by fascism, dictatorships, and communism, but *by all forms of state intervention that substituted collective judgements for those of individuals free to choose.*"[23]

The neoliberal economic values of individualism, privatization, and freedom have been extended as values to everyday dimensions of people's lives. In neoliberalism, settler colonialism works in conjunction with spatially dispersed agencies and is not confined to state institutions.[24] Private property became central to social control and reproduction, developing individualist "entrepreneurial subjectivities" in a "grid of economic intelligibility" where the abstract relations of money, interest, commodities, and value are embodied in the material transformations of everyday life.[25]

Neoliberalism claims that everyone has an equal opportunity to work hard and succeed in life by making smart economic or entrepreneurial choices. However, these opportunities are perpetually structured by hierarchies of race, class, gender, and sexuality. As a cultural discourse, neoliberalism uses the "privatizing language of rights, the morality of the marketplace, and the rhetoric of economic efficiency" to "recast social problems—power and inequity—as personal troubles."[26] Settler culture structures the discourse of neoliberalism and is invoked in a corporation's claim to eminent domain and the "rule of capture,"[27] just as it is invoked in white settler residents' claims to "grandpa's land." Neoliberal ideology thus upholds white supremacy as a structure that privileges white settler property relations, even at the cost of an individual settler's property.

The next section explores how the structures of settler colonial culture were expressed in interviews about the MVP and ACP projects. Residents of counties crossed by these planned pipelines were subjected to forced expropriation by eminent domain. Their inhabitation of the place was threatened by the imperative of capitalist accumulation and resource extraction. In this context, residents expressed two main contradictions embedded in what it means to be "of place" within the limits of settler colonial culture. First, interviewees expressed an affective relationship with place. This relation is bound by settler colonial possessive logics of private property expressed in the future anterior of "grandpa's land" that minimize Indigenous original and ongoing relations to place, rights to territories, and sovereignty. Second, residents expressed the pain of the limits of ownership in light of the imperative of neoliberal economic improvement and development under settler colonial sovereignty.

EXPRESSIONS OF SETTLER COLONIAL CULTURE AND FUTURITY IN THE PIPELINE FIGHT

In 2018, Rebecca Scott interviewed white residents in West Virginia affected by the construction of natural gas pipelines and the use of eminent domain. These residents were being forced to allow pipeline construction on their property against their will. Many expressed a sense of moral outrage at this imposition.

For example, Grace, a resident of a county in the path of a pipeline, described the community's reaction to the pipeline construction via eminent domain this way: "It's grandpa's land. And I think the issue is that you don't have any control over it. They're taking, you know, the land. I mean, you remember the scene in *Gone with the Wind*, when Gerald O'Hara says, 'Land, Katie Scarlett, land. It's the only—' I'll cry. 'It's the only thing worth fighting for. It's the only thing worth dying for.' They're taking our land [and] that knows no politics. That's just wrong."

Even though the speaker's own property was purchased, not inherited, white settler possessive logic asserts a general feeling that the land belongs to "grandpa." Moreton-Robinson describes white settler possessive logic as a mode of rationalization underpinned by an excessive interest in reproducing a nation-state's sovereignty, ownership, and the economic logic of capital.[28] The settler possessive logic circulates meanings about race, power, and ownership to condition "common-sense" decisions and socially accepted norms. Describing the land as "grandpa's" asserts a white settler possessive logic that implies that land rightfully belongs to an imaginary, historical white settler patriarch. This normalizes the erasure of Indigenous Peoples and their rightful connection to the land because it implies that the land was empty, or at best without value, before he took possession.[29] White settler possessive logics "discursively disavow and dispossess the Indigenous subject of an ontology that exists outside the logic of capital," exclusively operating in hegemonic terms they control and define that uphold white supremacy.[30]

White settler possessive logics exist within "settler time," in which the eternalization of the settler state makes the possession of stolen land always already a sacred inheritance for a white family.[31] Rifkin defines *settler time* as a linear conception of time that structures colonial memory in a way that narrates events in the space of the United States as unfolding within an atemporal container of history. This atemporal container evades Indigenous Peoples' existence before the United States and thereby erases claims to territories, self-determination, and sovereignty. In settler colonial memory, Indigenous Peoples are represented as absent, static, or disappeared and are thus "not allowed modernity."[32] Settler time assumes the nation and its economy to be a normative and political fact that must be defended against all threats, both past and future. As Jodi Byrd notes, the US empire has an unacknowledged birthing point, in which European colonialist agendas inflicted death and destruction upon Native Peoples and then appropriated Indigenous lands, knowledges, presences, and identities for its own use; to acknowledge this origin is to put into question national identity and legitimacy.[33]

Grace's reference to the 1939 Hollywood film *Gone with the Wind* (*GWTW*) demonstrates how white settler possessive logics and settler time are (co)produced and (re)produced through cultural artifacts, such as books and films, in ways that perpetuate white settler societal "common sense." In the scene referenced from *GWTW*,[34] the master-enslaver patriarch of the plantation instructs his white daughter on the importance of property ownership. Significantly, the marked Irish roots of the patriarch in this book and film suggest the social mobility afforded to those considered white by settler colonialism in the so-called New World. The film (re)produces discourses that have attained meaning through their iteration in laws, violence, and representations of history.[35] These discourses concretize the ideology that whiteness and property are interrelated concepts.[36] The whiteness of the characters and their love of the plantation they own are supported by the expropriation of Native American land and the enslavement of Black people. The invocation of *GWTW* in the context of the pipeline fight evokes an emotional response surrounding white settler possessive logics of private property experienced by many Americans. Grace's reference to the specific historical Civil War era, as part of her plea for private property rights, appeals to a significant, historical marker of white settler progress in the linear narrative of national history.[37]

The father-daughter scene invoked by Grace also underlines how white settler colonial logics rely on heteropatriarchal constructs that situate biological kinship within a monogamous nuclear family as the epitome of civilization. Biological family inheritance is also the goal of individual property accumulation.[38] Healthy families—those who follow the law, make "common-sense" decisions, live "respectably," and pass their property on to their children—are those who are meant to thrive in the settler colonial American system. Rifkin argues that settler culture creates a feeling of normalcy through "mechanisms like property law, zoning ordinances, rules of inheritance, regulation of commerce, police presence, and the construction and maintenance of infrastructure." Additionally, he contends that "such state-enacted geographies . . . help provide shape and structure" to the otherwise fragile construction of settler colonialism.[39] Settler possessive logics, settler time, and heteropatriarchy create an expected future for the white family. Property, once attained and owned, represents the hoped-for and expected future in which the children "will have been" able to enjoy their parents or grandparents' economic security.

The expectation of control of a piece of property in the hands of an exclusive biological kinship lineage expresses the American dream of US settler colonialism.[40] The grievances of residents in West Virginia thereby express the pain of losing control, money, expectations for the future, and a vision of the family. Here, Grace explains why she opposes the pipeline:

> We own property, um, across the road . . . twenty-five acres was the plot. And we haven't owned it very long. It's very difficult to find land . . . because nobody in this county wants to sell. And it's been in families for a long time. And we were just lucky that the fella that owned it, um, needed money. And so he sold it and he sold it at a good price. I mean he, he certainly didn't, um, it wasn't a bargain, but because it's so infrequently available, we went ahead, put our house up to borrow the money, and did so. Well we're still making payments on the land, but the pipeline is gonna come across three hundred plus feet. Doesn't sound like much, but it's coming across. And the one flat place that we had hoped our youngest daughter and her husband would build a house. . . . We had hoped they would come back. . . . We would be able to enjoy our grandchildren there . . . but the pipeline coming through the property, they're not, we wouldn't want them to build on a pipeline. So, of course, the value of the property will plummet. So, we are not optimistic about being able to sell it and get the money back in order to pay for it. So, it impacts us emotionally because our kids can't use it for home sites, and it impacts us financially 'cause we're still making payments on it . . . and will continue to do so without any assistance. We didn't wanna sell it. I have been bold enough to say that there's not enough money minted in this world to buy our property.

This attachment to the land she was unwilling to sell defies the neoliberal discipline of the market that says everything should be for sale. Nevertheless, many interviewees in this study expressed what Huber calls a "neoliberal subjectivity": assumptions, practices, and "common-sense" beliefs shaped by market values.[41] It is thus evident that neoliberal logics present several contradictions for the white settler property-owner citizen. For example, a neoliberal ideal is that state intervention in markets should be kept at a minimum to prevent powerful interest groups from exploiting the market for their own benefit. The need for state-enforced eminent domain to enable private natural gas companies to get their product to market thus challenges the expectations of the neoliberal subject. However, it is the state-enabled market that creates the privatization and commodification of land and labor. These contradictions structure neoliberal subjectivity and social life in ways that create an alienating and alienated possessive individualism. In other words, the individual's freedom to choose (labor, lifestyle, beliefs, etc.) is held as one of the highest values. Yet within the market, individual "freedoms" are entangled in racialized, heteronormative, and nationalized structures that actually limit freedoms in order to uphold the bottom line of capitalist accumulation and white supremacy. As Byrd et al. argue, under neoliberalism, "austerity discourse recycles and modifies repertoires of racialization, heteropatriarchy, and colonialism by articulating them in registers of economic necessity."[42]

Although Rose and Grace and many others in this study opposed pipeline construction, some accepted the new market for natural gas as inevitable for economic progress, specifically referencing the jobs brought to the area. Some interviewees lamented the material and cultural death of older forms of labor alienation in the coal industry at the same time as imagining a future marked by economic progress and labor in the natural gas industry. For example, Ellen describes the transition from coal to natural gas this way:

> It . . . is a sad fact of life . . . it's really sad what's happened in the coalfields. Those . . . people worked in the coal mines for years and years and years and that's all they knew, that's

all they did, and even now today, the ones that are still in the mines, you wouldn't get them to do anything else. . . . As natural gas has taken over, coal and the coal mines have shut down. There's still coal being mined in West Virginia but the towns, they're dead. There is nothing for them, nothing. And it's so sad and I guess maybe they thought coal would be mined forever. . . . I didn't like the fact that they quit burning coal, but it is what it is. You know, that pipeline works for the public good because many people in this county work there.

Workers under neoliberalism are mere factors in production, as is revealed in the natural gas industry, where laborers are often contracted temporarily, with little or no long-term job security or benefits. "Commodification presumes the existence of property rights over processes, things, and social relations, that a price can be put on them, and that they can be traded subject to legal contract."[43] In the neoliberal "grid of economic intelligibility," where abstract relations of money, interest, commodities, and value take priority in the name of progress, people are willing to sacrifice communities, job security, and land in the name of economic progress.

At the same time, many residents ask, "Progress toward what future?" Residents express the obvious tension that emerges from the contradictions between the need for human inhabitation and the desire for improvement (i.e., economic growth). The social and environmental consequences of economic development are assumed to be fully acceptable in the name of the continuation of the nation-state and of economic progress, despite ongoing destruction, alienation, and death. Neoliberalism embraces the uninhibited and unregulated freedom of markets and assumes a limitless future of economic development while accepting devastating costs to humans, nonhumans, cultures, and ecologies as a given. The emphasis on individualism further impedes organized opposition, including democratic collective associations and institutions working for justice, equality, and social solidarities (such as labor unions or environmental justice coalitions).

Ellen's comment that "it is what it is" expresses the contradiction inherent in the classical liberal ideal of the American nation as made up by white, independent acquisitive individuals and formed by a social contract to protect the source of their independence, their property. As the property-owner patriarch passes property to his inheritors, the family remains intact and in place within the nation.[44] However, the neoliberal "free market" created by this imagined social contract regularly promotes economic activity that destroys the grounds on which these independent individuals and families stand. As natural gas replaces coal, West Virginians seem to have no option but to try to get some benefit from this "economic progress," despite the fact that their expectations of the future are destroyed by the imperative of economic growth and environmental destruction. In the next section, we conclude with a reflection on how these settler structures are perpetuated by respectability politics that inhibit radical action against extractive economic practices like the MVP and ACP.

RESPECTABILITY AND POSSIBILITIES FOR ALTERNATIVE FUTURES

Social regulations such as normative heterosexual marriage, family structure, and their connection to property ownership "help define and delimit the horizon of the possible, providing a nonconscious frame that informs and guides the phenomenological experience of selfhood, situatedness, and connection to others."[45] Respectability is critical to both property ownership as a claim to citizenship and the health of the nation. In some parts of rural West Virginia, respectability is expressed in the conflict between "locals" and "hippies" or the back-to-the-land baby boomers who "moved in" in the 1960s and 1970s.

While discussing the lack of traction that environmentalism seems to have in the area, Ellen recalled a successful struggle from years ago against a development project planned for her rural county: "So you know about what they call the hippies that move in? A lot of the people that got [the project] stopped was the hippies, so a lot of the people that got involved in [the pipeline fight] were the hippies. And . . . so those people who say 'It's going to happen anyway' don't want to be associated . . . with the hippies."

Settler culture depends on an assumption of the European norms of civility, the respectability of rights-bearing citizens, and their expectation of legal protection in settler law.[46] In Ellen's statement above, she underlines the way that some rural Appalachians resist "making a fuss" because "it's going to happen anyway," indicating that those who do raise a fuss are often considered outsiders, even after fifty years in the community. "Hippies"—those countercultural activists who challenged middle-class norms of respectability in the 1960s and 1970s—in many cases created alternative lifestyles and political practices that continue to resonate in the present. Respectability in this context becomes resignation to the labor market and legal structures of a state long dominated by extractive industry, structures in which battles waged on the terrain of rights are understood as being unwinnable. Nevertheless, the collective investment in the settler state creates an expectation that this system "will have been" just.

However, radical environmental action against pipeline construction is going on across what is currently known as North America, challenging the dominant imagination of what futures can take place here. These interventions highlight the foreshortening of the "horizon of the possible" through their creative civil disobedience and direct actions that offer alternatives to the status quo.[47] In Appalachia, groups like Radical Action for Mountains and

People's Survival (RAMPS), Appalachians against the Pipeline, and others have employed tree sitting as a way to stop the pipeline.[48] As expressed by others in this volume, these actions open up imaginations of alternative futures to the one set in motion by settler colonialism and fossil fuel extraction.[49]

Expressing her admiration for such activists, Grace highlights normative middle-class expectations of the life course while suggesting the unlikelihood of such actions in her own life: "They're unarmed. They are nonviolent. They are mostly vegan and vegetarian. They are not aggressive people. They are just trying to save the Earth. And they're very dedicated to it. It's . . . a wonderful lifestyle. If I could grow up and be . . . a tree sitter or an activist I think I might. I mean, to go from place to place to fight for right and justice and to protect the Earth . . . I'm just so proud of them. I really am."

Despite individual landowners' opposition to the pipeline and their desire to save their land, settler colonial logics of possessive individualism and private property rights can stand in the way of a radical response. Heteronormative nuclear families rely on the inheritance of "grandpa's land" as a stake toward a future of security in the settler state. The activists who "go from place to place" to fight fossil fuel extraction necessarily have to give up this normative path to respectability. Settler culture works to limit each property owner to an individual effort to protect their own. This has the effect of miring them in an asymmetrical struggle over sovereignty with the state, whose interests lie in the promotion of economic development. Meanwhile, the state tries to shut down and mark as uncivil all efforts to respond to the natural gas boom through an anticolonial and collective approach.

Settler sovereignty endows individuals with the possibility of forming an exclusive right to a piece of land. Legal inheritance through biological kinship allows that land to be passed down to future generations. However, this individual right is both granted and limited by the ultimate sovereignty of the state, as expressed by eminent domain, to take the land for a "higher" purpose. In the end, the market determines both the worth and "highest use" of the land. The state's right to take the land is articulated through the same logic of improvement used by colonizers to negate Indigenous sovereignty. In other words, the contemporary appropriation of "grandpa's land" relies on the historical precondition of Indigenous dispossession.[50] The national narrative of economic development through natural gas extraction, pipeline construction, and petrochemical processing imagines the past and future of the settler state in perpetual progress. However, this progress ironically presupposes the sacrifice of the settlers' expected futures in place. As Grace suggests, living otherwise, outside the constraints of heteropatriarchal settler attachments, is one way to imagine an alternative.

NOTES

1. The proposed Appalachian Storage Hub is a network of cracker plants, natural gas storage, and chemical plants including plastic pellet manufacturers along the Ohio River. Kate Mishkin, "The Appalachian Storage Hub Is Mired in Secrecy. Residents Say They're Already Worried about What They Do Know," *Charleston Gazette-Mail*, August 3, 2019, https://www.wvgazettemail.com /news/the-appalachian-storage-hub-is-mired-in-secrecy-residents-say/article _91b8fb7b-8d49-5170-afc8-54338239a090.html.

2. Scott DiSavino, "New U.S. Pipelines to Drive Natural Gas Boom as Exports Surge," Reuters, April 12, 2017, https://www.reuters.com/article/us-usa-lng-pipelines -analysis/new-u-s-pipelines-to-drive-natural-gas-boom-as-exports-surge -idUSKBN17E2CH; Kathiann M. Kowalski, "Appalachian Gas Storage Hub Seeks Federal Clean Energy Loan Guarantee," Energy News Network, May 31, 2019, https://energynews.us/2019/05/31/midwest/clean-energy-loan-guarantee -could-be-a-stretch-for-natural-gas-liquids-hub/.

3. Justin Mikulka, "Struggling to Make a Profit, Fracking Investors Are Searching for the Exit," Nation of Change, May 26, 2021, https://www.nationof change.org/2021/04/26/struggling-to-make-a-profit-fracking-investors-are -searching-for-the-exit/.

4. The term *sacred* is often used to describe non-market-based place relations, as in "this place is sacred to me." Sisseton Wahpeton Oyate scholar Kim TallBear argues that the term inadequately translates a set of Indigenous concepts that are better expressed as being in relation with other human and nonhuman landforms and beings. Kimberly TallBear, "Caretaking Relations, Not American Dreaming," *Kalfou* 6, no. 1 (May 2019), https://tupjournals.temple.edu/index.php/kalfou/article/view/228.

5. Cheryl Harris, "Whiteness as Property," *Harvard Law Review* 106, no. 8 (1993); Scott Lauria Morgensen, "The Biopolitics of Settler Colonialism: Right Here, Right Now," *Settler Colonial Studies* 1, no. 1 (January 2011): 52–76; Stephen Pearson, "The Last Bastion of Colonialism: Appalachian Settler Colonialism and Self-Indigenization," *American Indian Culture and Research Journal* 37, no. 2 (January 2013): 165–84.

6. Patrick Wolfe, "The Settler Complex: An Introduction," *American Indian Culture and Research Journal* 37, no. 2 (January 2013): 1–22; J. Kēhaulani Kauanui, "'A Structure, Not an Event': Settler Colonialism and Enduring Indigeneity," *Lateral* 5, no. 1 (2016), https://csalateral.org/issue/5-1/forum-alt-humanities-settler-colonialism-enduring-indigeneity-kauanui/.

7. Roxanne Dunbar-Ortiz, *An Indigenous Peoples' History of the United States* (Boston: Beacon Press, 2014).

8. Eugene Thoenen, *History of the Oil and Gas Industry in West Virginia* (Charleston, WV: Education Foundation, 1964).

9. Harris, "Whiteness as Property."

10. Matthew T. Huber, *Lifeblood: Oil, Freedom, and the Forces of Capital* (Minneapolis: University of Minnesota Press, 2013); Amy Lind, "Querying Globalization: Sexual Subjectivities, Development, and the Governance of Intimacy," in *Gender and Global Restructuring: Sitings, Sites, and Resistances*, ed. Marianne A. Marchand and Anne Sisson Runyan (New York: Routledge, 2011); Julie Guthman, *Weighing In: Obesity, Food Justice, and the Limits of Capitalism* (Berkeley: University of California Press, 2011); David Harvey, *A Brief History of Neoliberalism* (New York: Oxford University Press, 2007).

11. Harvey, *Brief History of Neoliberalism*, 2.

12. Eva Mackey, *Unsettled Expectations: Uncertainty, Land and Settler Decolonization* (Black Point, NS: Fernwood Publishing, 2016); Paulette Regan, *Unsettling the Settler Within: Indian Residential Schools, Truth Telling, and Reconciliation in Canada* (Vancouver: University of British Columbia Press, 2011).

13. Bruce Erickson, "'Fucking Close to Water': Queering the Production of the Nation," in *Queer Ecologies: Sex, Nature, Poltics, Desire*, ed. Catriona

Mortimer-Sandilands and Bruce Erickson (Bloomington, Indiana University Press, 2010), 323.

14. Mark Rifkin, *Beyond Settler Time: Temporal Sovereignty and Indigenous Self-Determination* (Durham, NC: Duke University Press, 2017); Greta Gaard, "Toward a Queer Ecofeminism," in *New Perspectives on Environmental Justice: Gender, Sexuality, and Activism*, ed. Rachel Stein (New Brunswick, NJ: Rutgers University Press, 2004), 21–44.

15. Rifkin, *Beyond Settler Time*; Mackey, *Unsettled Expectations*.

16. Imani Perry, *Vexy Thing: On Gender and Liberation* (Durham, NC: Duke University Press, 2018).

17. J. Kēhaulani Kauanui, "Marriage Is a Colonial Imposition" (video, Barnard Center for Research on Women, New York, 2013), https://www.youtube.com /watch?v=u6ySbk35Y-k.

18. Royal charters made no statements on Native rights in (or to) land, which, as in the case of the Algonquin People of New England, were transitionally fixed. The Algonquin People in what became known as New England traveled seasonally among different regional locales for access to resources such as wild game and other plant-based food resources. See William Cronon, *Changes in the Land: Indians, Colonists, and the Ecology of New England* (New York: Hill and Wang, 1995), and James Warren Springer, "American Indians and the Law of Real Property in New England," *American Journal of Legal History* 30, no. 25 (1986): 25–58. Acquisition of these lands took place through arrangements that were viewed through the incompatible lenses of the British Crown and Indigenous Peoples. The Crown viewed land acquisition as a transactional arrangement and did not recognize tribal sovereignty, while Indigenous Peoples viewed the process as a bilateral agreement on use rights. See Cronon, *Changes in the land*; Mackey, *Unsettled Expectations*. This form of private property limited not only Native sovereignty but also that of the individual settler, who was not allowed to make individual purchases not sanctioned by the courts. In contrast to British and American sovereignties, Indigenous sovereignty is often structured by collective relations that are inalienable. The indeterminacy of private rights and public benefits under settler sovereignty are highlighted here, as these land takings dispossessed Indigenous Nations and some individual settlers.

19. Jodi Byrd, *The Transit of Empire: Indigenous Critiques of Colonialism* (Minneapolis. University of Minnesota Press, 2011).

20. Daniel P. Dalton, "A History of Eminent Domain," *Public Corporation Law Quarterly* no. 3 (Fall 2006): 1–20.

21. Dalton, "History of Eminent Domain," 3. While the notion of "improvement" was critical to the social, political, and economic fabrics of Revolutionary America, its roots trace back several centuries. Polanyi traces the discourse of improvement to the spread of enclosures across the English countryside. Enclosure privatized large estates, which were then available for use by the sole right of the owner. This meant that lands previously held in common were no longer available for community use or benefit. By the seventeenth century, Polanyi argues, the Enlightenment ideology of economic liberalism, private property, and improvement had taken a strong hold among English elites in Karl Polanyi, *The Great Transformation* (Boston: Beacon Press, 2001).

22. Dalton, "History of Eminent Domain," 4.

23. Harvey, *Brief History of Neoliberalism*, 5 (emphasis added).

24. Jen Preston, "Racial Extractivism and White Settler Colonialism: An Examination of the Canadian Tar Sands Mega-Projects," *Cultural Studies* 31, nos. 2–3 (2017): 353–75; Eve Tuck and K. Wayne Yang, "Decolonization Is Not a Metaphor," *Decolonization, Indigeneity Education and Society* 1, no. 1 (September 2012): 1–40.

25. Huber, *Lifeblood*, 22–23.

26. Michael Mascarenhas, *Where the Waters Divide: Neoliberalism, White Privilege, and Environmental Racism in Canada* (New York: Lexington Books, 2012), 19.

27. The rule of capture allows ownership to "capture" a resource such as natural gas, oil, or groundwater. As global dependency on petroleum advanced during the twentieth century, land access became an especially critical issue where mineral resources were concerned (Brian C. Black, *Crude Reality: Petroleum in World History* (Lanham, MD: Rowman & Littlefield, 2012); Huber, *Lifeblood*. The United States upheld the "rule of capture," a carryover from British common law, creating settler colonial frontier-like struggles for resources and requiring government intervention to regulate supply and pricing. Such public-private partnerships are shaped by the logic of improvement that sees privatized resource extraction as a necessity, regardless of its effect on human habitation.

28. Aileen Moreton-Robinson, *The White Possessive: Property, Power, and Indigenous Sovereignty* (Minneapolis: University of Minnesota Press, 2015).

29. Patrick Wolfe, "Settler Colonialism and the Elimination of the Native," *Journal of Genocide Research* 8, no. 4 (December 2006): 387–409.

30. Moreton-Robinson, *White Possessive*, 191.

31. Rifkin, *Beyond Settler Time*.
32. Rifkin, *Beyond Settler Time*; J. Kēhaulani Kauanui, *Paradoxes of Hawaiian Sovereignty: Land, Sex, and the Colonial Politics of State Nationalism* (Durham, NC: Duke University Press, 2018), 53.
33. Byrd, *Transit of Empire*.
34. This beloved but controversial American novel and film about the Civil War and Reconstruction represents a love of the land but from an (unacknowledged) settler perspective that naturalizes slavery, perpetuates anti-Blackness and white supremacism, and attempts to sanitize historical acts of violence systematically committed by white people.
35. Bruce Braun, "'On the Raggedy Edge of Risk': Articulations of Race and Nature after Biology," in *Race, Nature and the Politics of Difference*, ed. Donald S. Moore, Jake Kosek, and Anand Pandian (Durham, NC: Duke University Press, 2003), 175–203.
36. Harris, "Whiteness as Property."
37. Rifkin, *Beyond Settler Time*.
38. Kauanui, *Paradoxes of Hawaiian Sovereignty*.
39. Rifkin, *Settler Common Sense*, 14.
40. TallBear, "Caretaking Relations, Not American Dreaming."
41. Huber, *Lifeblood*.
42. Jodi Byrd, Alyosha Goldstein, Jodi Melamed, and Chandan Reddy, "Predatory Value: Economies of Dispossession and Disturbed Relationalities," *Social Text* 36, no. 2 (2018): 9.
43. Harvey, *Brief History of Neoliberalism*, 165.
44. Perry, *Vexy Thing*.
45. Rifkin, *Settler Common Sense*, 14.
46. Kauanui, *Paradoxes of Hawaiian Sovereignty*; Mackey, *Unsettled Expectations*; J. Sebastian, "Already Something More: Heteropatriarchy and the Limitations of Rights, Inclusion, and the Universal," *Abolition: A Journal of Insurgent Politics* 1 (2018), https://abolitionjournal.org/already-something-more/.
47. Nick Estes, *Our History Is the Future: Standing Rock Versus the Dakota Access Pipeline, and the Long Tradition of Indigenous Resistance* (New York: Verso, 2019); Jorge Barrera, "RCMP Arrest 14, Clear Road on Wet'suwet'en Territory in Ongoing Dispute over Land Rights, Pipeline," CBC News, November 19, 2021, https://www.cbc.ca/news/canada/british-columbia/rcmp-wet-suwet-en-pipeline-resistance-1.6254245.
48. "RAMPS Campaign" Radical Action for Mountains' and People's Survival. A direct action campaign based in Appalachia, accessed June 29, 2020, https://

rampscampaign.org/; "Appalachians against Pipelines—Home," accessed June 29, 2020, https://www.facebook.com/appalachiansagainstpipelines/.

49. Pancake, "Arboreal Blockaders: 'Queer/Trans Moments of Critical Appalachian Eco-action,'" this volume.

50. Kauanui, "'Structure, Not an Event.'"

EDIBLE KENT

Collaboration, Decentralization,
and Sustainable Agriculture in
Urban Food Systems

Lis Regula and MJ Eckhouse

E dible Kent utilizes land that is publicly owned or accessible to
the public and grows food free for the public without barriers
or gatekeeping mechanisms. Maintenance is done by volunteers,
there is no private ownership, and the resources are situated in
areas with the highest need (local food deserts) rather than the
most profitable locations. It is a queer project in the oppositional
sense put forward by Halperin, where *queer* "acquires its meaning
from its oppositional relation to the norm. 'Queer' is whatever is at
odds with the normal, the legitimate, the dominant."[1] In addition to
successfully deconstructing normative views of community, local
agriculture, and land use, the community-based model is replicable
in a range of communities assuming there exists need and willing-
ness to address these issues in a progressive fashion. Edible Kent
queers geographic divides by challenging the idea of rural, urban,
and suburban spaces and bringing agriculture into the city. Edible
Kent also queers socioeconomic divides by putting resources that
are necessary for life and often subsidized via nonprofit and government organizations to work in areas of economic development and

locations close to downtown. The goal of this chapter is to serve as a case study in addressing food sovereignty through a perspective that is based in queer theory and attempts to apply a social justice framework.

The city of Kent is a "queer space" in the sense used by Jaffer Kolb, who explains queerness as "an open mesh of possibilities, gaps, overlaps, dissonances, resonances, lapses and excesses of meaning."[2] Kent, like many college towns, is a place of breaking binaries, be they geographic, social, economic, or otherwise. For this paper, Appalachian queer ecology is reimagining the natural and constructed landscape in ways that seek to break heterosexist and colonial systems. It is geographically a few miles outside of Appalachia, lying in Portage County, Ohio, which is adjacent to the western border of Trumbull County, Ohio, the western edge of the northern subregion of Appalachia. It also lies about fifty miles north of Carroll County, Ohio, which also makes up the western border of Appalachia. Economically and socially, Kent has significant influence coming into it from these and other regions of Appalachia, connections that are reinforced by the city's annual folk festival and vibrant folk art community. Kent is functionally Appalachian in that the space is colonized metaphorically by the university and literally by the Western Connecticut Land Reserve before that. Geographically, Kent is queer in many regard: it does not fit the model of rural, urban, or suburban very well, and it is land that has been claimed by many cultures over the course of its existence. Between its location adjacent to Appalachia as defined geographically and its history as a colonized colony (colonized first by settlers and later by the university and those in the upper socioeconomic level that is associated with it), Kent is undeniably an Appalachian space.

Some of the principles of queer liberation state that people have a right to a life free of oppressive forces, that individuals have the right to the means to meet their needs for a thriving life, and that there should be no judgment or shame in meeting one's needs as one can. These principles queer the standard nonprofit model by taking away administrative and bureaucratic processes that act as gatekeepers between the organization and the individuals being served, as those processes functionally judge and can shame individuals attempting to access the resources provided by Edible Kent. As Edible Kent is providing necessities, it is the organization's belief that these resources should be available without judgment to anyone. Edible Kent attempts to live by these principles in its organizational structure and in its interactions with other community members. While these last principles are in line with many modern nonprofit organizations, Edible Kent works to use equitable and just practices in its organization. By *equitable* here, the author is talking about treating people without bias and doing the emotional work of addressing implicit bias proactively. *Just practices* in this sense means recognizing the fact that our current system is structurally biased and working to break down those structures of inequality where possible.

SOWING AN IDEA

Kent has a population of nearly thirty thousand, slightly exceeding the population of twenty-five thousand students attending Kent State University. The university remains noteworthy as one of the few places in the United States where the military has opened fire on civilians since the Civil War. Because of its sizable college population and its prominent antiwar history, Kent's reputation as a town far more progressive than its surrounding rural Ohio county is not entirely unwarranted. This is not something unique to Kent but is a common feature of rural college towns.[3]

More recently, Kent State University has been lauded for its LGBTQ+ Center on campus and its inclusive, supportive, and accepting atmosphere. The campus LGBTQ+ Center has attracted a growing LGBTQIA+ population to the city of Kent. The university and the city house many diverse and inclusive organizations serving various faiths, ethnicities, and racial groups, with active Jewish and Muslim religious communities, an African studies program, an African drum group, and Black United Students at Kent State University.

Kent, like most areas, is neither a sanctuary of progressivism nor a backwoods bastion of conservatism; however, there is a stark contrast between Kent and the surrounding county. Portage County, Ohio, is primarily rural, one of nine Ohio counties that flipped to back President Donald Trump in 2016 and 2020 after supporting President Barack Obama in 2008 and 2012. As a reliably Democratic stronghold, like many college towns, Kent has a more progressive character than its surrounding towns and townships.[4] The Edible Kent project challenged the identity of Kent as a liberal city. The project's focus on agriculture, mutual aid, and community-driven land usage was met with obstacles and increased regulations from the city's community development department, which revealed inconsistencies in local leaders' and stakeholders' perceptions of the city itself, as well as demonstrating the common pattern of "progressive" signaling serving as a convenient public relations strategy without extending cohesively throughout a policy, community, or organization. This pattern of "pinkwashing" (appealing to the LGBTQIA+ community) or "greenwashing" (appealing to the sustainability community) are not unique to Kent and, in fact, are seen in multiple places throughout the United States as ways to benefit economic development through virtue signaling progressive causes.[5]

Food production in Kent has been a growing and developing culture for much of its existence, and it has a history of small-scale, subsistence agriculture within the city limits, especially on the south side. This neighborhood is predominantly populated by African Americans and immigrants. Here, kitchen gardens and backyard small livestock were common into the middle of the twentieth century. Now that the area has a higher proportion of rental properties, there are fewer gardens, and food insecurity is common.[6] The town has had a thriving farmers' market since 1994, and although many of the producers at that market have typically been farmers from outside the city, a growing number are coming from within Kent itself, including companies that are owned and run by people of color or women. Embedded in northeast Ohio's local-, organic-, and artisanal-foods network, Kent has benefited from this regional context significantly in recent years.[7] In addition to the interest in high-quality food for retail purchase, Kent and the greater northeast Ohio region have seen a growing interest in community gardens and school gardens.[8] These practices also include incorporating gardens into classroom education, building gardens with Parks and Recreation after-school groups, and creating more traditional community gardens. Edible Kent helps to merge these two things—making food available, without barriers, to low-income residents in areas where they live and also using sustainable models in public spaces that aren't typically seen as agriculturally productive.

In the early spring of 2013, in Kent, Ohio, several local friends interested in sustainability started talking. The group originally consisted of Lis Regula, biologist; Katie Young, writer; Lynn Gregor, professional gardener; Debra-Lynne Hook, photographer; Julie Morris, outreach coordinator; Fred Pierre, librarian; Terri Cardi, teacher educator; and Jennifer Marks, public health graduate. We represented multiple marginalized communities, including women, LGBTQIA+ individuals, low-income folks, and people of color. Our diverse representation was an example of collaboration across marginalized subcommunities, or queer solidarity. This stands in sharp contrast to the dominant, paternalistic nonprofit industrial complex.[9]

Early discussions focused on the needs of the city residents, including the student population. One of the major needs was economical fresh produce. The city offered few grocery options, including only one grocery store on the edge of town and a small food co-op downtown. Food insecurity is not unique to Kent but prevalent across the United States, in both rural and urban areas.[10] We pursued a new community garden, based on the free food forests common in the Pacific Northwest.[11] One of the other points of discussion within the early stages of Edible Kent was that of individuals' relationship to land that they do not own. While Edible Kent periodically would have educational programming that included the history and construction of "seed bombs" for adding beneficial seeds to inaccessible spaces, we eventually decided to stick with the more conservative approach and refrain from using seed bombs or other forms of guerilla gardening at first. Instead, Edible Kent used plots with the permission of the owner, whether public or private, and opened up that land to a more public space based on the community's relationship to the land. This change in focus from the ownership of land to a relationship with the land is more of an incremental approach than a revolutionary one, and the thinking was that, as with a violin string, the appropriate pressure must be applied to a system so as to build tension and make music without breaking the string entirely. With the tension between Kent's perception as progressive and a less progressive reality, between the town and the university, and between the city and the conservative surroundings, this incremental approach was thought to be the best action at the time.

Kent is a small city in northeast Ohio, lying south of Cleveland, east of Akron, and west of Youngstown. These three major cities near Kent are all solid Rust Belt cities (Cleveland is the home of Belt Publishing, specializing in Rust Belt anthologies), and Portage County, where Kent resides, borders the western edge of Appalachia in northern Ohio. Kent itself has a history of some small-scale manufacturing and industry, although the economy is now associated more with the Kent State University predominantly, followed by retail and service industries. It is one of two major population centers in Portage County, a county of 110,000 that is predominantly rural, with most of its population residing in the unincorporated townships. Both Portage County and Kent have higher than average poverty rates. While Portage County skews older than average, Kent's population skews younger than average because of Kent State University, Ohio's second-largest public university system.

Kent follows the pattern of Rust Belt city decline with recovery, including a focus on sustainability. Edible Kent fits in the framework of moving toward sustainability while also addressing economic needs for low-income folks, while the city's economic recovery and development strategy has been so focused on gentrification that one could call its view of sustainability anti-poor.

Revitalization in Kent focused largely on reinvesting in parks and emphasizing sustainability in the development projects downtown. One of the efforts in this period of rebuilding was a downtown beautification project filling flower beds. These flower beds became the target of our efforts when we were citing a novel form of community garden in the city. The city's community development department saw them as a way to help attract new visitors and residents and to build on their theme of "Destination Kent," used to describe the renovations occurring downtown and in the more affluent neighborhoods closely connected to the Kent State campus. The issue of gentrification around the city was seen by many as a form of settler colonialism, with the attraction of out-of-town interests (including those catering more heavily to students) providing the path to prosperity in the view of local government officials. Edible Kent's use of public land and their encouragement of locals to develop underutilized and functionally abandoned spaces in these more inclusive and social justice-focused ways built the foundation for a discussion of the commons that contrasted heavily with the official actions of the city.

TRANSPLANTING TO THE GARDEN

During the first year of Edible Kent, we focused our initial public effort on identifying the food needs of the city residents via survey at the Haymaker Farmers' Market. This farmers' market, founded in 1994, was a highlight of the city and a hub of civic activity. In the beginning, our idea was simple: to respond to the needs of Kent residents by providing sustainably produced food and education to those in need with as few barriers as possible, and to do so in a publicly accessible place, free of shame or stigma. To do this, we needed a few things, including volunteers, land, raw materials, outreach, and funding. We wanted to work specifically with other organizations and individuals who shared our values of communitarianism, resilience, and respect for autonomy. This form of like-minded collaboration would not just make sure that we were exemplifying our ideals but also promote solidarity among similarly aligned entities.

The first task was to locate a space. We first prioritized city-owned land, believing that we could urge the city to grant us its use since they would save money by allowing us to conduct land maintenance. We compiled a list of city-owned properties based on the county recorder's office data and then filtered those results on the basis of their location and size. We visited each site to narrow our selection down before approaching the city council. We also came around to the idea of using guerilla gardening (covertly planting in unused spaces without permission) to utilize neglected, blighted, or otherwise unused spaces, and we organized a campaign to encourage front-yard gardening. We did so to normalize and promote food production as a more favorable option than unkempt lawns or overgrown weeds. Our goals centered on the understanding that there is untapped potential for land use that serves aesthetic and functional purposes, including food production and the improvement of food sovereignty. This stands in contrast to the ways in which land is typically used—either as a standard-issue front yard with an acceptable, manicured garden or as a neglected, weedy lot. These two dominant residential-area land uses lead to artificial food scarcity, which increases food costs and exacerbates negative environmental impacts.

We eventually settled on two initial gardens that were close together near a public parking lot at the edges of downtown, close to the south side of the city, where average incomes were lowest. Together, the sites were less than a tenth of an acre, but this small size was more manageable in our infancy as an organization. We reasoned that we could also help increase food production in the city through our alternative pathways—guerilla and front-yard gardening—while we built capacity and relationships around town. The sites were also near the Haymaker Farmers' Market. By speaking with the city and the farmers' market, we secured those beds for the first iteration of our gardens. As the garden had the potential to take business away from the farmers' market vendors, we expected to face reservations, if not flat-out opposition, from them but instead received a warm welcome and encouragement. The market and its vendors supported this effort, which laid the groundwork for long-standing relationships between Edible Kent and the farmers' market vendors.

Our first opposition came from the city administration. In 2013, Kent began a period of revitalization and attempted to gain a city beautification award to attract commerce to the downtown area. The city's elected officials and its upper administrators expressed a strong preference for conventional urban plantings and a fear that food production would be unsightly and incongruent with the rest of the downtown garden areas. We addressed this fear by giving examples of food gardens and by enlisting help from permaculture enthusiasts. We added pollinator plants and herbs alongside our primary, food-producing plants. Shifting away from an exclusive focus on food production both made the project more amenable to the city and gave us additional opportunities for engaging the public. With the addition of these new types of plants, we could more explicitly focus on the importance of sustainable practices in urban agriculture. By appealing to the community identity of Kent as a sustainability-minded city and framing the project as bolstering the city's aspirations of economic revitalization, we eased opposition.

Having located a site and developed a list of desired plants and food crops, we began gathering these plants and seeds. For the first year of Edible Kent's existence, many of our plants came from those we had already started on our own and from organizations like the Kent State University Child Development Center, Green Sprouts (a local nonprofit organization building sustainability curricula and lesson plans and teaching educators how best to incorporate sustainability into their existing curricula), Holden Elementary School's garden, and Kent Cooperative Housing. We also obtained starts in various years through donations from Birdsong Farms, Crown Point Ecological Center, and members of the Kent Community Time Bank. Seeds also came from the Kent Free Library's seed bank, which highlighted local plant varieties, like the endemic-to-Kent Hobbs's goose beans. The reliance on free seeds adapted for local microclimates helped cut costs for low-income gardeners, promote resilience, and increase reliance on the local community instead of larger businesses without community ties.

The major detraction of this initial site was the lack of water. The first year, the limited water access stunted our plants and reduced food production but did not stand in our way. We adjusted the crops that we planted to focus on drought-tolerant varieties and plants. After that first year, a local lawn-care company, Freedom Lawn Care, offered to help by once a week filling a rain barrel that we located on-site. The company is run by clients served by Freedom House, a shelter for homeless veterans, and it employs those vets and assists their return to civilian life. Some of the vets had been using the garden and wanted to help, and in the same year, the city contracted

Freedom Lawn Care to maintain the city-owned beautification sites. The rain barrel was funded by a grant from the Kent Environmental Council. This collaboration was perhaps our most surprising, and eye opening, as Kent Environmental Council and Freedom Lawn Care were so different from each other, demographically speaking. The members of Kent Environmental Council were primarily older white people with a high level of educational attainment, while the individuals with Freedom Lawn Care were primarily younger male veterans of color without college degrees. Out of this collaboration, we saw an increased mutual respect between the two groups and a general increase in compassion (as informally self-reported) between the individuals.

We also needed volunteers to help plant and maintain the gardens. For this, we heavily utilized the Kent Community Time Bank. Time banks are a novel economic model that is both decentralized and more egalitarian than typical monetary-based economic systems. Time banks have been growing in popularity across the United States, and one was adopted in Kent in 2010.[12] The core concept of a time bank holds that every person's time is equally valuable. Under this model, the currency is time instead of dollars. This model fits well with Edible Kent because of its anti-oppressive structures and its core alignment with liberation principles. The time bank allowed us to compensate volunteers for their time, thus attracting more volunteers to Edible Kent without incurring monetary expenses. We also managed to attract more volunteers through collaboration with Scratch Local Food, a food truck vendor in Kent. Scratch donated a meal for every Edible Kent volunteer on planting day in the spring and on harvest day in the fall. Connecting these for-profit, public, and nonprofit—many of which function by anti-capitalist principles—resources helped advance discussions of creating an equitable and sustainable community, as well as highlighting which of those structures already existed.

One major communication challenge was clarifying the goal of the project. Residents were unfamiliar with the concept of a free-use community garden, in which food was literally free, without any barriers, verifications, or requirements. Some well-intentioned citizens began policing the garden spaces by attempting to prevent people from taking the food. One gentleman approached a cofounder of the project to let them know that "this isn't for you; these are Edible Kent's gardens." After they explained the purpose of the garden, he left the conversation with an understanding of the project, as well as a bunch of mint and basil from the garden. After that incident, we added new, more explicit signage declaring, "Take what you need, Give what you can," and we included a QR code that directed smartphone users to the page on our website that described the function of the gardens and encouraged folks to take produce as it ripened.

WATERING COMMUNITY

Our educational outreach originally aimed to help inform the public about gardening in urban spaces; cooking with fresh produce, especially the types of produce in the gardens; identifying pollinators and understanding the importance of those organisms; seed-saving; and practicing some of the rudiments of permaculture and sustainable agriculture. Our educational events provided time to interact with folks who may have had some misconceptions or misunderstandings about the purpose of the community gardens. To keep the public engaged, we organized these educational events at regular intervals as well as at key points in the growing season, such as prior to planting day and harvesting day, and around special events occurring in the downtown Kent area. We kept the special-event educational outreach focused on the gardens and our mission and included activities to spark interest in the project and the events. Outreach around the bigger seasonal events tended to focus on upper-level topics with an activity of some sort, while for the regular outreach events we focused on very basic gardening and sustainability topics. This practice of providing educational opportunities at introductory through advanced levels helped to bring in volunteers at all gardening-proficiency levels. Because of our focus on sustainability, many of these educational events challenged the model of the normative US concept of "lawn and garden," and wherever possible, we uplifted viewpoints from traditional Indigenous agricultural practices. This paradigm, in addition to permaculture theories, provided a stark contrast of functional, sustainable, and high-biodiversity garden systems to the homogeneity of the manicured ideal typical of US culture.

For our regular educational events, we often collaborated with the Kent State University Child Development Center, which prompted us to focus on children's activities. One particularly successful example was our seed-bomb demonstration. Seed bombs are small projectiles made of clay, soil, and seeds all mixed together and dried. The projectiles are thrown at the ground from a distance, and when they get wet with the next rain, they begin to germinate, with a small packet of soil ready to start nurturing the seedlings. We taught the attendees how to make a seed bomb and discussed the legacy of guerilla gardening in blighted areas. We used common household items like plain clay cat litter to make the seed bombs, provided materials for children to make one of their own, and then sent them off with samples and literature providing additional information.

Outreach efforts allowed us to raise public awareness of our project and provided critical collaboration opportunities with other local organizations. This additional engagement helped us obtain funds to sustain our efforts and find volunteers and space to expand the reach of our small, grassroots nonprofit project. We also expanded to help the Child Development Center build a classroom garden for their students, reach students through their summer program, and fill snack and educational needs.

We brought cooking classes to the local hot-meal site and planted our largest garden in front of their building. In addition to providing produce for the hot-meal site, we spoke with the patrons and recipients of Kent Social Services about poverty and food insecurity, which helped deconstruct the stigma of using this freely available food resource. The Kent Social Services garden had considerable input from the head chef of the kitchen, Bill Bowen, and Kent Cooperative Housing, a tenant-owned housing cooperative. Kent Social Services has run their current kitchen space since the late twentieth century and have worked with Kent City Parks and Recreation for much of that time to bring educational summer activities to the Kent Parks and Rec day-care program through the gardens maintained by Kent Cooperative Housing tenants on Kent Parks and Rec land. These gardens helped to tie in with the Kent public school system, giving teachers a place to incorporate educational curricula with experiential learning. Over the summers, we introduced children to gardening and nutrition, and the elementary students and teachers helped to plan and plant the garden. In the fall, the returning students took over care and harvest, while the summer day-care students partook in the produce until the new school year began. These collaborations focused on the underserved in Kent and helped build lower-socioeconomic solidarity and educate people on food sovereignty.

While many of the board and founding members of Edible Kent were members of the LGBTQIA+ community themselves, Edible Kent extended little concerted outreach to specifically LGBTQIA+ groups to collaborate and work on the gardens. One factor in the lack of this targeted outreach was the paucity of specifically LGBTQIA+ groups in Kent other than Kent State University's LGBTQ+ Center. Considering the disproportionate incidence of homelessness and poverty among the LGBTQIA+ community compared to the non-LGBTQIA+ population, it is highly likely that our efforts to help the economically marginalized communities in Kent touched and helped LGBTQIA+ individuals as well. Additionally, throughout its time, Edible Kent has made a point to use inclusive language and be as accepting as possible. Edible Kent was not the only LGBTQIA+-led agricultural organization in Kent or the surrounding area, a feature that made the area an interesting space to work and differentiated the sustainable agriculture scene in the area from that in much of Ohio, aligning it more with Appalachia's sustainable agricultural scenes (as an example, look at the work by the annual Queer Farmers' Convergence).[13]

GROWING RESULTS

Funding for these events and the gardens themselves came through private donations and grants. Both the City of Kent and the Kent Environmental Council helped support Edible Kent. These funding opportunities resulted from data collection on the types of plants desired, the amount of food harvested, and our revenues and expenditures. In the fall of 2015, we sought and received our official 501(c)(3) nonprofit status, which opened up additional sources of funds for us and the ability to provide charitable contribution receipts to our donors, giving them an additional incentive to donate to our cause. This bureaucratic hurdle, while it has its advantages, also serves as a gatekeeper that makes starting a new nonprofit organization more difficult, especially for those of limited means or with less privilege than others.[14]

For the city's community development block grant, this legal status was far less relevant as Haymaker Farmers' Market was willing to act as our pass-through organization before we completed the 501(c)(3) application, but neighborhood need and utilization data were critical. The requirement of a formal, legal nonprofit fiscal agent is another example of gatekeeping, as without this complicated administrative process the grant could not be awarded. If we hadn't had a relationship with someone in power, in this case the market manager and several board members, the farmers' market would have likely been unwilling to risk serving that role for Edible Kent. To prove that we were filling a need and doing so efficiently, we used our initial surveys of community needs assessments and our door-to-door surveys about community support for the project. We also collected survey data about utilization rates from educational events, outreach days at the market, and social media engagement, as well as data on the gardens' annual production. The need for data collection, promotion of the survey, and data analysis created additional tasks on harvest day each year, along with packaging, weighing, and delivering the final produce to a food distributor.

Additionally, we informally tracked the utilization of the gardens for food obtainment. Especially after the addition of the Kent Social Services garden site, volunteers had regular interactions with unhoused folks who were using the garden to supplement their diet. Many of these people came to the site for the hot meals, and after an introduction to the gardens, they used them for sustenance when the kitchen was closed. These were generally pleasant and fulfilling interactions for the volunteers, as they got to connect with the community members who most needed this resource and affirmed the importance of the work. Many unhoused individuals took a personal interest in and responsibility for the gardens—pulling weeds, asking questions, picking up trash, and informing others about the garden. On multiple occasions, Edible Kent executive board members personally heard remarks from the Kent Social Services clients about the clients' feelings of pride in alerting the kitchen staff when produce looked ripe or discouraging others from littering in the garden. Some indicated that the access to fresh, nutritious produce without bureaucratic and judgmental gatekeeping offered them a feeling of personal autonomy. Others simply enjoyed the act of gardening or appreciated the garden as a space for relaxing.

All these metrics demonstrated the benefits of the garden project so we could continue to secure funding for our mission.

However, the cost of time and effort was substantial, and, for the first couple of years, it detracted from our board's ability to do the work. To mitigate this, we enlisted help from student interns at Kent State University's business and nonprofit management classes. We also utilized assistance from a certified public accountant at the Canton, Ohio, SCORE office (Service Corps of Retired Executives, a volunteer organization that provides small business mentoring and other services). This national organization offers free and low-cost small business and accounting advice to start-ups and nonprofit organizations. The service was provided for free through the Kent State University Stark campus office of SCORE. The use of data-driven neoliberal nonprofit models, communitarian-based resources, and vulnerable personal narratives all combined to ensure that we were able to make Edible Kent a success.

FRUITS OF OUR LABOR

As we reflect on the factors that facilitated the successes of the Edible Kent project, several key takeaways emerge, which may offer useful and applicable insights to those undertaking similar projects. First, successfully challenging and transforming social structures requires community collaboration. Edible Kent's successes were heavily reliant on collaborating with various groups whose missions complemented one another, as opposed to groups whose missions overlapped. By harnessing the help of our community, all involved were able to leverage our collective array of talents, resources, and perspectives to lay the crucial groundwork for building and strengthening the sense of community, solidarity, and justice that informs successful liberation efforts.

The proviso to this lesson is that while grassroots efforts may provide an effective mechanism for creating change, there won't always be much of a root to start from. In cases like this, where there is a depauperate beginning community structure, or where a need for change is not seen by most people in the community, grass-tops organizing efforts may be more appropriate and have a better chance for success. The danger here is that these grass-tops methods cannot become astroturf movements; there must be at least some root of change there from the beginning. In the case of queer liberation in rural America or food liberation anywhere, this initial root may be exceedingly small. The small roots do tend to make community-based organizing in order to challenge social structures slow and difficult work in these areas. Some of the causes for this slow pace of change are due to the long-standing perpetuation of cycles (cities are more inclusive, so queer folks flee rural communities for urban and suburban centers), and some are simple reality (economic disinvestment in rural areas has left gaps in services that make rural communities less attractive than their urban and suburban counterparts). In either case, the result is that social change in rural areas tends to be tedious work.

Another key takeaway is the need for conscientious and proactive planning. While these projects often begin as simple conversations among friends and neighbors or as part of a larger service project by an established organization, they have better chances for success if enough planning goes into the early stages of the project. In advance of the launch date, try to foresee what problems or objections may come up. Look at what resources are most needed in the community and what resources are currently found there. A good needs assessment may show that there is not a current need for better food availability but instead a need for dissemination of information about existing resources. Research and data collection becomes far easier when conducted by individuals with strong connections and knowledge bases in the community served. In the absence of such community ties, or as a supplemental measure, community surveys can fill that gap.

Additional lessons include the necessity of internally practicing principles of equity and justice, particularly as they apply to the distribution of labor. Many community organizers are themselves a part of a marginalized community, and as such, they often face the impacts of economic inequality, interpersonal and systemic expectations of emotional labor, and fewer opportunities for necessities such as stable housing, nutrition, and childcare. For this reason, it is critical to uphold and respect individuals' boundaries while maintaining a base of support that aligns with members' goals (or vice versa) to ensure that labor is spread equitably throughout all involved in a project.

Our initial group of organizers was predominantly, though not exclusively, white. Women and LGBTQIA+ people were strongly represented. The group included an array of backgrounds in terms of disability/ability; neurodiversity/neurotypicality; educational attainment; and income levels.

This variety of perspectives gave us a broad depth of understanding but may depend on the local population in each geographic area. In Ohio, as in twenty-eight other states, there is not a statewide comprehensive statute to protect people from discrimination in employment, housing, or public accommodations. Without a federal level of protection either, LGBTQIA+ people in Ohio are left to the whims of local ordinances and their often underfunded or nonexistent enforcement for protection against discriminatory practices. With Ohio's patchwork of incorporated areas and townships and the disparate legal entities in each space, legal equality for LGBTQIA+ Ohioans is far from reality. At present, there are fewer than thirty cities, towns, and villages in Ohio with something like the Ohio Fairness Act, legislation that would enact legal equality for LGBTQIA+ Ohioans even without a federal mandate. Since the June 2020 *Bostock v. Clayton County* Supreme Court decision, employment discrimination (at least) has been ruled unconstitutional, although there still is a lack of statutory protection at the federal and state level in Ohio.

In socialist and justice-oriented circles, there is often talk of the means of production, from a perspective of either acknowledging who owns these currently or considering how to reclaim these things in the creation of a more equitable world. At the same time, personal and anecdotal experiences have led to a not-uncommon belief that cities provide more and better support systems for queer folks in America today and a better chance at both lived and legal equality. Agriculture, or food production, is a vital component in the means of production, and currently the bulk of this component resides in rural areas, the very areas from which many queer folks flee. This functionally cedes that part of the means of production to people and places that are less inclusive and less accepting. To seize the power of food security again, we must find ways to increase urban agriculture while we work on improving the landscape of equality, a far larger and longer-term task than building infrastructure and knowledge in areas that are already more inclusive.

To fully function as a community and integrate into American culture, LGBTQIA+ folks cannot continue to simply take a back seat and decide to disengage from rural life. Instead, full integration into society requires that we continue to fight for both the legal and lived equality that other folks can more readily access. This means being in the public, even in relatively rural areas and those areas that might be less conducive to complete recognition of the humanity of LGBTQIA+ individuals.

NOTES

1. D. Halperin, *Saint Foucault: Towards a Gay Hagiography* (Oxford: Oxford University Press, 1995).
2. Jaffer Kolb and Aaron Betsky, "The End of Queer Space?," *Log* 41 (2017): 85–88.
3. B. Gumprecht, "The Campus as a Public Space in the American College Town," *Journal of Historical Geography* 33, no. 1 (2007): 72–103.
4. Jennifer Mapes, "The New Main Street: Planning, Politics and Change in Downtown Kent, Ohio," in *Urban Transformations*, ed. Nicholas Wise and Julie Clark (New York: Routledge, 2017), 62–78.

5. K. E. Portney, *Taking Sustainable Cities Seriously: Economic Development, the Environment, and Quality of Life in American Cities* (Cambridge, MA: MIT Press, 2013); E. Berisha, M. Sjogren, and J. St. Ive, "Pinkwashing or Pro-diversity?," *LBMG Strategic Brand Management—Masters Paper Series*, 2015.

6. Lisa Henry, "Understanding Food Insecurity among College Students: Experience, Motivation, and Local Solutions," *Annals of Anthropological Practice* 41, no. 1 (2017): 6–19.

7. Myra Moss, "The Power of Sustainability: The Story of Kent, Ohio," in *Sustainable Cities and Communities Design Handbook*, ed. Woodrow W. Clark (Oxford: Butterworth-Heinemann, 2018), 521–36.

8. Jacqueline Ann Luke, "Urban Community Gardens in a Shrinking City: Community Strength and the Urban Community Gardens of Cleveland, Ohio" (PhD diss., Kent State University, 2013).

9. Kelly LeRoux, "Paternalistic or Participatory Governance? Examining Opportunities for Client Participation in Nonprofit Social Service Organizations," *Public Administration Review* 69, no. 3 (2009): 504–17.

10. Christopher B. Barrett, "Measuring Food Insecurity," *Science* 327, no. 5967 (2010): 825–28.

11. M. McElhinny et al., "An Educational Permaculture Experience in the Vancouver Westside Community Corridor," *ENVR*, 2019–2020.

12. C. Valor, E. Papaoikonomou, and C. Martínez-de-Ibarreta, "Consumer-to-Consumer Exchanges: A Goal Theory Approach in the Time Banking Context," *Spanish Journal of Marketing—ESIC* 21, no. 1 (2017): 14–24.

13. Queer Farmer's Convergence, "Humble Hands," accessed August 14, 2023, https://humblehandsharvest.com/queer-farmer-convergence/.

14. Z. Rezaee, *Corporate Governance in the Aftermath of the Global Financial Crisis*, vol. 3, *Gatekeeper Functions* (Hampton, NJ: Business Expert, 2018).

.

ARBOREAL BLOCKADERS
"Queer/Trans Moments of Critical Appalachian Eco-action"

Chet Pancake

INTRODUCTION

In fall 2018, I twice visited an arboreal blockade site, Yellow Finch, constructed in the path of the Mountain Valley Pipeline (MVP) project in Southwest Virginia. The arboreal blockade site comprised a cluster of hardwood trees holding wooden tree-sit platforms built high in the canopy, where eco-activists lived in tents with a base camp that supported the tree sitters, or "arboreal blockaders," with food, medical care, and communication with friends and family. The visit was prompted by an invitational fine art exhibition at the Hicks Art Center in Bucks County, Pennsylvania. The exhibition, *And This Is How You Are a Citizen . . .*, highlighted intersectional feminist themes inspired by the book *Citizen: An American Lyric*, by Claudia Rankine. My purpose in visiting Yellow Finch was to record video and audio portraits regarding experiences of activism on the ground to block natural gas infrastructure, including arboreal blockading (tree sitting), locking down on equipment, and walking onto active construction sites to slow the progression of pipeline construction in Appalachia. My particular interest was the impact of blockading on the activists' sense of embodied knowledge. I wanted to learn how their physical bodies sensed, reacted, felt, changed, or potentially experienced trauma during blockading and how this might provide personal insight or intelligence to share with others witnessing or engaged in this direct activist work.

To visit the Yellow Finch camp, I was completely reliant on a guide who drove me through Southwest Virginia to the unmarked site. This constituted a novel embodied orientation for me while performing creative research. I sensed a loss of control and a feeling of vulnerability, perhaps preparing me for the perspective of the activists.

I patiently observed as my perspective evolved from surveyed, sited, and engineered roadways to the rolling geography of a private landowner and then onto a path into the forest. As I traversed the Appalachian hill terrain so familiar to me, my sight lines were lost in steep hollows, where perspectival horizons blur into complex iterations of flora, both alive and dead, displacing one's gaze into the network of forest limbs, the dense rhododendron thickets, the shifting ground cover, the refracted light, the flicker of animal movement, the fungi, and the loam. For some, including myself, this sensual experience connects deeply to my embodiment as "my safe home." My body relaxed, my senses opened, and I felt more focused.

As we moved up a steep hill to the blockading site, I climbed and slipped on the muddy path while clutching my gear. When we reached the camp, I wandered around before finally asking where the blockades actually were. A helpful activist pointed toward the sky, and I realized I had been standing beneath the tree sits the entire time. I craned my head back uncomfortably to see the sites far above. My hike through the tangles of a forest ridge without clear figure or ground gave way to a new horizon peering awkwardly directly above my head, momentarily lost in the gentle oscillation of the canopy leaves marked by the tree-sit planks, tents, and banners over fifty feet above.

I write as a queer and male transgender person who spent my formative years outdoors with five siblings engaging in imaginative play or doing chores in contact with rural Appalachian land, forests, streams, rivers, and mountains. Our bodies took shape in reach of, proximity to, and daily skin contact with the natural elements of a particular local ecosystem and region. Our reality was constructed through these intertwined networks of sensual contact, complex sibling relationships, and the sense of a stable, well-traversed ecosystem frequently accessed for me as a source of solace and recuperation from a physically abusive mother, gender dysphoria, and a simple need for peaceful, meditative alone time. Being alone in nature for me was "queer time and space," a lacuna for a nonnormative child to seek hours of solace and connection with my human senses to commune with nonhuman life and the material contours of path, ridge, valley, and stream in resistance to the power dynamic of a particular Christian patriarchal family structure that was difficult and often traumatic to navigate. When I use the term *queer*, I am describing positions that resist normative patriarchal gender binary power structures as well as a sexual identity that is not heterosexual. As with many people, these qualities of "queerness" can ebb and flow over time and personal development. For me, my queer trans identity is inextricable from my Appalachian identity I formed in deep embodied contact with my immediate natural surroundings.

As I completed my creative research in the Yellow Finch camp, I found female/nonbinary/trans activists who expressed queerness in terms of identity and also in terms of resistance to normative power structures. The activists further articulated their experience grappling with how to express their personal relationship to the protection of land, forests, water, and wildlife, which felt so queer, so subversive, and so unacceptable to economic planning and the fossil fuel industry as to provoke threats with chain saws and forcible extraction by law enforcement and private security. Not only do queer eco-activists cope with the stress inherent in disorienting social marginalization but their blockading activities additionally point to a novel embodied queer/trans eco-phenomenology. I posit through analysis of my creative research that the desire, impulse, and bodily orientation to protect Appalachian ecosystems through embodied blockading activities appear to constitute a notably productive queer response to phenomenological disorientation from climate change, ecological trauma, and nonconsensual large-scale industrial fossil fuel extraction.

In *Queer Phenomenology*, Sarah Ahmed states that she aims to put queer studies in closer dialogue with phenomenology. She discusses how the concept of "orientation" is central to both those marginalized by sexual orientation / identity and also the general philosophy of phenomenology. The centralizing of orientation in both cases brings up questions about how groups made different by their identity orientation via sexual orientation, gender, or race might pose important questions to the history and understanding of phenomenology.

Ahmed describes how phenomenological theories explain that our bodies take shape while tending toward material objects that are in reach or within our bodily horizon. She further explains how phenomenology can offer a resource to queer studies "insofar as it emphasizes the importance of lived experience, the intentionality of consciousness, the significance of nearness or what is ready-to-hand, and the role of repeated and habitual actions in shaping bodies and worlds."[1]

Ahmed introduces Maurice Merleau-Ponty's additional interest in disorientation as a potentially productive event that she posits can queer phenomenology. Phenomenological orientations address the "intimacy of bodies and their dwelling places."[2] The body is the place where central perspective begins within our most immediate dwelling, our home. Our visual and sensual horizons connect back with our bodily senses, constructing our foremost reality, which is deeply influenced by what is within our touch, what we can seek or reach for, what eludes our grasp, and what is kept from our immediate horizon.

Appalachians have historically grappled with ongoing environmental and human catastrophes induced by fossil fuel (coal and natural gas) extraction, industrial chemical production, and legacy infrastructure failures that have caused long-term health problems as well as water, air, and soil contamination. Narratives regarding citizens' sensory experiences of these ecological abuses or traumas may be officially recorded through the health-care system if there are symptoms to report or evidence of physiological disease from toxicity.[3] In reaction to the stress, citizens may also present mental health and substance abuse symptoms for traditional medical intervention.

In my experience as a documentarian, citizens frequently use very personal ways to describe how they feel in their mind, body, and being when immediate ecological contexts are put into danger or threatened with destruction. These ecological perspectives wrought first from the private, personal, and body senses carry a primary knowledge, as Merleau-Ponty might say, that perceptually *constitute the world* for this person.[4] This would be an alternative view to the idea that our personal senses or feelings are subjective and always fallible and that thus we must seek to find objective reason through scientific study and engagement with civil law to assert a valid perspective of objective reality to protect ourselves. When an immediate natural ecosystem is experiencing or being threatened by industrial harm, a person's feeling of interconnection with the sensed world can seem to be under a devastating assault. The denial of what a citizen's body or senses are saying in terms of environmental harm to their health and well-being can be weaponized through portrayal of these reactions as overly emotional or false. Meanwhile, extractive industries greatly harm citizens as they wait for months or years for normative research or civil lawsuits to "prove" their personal experience of a traumatizing loss of home that is interlocked with family, land, forest, animals, and ecological context.

I want to posit as an inclusive statement that for any Appalachian person the queerness of a particular phenomenological felt sense of ecological place (largely unrecognized by governmental economic planning and extractive industries), when under assault, can become the queer disorientation that leads average citizens to engage in recuperative radical embodied activism they would never have considered before. Scientific practices have a critical role in environmental justice, but when a local citizen says that she is blockading because the trees scheduled for a clear-cut for a pipeline on her property against her will are actually her family just as her children are, normative strategies fall short. By turning to the work of Ahmed, Merleau-Ponty, and Gayle Salamon, I will relate discussions of queer and trans phenomenology to my creative research at Yellow Finch. I hope to contribute clarification and additional understanding of the activists' ineffable, difficult-to-express perceptions and feelings, along with their context in Appalachian queer/feminist/trans radical ecological activism.

QUEER ACTIVISM AND APPALACHIAN ECO-CONNECTIONS

Queer activism and histories have notably been movements centered on or led by people with identities considered at the fringe of gay or lesbian rights movements from the Stonewall Uprising to ACT UP (AIDS Coalition to Unleash Power), Queer Nation, Lesbian Avengers, and currently the queer female Black activism central to the Black Lives Matter movement. These movements feature direct activism in which somatic bodies are discussed, defended, and frequently placed in the direct path of power via civil disobedience or in-person protests. These organizations address not only marginalization but also direct violence against Black bodies, BIPOC (Black, Indigenous, and people of color) bodies, and openly queer bodies in the form of bar raids and incarceration; AIDS and HIV illness and death; police violence toward AIDS activism; violence, murder, and damaging invisibility targeting lesbians; and police, state, and institutional violence toward trans bodies and particularly trans Black bodies. Embodiment is inevitably tangled in queer activist resistance as the literal physical survival of contested bodies is frequently at play.

LGBTQIA+ ecological activism in rural areas has spanned from lesbian movements to purchase and live collectively in peace on communal land to LGBTQIA+[5] representation in rural environmental movements. Recent activism by Beth Stephens and Annie Sprinkle celebrates "ecosexuality" as a queer-embodied and sex-affirming approach with focused goals such as saving Gauley Mountain, West Virginia, from mountaintop-removal coal mining. Cynthia Belmont lauds Stephens and Sprinkle's work in which nature "is seen as an active agent and erotic partner for humans, who are likewise drawn emotionally, physically, spiritually, and politically to its eroticism, which they celebrate and work to protect through diverse activist and educational endeavors, including performance and other art, such as street theater, photography, and pornography."[6] Belmont makes a strong case for the subversive power of this work generally focused on the coal industry while also briefly questioning the anthropomorphizing of the earth if this work's thrust is to emphasize the nonhuman as an active and empowered partner to move toward a radical queer ecological position.

From my observations while visiting Yellow Finch (albeit as an outsider), the principles of centering diverse female, queer, trans activists and voices were very evident at the site. The physical camp, blockade, and frequent documentation of activities on the Appalachians against Pipelines social media presented no hierarchical leadership or official organizing principle. Diverse activists spoke for themselves directly on social media posts and requested funds only for bail costs for jailed activists. The subjects I interviewed for this project overtly stated the following as influences: #NODAPL, Black Lives Matter, Camp White Pine tree sit,[7] the monopod tree sit on Bent Mountain,[8] and Peter Kropotkin. #NODAPL refers to legal actions taken by the Standing Rock Sioux and supporting organizations to block the Dakota Access Pipeline (DAPL) in the northern portion of the United States. A defining feature of the case was the large protests on the proposed sites of the pipeline regarding burial lands and water preservation. A large-scale social media campaign with the hashtag #NODAPL, started by Standing Rock Sioux youth, engaged mass international social media attention on the conflict. Additional details from the Yellow Finch site regarding Appalachian queer identity and community can be found in the words of Chessie Oak, who wrote a first-person manifesto regarding blockading in the text "Y'all Means All: Queering Appalachia in the era of 'Trump Country.'"[9]

MVP BACKGROUND AND RESISTANCE

On October 23, 2015, Mountain Valley Pipeline (MVP) LLC filed with the Federal Energy Regulatory Commission (FERC) to begin building a 301-mile natural gas pipeline through rural West Virginia and Southwest Virginia. Company press releases promised significant production income, employment, and tax revenues for both states with plans to serve local communities as well as industrial power plant clients.[10]

As pipeline construction proceeded, documented community resistance to the MVP began in early 2018. Civil disobedience activity (sitting on arboreal platforms, locking down on equipment, and physically disrupting labor on-site) began to be announced and documented on the Appalachians against Pipelines Facebook page on February 27, 2018. This social media site documented eighty-six individual acts of civil disobedience disrupting the MVP construction in Southwest Virginia between February 2018 and March 2020. Many of these actions were performed by local families whose property was disrupted by pipeline construction.[11] Numerous environmental violations and problems were reported by the local press,[12] and area families also filed eminent domain lawsuits to disallow the pipeline from crossing private properties.[13]

NORMATIVE RESEARCH IN PERSPECTIVE

Normative social science research addressing the impact of Appalachian natural gas pipelines has been published by Martina Angela Caretta and Kristen Abatsis McHenry regarding the MVP and Finley-Brook et al. regarding the Atlantic Coast Pipeline. Normative research to date on the impact of pipelines on communities and environments in West Virginia and Southwest Virginia is scant. The normative environmental research context for citizens coping with impending industrial extraction near their homes and property is frequently an impossible "chicken and egg" scenario wherein empirically measured impacts can't be known until the environmental damage is done and has already harmed affected citizens.

Caretta and McHenry use qualitative data analysis to make evident a number of individual citizen complaints for those living in proximity to the MVP infrastructure,[14] distilling the initial reportage into three predominant citizen issues:

- Economic stress from tax burdens on land rendered useless by gas infrastructure, eminent domain, and "quick-take" actions that allow for industrial surveying and construction on private land before the landowner receives any compensation for the land
- Public health stress from the lack of a sense of safety and security caused by histories of pipelines leaking, exploding, and killing citizens, as well as by the resulting air pollution, noise pollution, and increase in traffic accidents
- Environmental damage to properties from erosion that causes flooding, flash flooding, water contamination, and negative health impacts on livestock

Finley-Brook et al., while studying community impacts and resistance to the Atlantic Coast Pipeline, propose a "framework for critical energy justice" that emphasizes the intersectional and interconnected nature of various sites of injustice spanning not only geography but coalition identification, social identity, class, race, and other characteristics. "Critical energy justice" appears to present a rhizomatic and networked sense of environmental justice resistance rather than a binary opposition of local citizen versus anti-gas activist.[15]

Finley-Brook et al. also provide a useful typology to describe and acknowledge a continuum of "infrastructure encounters, frictions, and forces" in community resistance to harm from natural gas infrastructure. Within their category "Oppositional Encounters," recognition frictions include "public displays of agency and opposition" (e.g., rallies, petitions, and civil disobedience) in response to "Structural Inequalities."[16] The inclusion in normative research of civil disobedience as a recognized and legitimate strategy to work toward justice is an important step to adding complexity to the normative scientific framing of activism. Yet this research might fall short in recognizing that, as ecological damage worsens, abates, or ends, the same individuals and families can fall across a continuum of these roles, frequently representing more than one at a time (affected citizen, civil disobedience activist, dues-paying coalition member, industry employee), depending on their personal perceptions, feelings, and relationships and on the evolution of their ecological ties to the land.

MVP AND #NODAPL

The influence of #NODAPL actions on the MVP blockading resistance is documented in multiple posts on the Appalachians against Pipelines social media pages as well as in the personal narratives of one white transmasculine activist interviewed for this text, who described his personal exposure to protesting DAPL as a conversion experience to anti-capitalist beliefs caused by having watched with horror extreme police violence against peaceful protesters for the first time in his life.

The MVP protesters were also validated and supported by Indigenous leadership central to #NODAPL, Mama Julz, Oglala Lakota, and Cheri Foytlin, Afro-Indigenous, who visited and performed in-person blockading of the MVP with local activists on September 10, 2019, demonstrating visible solidarity between MVP blockaders and Indigenous pipeline activists.[17]

Because of the complex power dynamics of a white, rural upsurge in environmental activism drawing from a movement generated by the cultural heritage of the Dakota and Lakota Peoples of the Standing Rock Sioux Tribe, it is pertinent to explore scholarship from Native American perspectives, such as that of Kyle Powys Whyte, regarding decolonizing normative environmental justice.

Whyte describes the history of the Standing Rock Sioux members' ordeal with DAPL as beginning in 2012 when the tribe officially resolved to reject all current and future pipelines from their ancestral lands. Conflicts with the US Army Corps of Engineers and with Energy Transfer resulted in a gathering of tribal members at Standing Rock to prevent construction of DAPL across tribal lands.[18]

Imposed language such as *protest* or *standoff* failed to accurately capture the resistance, which was described by tribal members as an event of "ceremony, prayer, and water." *Ceremony* and *water is life* refer to Indigenous knowledge regarding respectful relations with water and other nonhuman beings and entities vital for human safety and wellness. Tribal members used the name *water protectors* for those participating in these sacred actions.[19]

Tribal members' advocacy of using the correct descriptive terminology for their work overlapped with the MVP blockades. Diverse and Indigenous blockaders raised banners citing their work as "water protectors." Indigenous cultures and spiritual practices present arguably the richest language and cultural support in North America for personal and communal perceptions of the relations between phenomenological embodiment and ecological systems. An assumption of ecological interdependence is culturally primary, with a deep and complex sense of embodied ecological knowing spelled out in daily ritual and life across diverse Indigenous practices. Scholars such as Patricia Locke have provided further phenomenological analysis of Indigenous practices within the Haida Peoples using Merleau-Ponty's concept of "Flesh" as a "between" concept a priori to binaries separating humans from animals, and other ecological features.[20]

In thinking about how Western philosophical analysis and my descriptions of the majority white MVP activism intersect with #NODAPL, I will turn to Whyte's definition of settler colonialism and environmental justice:

> Again, settler colonialism refers to complex social processes in which at least one society seeks to move permanently onto the terrestrial, aquatic, and aerial places lived in by one or more other societies who derive economic vitality, cultural flourishing, and political self-determination from the relationships they have established with the plants, animals, physical entities, and ecosystems of those places. Settler colonialism is an "environmental" injustice, for the US settlement process aims directly to undermine the ecological conditions required for Indigenous peoples to exercise their cultures, economies, and political self-determination. Ecological conditions refer to the complex relationships with place that are the substance of Indigenous governance systems.[21]

The majority of European-descent, white interviews analyzed in this chapter did not include claims, questions, or references to permanent status on the private land owned by a white family where the blockades were constructed. Activists did articulate later in interviews the desire for communal land "outside the system" but did not in my interviews interrogate the permanent status of the white farming family providing access for the blockading camp in an area notable for a history of European colonialism. The interviewees did not claim self-indigeneity as has been critiqued by scholar Stephen Pearson, wherein white Appalachian citizens articulate their own identity through a primary connection to the land and position their removal or flight from toxic land on par with the genocide of Native Peoples.[22] Additional research regarding settler or white identity would provide further clarity on MVP blockaders and the relations of Western phenomenological scholarship to Indigenous practices or influences.

Sarah R. Kostelecky provides an Indigenous perspective weighing the inclusion of nonscholarly material (social media posts or tags) in academic environmental or energy justice work.[23] Kostelecky created the DAPL LibGuide from an Indigenous perspective.

Kostelecky, aware of the Black Lives Matter movement LibGuide, the Beyoncé Lemonade LibGuide, and other such guides addressing social injustices, proceeded with the DAPL LibGuide at University of New Mexico. The DAPL LibGuide initially only included Indigenous voices and perspectives from Native American news sources and social media posts. Later, as the movement grew larger, she added news from major media outlets. Kostelecky's work demonstrates the near invisibility of Native American scholars or even Native Americans with advanced degrees in commercial media, as well as Native American public and academic discourses. She makes a strong case for the inclusion of a range of Indigenous knowledge to counteract the failure of most library systems to provide such narratives and to compensate for the many inaccuracies and gaps in library material and in classification systems.[24]

As the most extensive documentation of the blockading on the MVP is held on Appalachians against Pipelines social media pages and as a number of the public-facing activists are queer, nonbinary, or trans, I propose that the Facebook page itself stands as an important archival historical document, albeit currently on a private, corporate server.

ORIENTATION ON THE BLOCKADE

While visiting the Yellow Finch camp, I completed a series of conversational and wide-ranging audio interviews with activist volunteers. I discussed with each subject my primary interest in asking questions that would draw out ways of knowing, being, or learning explicitly guided by physical or somatic sensations and experiences. The resounding themes that seemed to arise from the interviews were descriptions of a series of critical personal embodied disorientation points (including trauma) that resulted in the activists leaving everyday life to position their physical bodies in the path of the rural Appalachian natural gas pipeline. Once the blockading activity began, phenomenological horizons continued to shift as new orientations toward nature and fellow activists altered previous personal boundaries. Actions that achieved a meaningful political objective resounded somatically in deeply validating as well as anxiety-provoking, life-changing ways.

INTERVIEW NOTES: NETTLE AND LAUREN—ECO-DISORIENTATION

Sarah Ahmed articulates in "Queer Phenomenology" descriptions regarding her concerns with phenomenology and objects of perception. This could mean an object in real time and space, or an object generated within one's mind as imagining or writing. The description of the existence of objects of perception validates philosophically the connection of the mind to the body in an on-going horizon of experience. Ahmed elaborates: "The radical claim that phenomenology inherits from Franz Brentano's psychology is that consciousness is intentional: it is directed toward something. This claim immediately links the question of the object with that of orientation. First, consciousness itself is directed or orientated toward objects, which is what gives consciousness its 'worldly' dimension. If consciousness is about how we perceive the world 'around' us, then consciousness is also embodied, sensitive, and situated."[25] Ahmed then goes on to discuss Edmond Husserl's descriptions (real or imagined) of his writing table at home in his text "Ideas." The warm, quiet domestic scene of his writing table is the event horizon upon which his perceptual investigations begin. The writing table, real or imagined, becomes the concept allowing Ahmed to connect with Husserl imagining a queer female subject in or around the writing desk of this notable male philosopher and the gendered insights regarding perceptual objects that might occur. Much as Ahmed centralizes Husserl's "table" as the site of phenomenological investigation,[26] I would like to propose for activists Nettle and Lauren extending this object horizon to the wooden platform of the aerial forest blockade as a starting point for exploring their queered eco-phenomenological orientation/ disorientation. As Ahmed longs for methods of describing the particularity of objects "beginning at home as Husserl describes," with a body writing at "home,"[27] the blockaders provided descriptions of inhabiting "a home" that was an uncanny forest horizon serving as a starting place for exploration and reflection. These activists turned their attention to the arboreal, the tree, and in that sense the tree-sit platform provides a stabilizing position. The proximity to the tree also appears as the establishment of a relationship of respect and protection.

Nettle is a pseudonym for an anonymous non-gender-identifying arboreal blockader who self-described as "recently not a student." Lauren is a local resident of Pulaski, Virginia, who was also recently a student studying wildlife conservation and who identifies as female and heterosexual.

Both students' motivations for ecological blockading stemmed from a sense of personal disorientation and helplessness that led them to seek out and personally observe blockading actions, notably those led by elder women in the community.

Nettle: I was in school, and I was very into sustainability and environmentalism as it related to the individual. I really thought the smaller choices that I made, my diet, my consumption, my purchases, were ultimately toxic because this made me think on a very individualistic level, which ended in a lot of helplessness.

I then found deeper movements full of passionate people working together mostly outside the system, imagining and creating the world that they wanted to see happen. In those ideas I felt a lot more strength and a lot more support and a lot more love. I was really inspired by Camp White Pine, an encampment that lasted years.

Lauren: I decided to study wildlife conservation in school because I felt very passionate about all of the environmental issues that I had become aware of. I felt as a conservationist especially that direct action is so incredibly important.

I saw they were asking people to come out and support [the tree sits] because they thought that the police might be attempting to extract the tree sitters that day. I dropped everything that I was doing that day. I was actually in the gym on my phone, and I stopped my workout in the middle of it and was like, okay, I, I don't think I could focus on anything else today after seeing all of this.

So I went out and saw the monopod for the first time and was blown away by it and very inspired and very motivated myself because I hadn't really ever seen anything like that before. It was just—it just seemed really crazy to me. It was just incredibly inspiring that there were still things that we could do to try and fight the pipeline. It just comes down to the power of knowledge, because I never realized that doing things like this were an option and I just felt very apathetic and very helpless.

Both blockaders broke with conventional wisdom and the known horizon to engage in a new orientation modeled by older female blockaders positioned on tree platforms out of reach of law enforcement and corporate security. This new orientation also blocked pipeline construction effectively for several months. A novel and reinvented visual horizon produced by blockading in the tree platform provided a stabilizing freedom from a disorienting lack of agency toward justice.

Nettle: My platform is four feet by seven feet, so it's even smaller than the last apartment I lived in, which was pretty close to this honestly.

It was interesting because this slope is really hard to walk up. We've been watching people stumble over this hillside for a month now. It was honestly kind of funny watching the loggers try to be really intimidating, holding their chain saws in an intimidating way and then stumble over the slope, like the rest of us getting their chain saws and gear, like, caught in the brush as they come up.

Lauren: The first day was pretty chaotic. MVP did show up with surveyors to see what was going on. As time went on, I got more comfortable in the tree. I started to adjust to being up so high all the time.

I wasn't really afraid of heights before I went up there, but I definitely wasn't afraid of heights afterwards. It's cool how your mind can adjust to these types of things. I think that kind of mental aspect of it all was also a little bit trying. It really took a lot of meditation. When you're not sure if they're [MVP] going to show up one day and also continuously not having anything happen at all, I had to practice being still and being content, not doing anything and just being up there reading and relaxing.

Inspired by Ahmed's text, I will suggest that one of the important implications of aerial blockading is the subjects' relationship to the "objecthood" of nature. Ahmed discusses critiques of Marx's distinction between matter and form—the difference between "the wood and the table." Marxist critiques of German idealism and phenomenology point out that simply passively observing an object could erase the fact that objects are the result of social actions associated with specific labor histories. Commodities are composed of matter and labor pulled from the natural world as man uses the natural materials for industrial or consumer goods.[28] One key critical quality of the arboreal blockaders' experience is their refusal to see the forest as simply "latent matter" that will end up as waste material removed to make way for carbon-based fuels or lumber for housing or goods. The birds, trees, landscape, and weather are neither background material nor aesthetic horizon for other tasks of daily life nor raw material for human consumption; they become a permeable boundary for queering orientation.

Both arboreal blockaders, particularly Lauren, describe the queerness or otherness of orienting toward nature not as a matter of possible instrumentation or objecthood but as interactive personal engagement, enlivened with emotional depth and personal grounding over the course of several months on the platform.

Lauren: I definitely didn't realize just how disconnected we are from the natural cycles of the day and weather patterns and just how disconnected we are from the earth. When you are outside, you really pay attention to when it's gonna rain or when it's super windy or when it's very hot. I mean you have to. These are just things that you don't think about or you take for granted when you're living in very comfy, cozy living conditions indoors. I definitely started to appreciate good weather more, and I think about three o'clock is when the sun was shining directly on my platform; that was a great time, use my solar charging device.

I think people thought I was a little nuts because I was always talking about the birds while I was up there. I would say, "I saw a female scarlet tanager earlier today, and it was so cool," and I would talk about what they were doing, and others didn't seem to have the same level of excitement. But I was always just so interested in it.

I've always had this connection to, to animals and wildlife. And I think, like, my mom thinks I'm crazy 'cause she's not really ever understood why I have so many animals or, like, why I feel such a deep connection to them. But yeah, a lot of these things I really don't know how to put into words, but it is what it is.

It's weird. I almost didn't want to go back to living inside because I just felt so connected and peaceful out here.

In Ahmed's notes in chapter "Inhabiting Spaces," she asks, "How do bodies matter in what objects do?" Ahmed's text provides context for Lauren's description of her time on the tree-blockading platform, in which particular experiences seem to merge physical embodiment with the uncanny. Ahmed cites Merleau-Ponty in further defining the "body not as an instrument, but a form of expression, making visible all of our intentions." Lauren has in some ways instrumentalized her body as a way to block environmental harm, but she appears to equally find that the body is a form of expression interlinked with the forest. Ahmed continues to posit that space is not a container for the body but that bodies are emplaced so that "they become the space they inhabit."[29]

In Lauren's descriptions of moments of more spectral, abstract body sensing of the weather, birds, temporality, and forest interactions, she uses language such as "very strange," "very weird," "crazy," and "hard to put into words." Her descriptions of the uncanny disorienting sense of her move from the tree-sit platform back to the "normal world" are not only striking and quite poignant but also open very personal insight to her own queer ecological phenomenology. Lauren discusses a sense of phenomenological merging with "nature" or the ecosystem that she is striving to "reorient," but it falls beyond easily accessible language.

> **Lauren:** I've had a really hard time adjusting back to the outside world, back to civilization. It's been very strange, and I haven't really been able to quite understand what's going on with me, but I just feel very out of place, and I don't really know what to do from here. Like, I just feel I used to have, like, this very strong sense of being very driven. I asked myself how much can I get done today and what can I be doing to progress my career?
>
> After coming out here, I just don't—I don't feel that anymore. I don't want any part of it anymore. And it's very weird. Obviously. I also have to have, like, some kind of self-preservation. I need to have a job and work, and, um, I've just kind of lost a lot of motivation for that.
>
> I think my days are just much slower. I want to relax a lot more and, um, just try and be present a lot more. I think just when you learn to be more present and more in tune with the natural cycles of the earth and you stop viewing yourself as an individual separate from, from the earth and you really start to kind of feel just like one being, it's very weird to explain.

"I want us to think about how queer politics might *involve* disorientation, without legislating disorientation as politics" says Ahmed. Later, she adds, "The point is what we do with such moments of disorientation, as well as what such moments can do—whether they can offer us the hope of new directions, whether new directions are reason enough for hope."[30]

At times, Lauren's respect or even love gained from weeks on the tree platform created a pleasurable loss of boundary between self and the ecosystem of the forest and animals. When she reencountered her peers, family, or community of origin, she felt a new sense of disorienting strangeness that fell beyond language and her ability to express this "queer" orientation to nature. Within the larger communal "queer table" of the blockading camp and in the community, Lauren found like-minded kin who share this queering of orientation in the name of preserving this particular ecosystem in a specific embodied way.[31]

TRANSGENDER/NONBINARY EMBODIMENT IN ECO-ACTIVIST ORIENTATION

My research interviews included two subjects on the transgender spectrum: "Anonymous" (name withheld), a trans man, and "Ember" (pseudonym), a transfeminine person who uses *they* pronouns. Both subjects were interviewed on the ground where they were providing support for the arboreal blockaders. Both subjects referenced other MVP civil disobedience actions that either occurred in the past or were planned for the future.

The interviews with Ember and Anonymous contained a strong orientation toward action but also a pondering of the stability of a material trans identity. In other words, the subjects were not positing how a "real" or "authentic" transitioned transgender person or body does or should do activism but rather were describing the ineffable embodiment of trans identity that merges with ecological concerns in a very personal way.

In *Assuming a Body*, Gayle Salamon examines the formation of the trans self from a psychoanalytic perspective via Freud and Judith Butler that jibes with the interplay of materiality, orientation, and desire that I found in the words of the subjects: "To affirm a materiality—or, to be less abstract, to insist on the livability of one's own embodiment, particularly when that embodiment is culturally abject or socially despised—is to undertake a constant and always incomplete labor to reconfigure more than just the materiality of our own bodies. It is to strive to create and transform the lived meanings of those materialities."[32]

This is not to say that a particular surgery or therapy can provide a "real" indication of an "authentic" prescribed gender—male or female—but rather that, according to Butler via Salamon, entirely new "alternate imaginary schemas"[33] for thinking beyond gender binaries altogether are required for a deeper analysis of trans experience and, from there, all human experience. I will propose to add to these "alternate imaginary schemas" the examination and revision of destructive human/ecological binaries actively pursued by the subjects.

TRANS ECO SENSES—ANONYMOUS AND EMBER

I found it notable in my research that both trans and trans spectrum subjects spoke openly about the trauma they had previously experienced or about violence that they had witnessed and assumed would be enacted on their bodies. This possibly speaks to the imminent threat of violence in daily life frequently felt by and enacted against trans people, particularly trans women of color.[34]

Ember: "I use they/them pronouns. I've been doing this for a little while, about, like, since January or so."

Over last summer, I had a very traumatic event happened to me at a antifascist rally, and make your guesses as to what, but it kind of gave you this frustration with a certain detachment that I was seeing from actual action, which is not necessarily inherent to academic circles but very common in them. I went from having felt very satisfied with reading and the writing that I was doing in school to feeling really, none of it was helping me. I guess I had a sort of a sense desire. I think I wasn't able to fulfill my desire [to act] through academics.

A lot of the things that I think about with my body are related to gender expression and identity. There's a very interesting confluence in terms of doing this work and gender. It's the most validating space that I've found in a sort of ironic way. It's also a space in which I have to wear clothing that is practical. Which ends up being gendered in a way that I don't necessarily desire. Living in the woods, a lot of those things are gendered masculine, and they shouldn't be. So it's ironic that this is the thing that actually helps me feel more at home in my body. I'm away from mirrors and societal expectations.

It's an experience that you feel in your body when you're able to reclaim power, especially if it has been, like, taken from you by trauma. Being able to do direct action and see results from it—it's a really powerful way to say even though I exist in a form that a lot of society would not think is something powerful, I am powerful, and I can do things if I desire to.

When you're in these places where you're maybe putting your body in front of machines or chain saws and you're exposing yourselves to the more directly oppressive structures of the state, like police, for me as someone who can maybe pass as feminine, but not necessarily like a trans woman, you're placing yourself, like, very much in a dangerous place. Right. But still it feels like much more freeing and a much better place than existing in the normal world because you're reclaiming space. Being a trans person in jail is a terrible experience. Interacting with, like, hypermasculine, chainsaw-wielding loggers is not a good experience, but it still is so much better to be in a place where the understanding of what is normal has been disrupted and deconstructed.

In his interview, Anonymous discussed his history of difficulty with fitting in, lack of formal schooling, and manual labor in a southern state doing seasonal maintenance on yachts as an early-twenties white person among majority immigrant labor of color from the Caribbean. His ongoing lack of a sense of purpose compelled him to travel to Standing Rock.

> **Anonymous:** I dunno, I was never really particularly in, like, social norms or in society. For me stepping out of that wasn't really a big step in general. I was really young. I was around eighteen and starting to hear about Standing Rock and these symptoms of capitalism. Pipelines, to be specific. After months of me going back and forth, should I go, should I stay, what am I doing with my life?
>
> I finally made a decision that I'm leaving, I'm packing one pack, and I am going to Standing Rock. I'm just leaving everything; I'm going in; I'm in. I hitched out of Florida in my first ride that picked me up, took me all the way up to Minnesota in twenty-four hours straight.
>
> I think why I'm so anti-this-society and anti-capitalism and the money system and stuff like that—it's like I came to a realization, like, there is so much brute-like force oppressing us at Standing Rock, like visibly, like right across the bridge. I just one day, I just thought to myself, they're killing us in everyday actions. So I'd rather die trying to stop them than to let them kill me. It set off my journey after that of I'm gonna

die fighting for this. Even if they kill me, like, I'd rather die fighting for this than just to sit here and let them kill me.

Both subjects also discussed embodied experiences of gender and suffering related to ongoing social stress from imposed binary gender hierarchies they both wished would radically change or cease to exist. Their language regarding the ontological experience of gender included a discussion of subjective phenomenology in addition to a thoughtful analysis of engagement with surgical and hormonal therapy.

> **Ember:** It's difficult to really even comprehend. Gender is just a simply nebulous thing. I think as a structure that it's oppressive and that, like, in an ideal world, gender would not exist. But in the world that we have, if portions of your essence are deemed either dominant or nondominant or normative or nonnormative either way that you want to talk about it, then gender is an important concept. Ideally, I would rather it didn't exist. It might be beyond words a little bit.

> **Anonymous:** I just kept thinking through my [gender] transition and if I was in a utopia, I wouldn't have to do this because it would just be normal. I'm just a normal human being. That's it. And I still feel that today. Like I can categorize myself as a trans man, but I just think I'm a human at this point and maybe society plays a big role in it. So I just think it's specific towards our society of having to come out like that [either male or female] and thinking that I'm different.
>   The first time I took a testosterone, I took it for like two years straight. I got off of it because I didn't want to be in the pharmaceutical industry and pay into that and stuff like that. So, when I first took it, I knew that I would undergo physical appearance changes. But what I realized is you go through

internal changes as well. You completely change inside and out. Everything about you changes. Then I got off of it, and the transition back into having estrogen in my body was difficult. I'm just a man because I'm a man. That's it. Not because of the hormones in my body.

Ember's description of being compelled by a "sense desire" into direct environmental action that is carried through with additional focus on personal desire. Salamon references the centrality of the phenomenological body in Merleau-Ponty's work and his focus on transposition and desire. "Through desire my body comes alive by being intentionally directed toward another, and I myself come into being through that desire."[35]

Salamon's text plays out a deeper analysis of trans sexuality and desire. Ember intertwines their embodied desire with political and collective action referencing at times Kropotkin's contrasting views to Darwin's evolutionary theory centered on competition rather than cooperation.

Ember: Some of the early anarchist philosophers like Kropotkin talked about mutual aid. There's symbiosis everywhere. A lot of the time animals could not survive if they didn't have the other parts of the ecosystem, which support them. To view it in terms of competition is something that reinforces the ways that humans act already, which is not necessarily a natural way. And I think if we're able to reclaim desire and think of it not as something that we need to repress and control but instead of something that probably is pretty good, then that's a really powerful thing.

Various experiences with trauma have helped me to understand that the body and the mind are very intimately connected and that it doesn't really make sense to separate one from the other. I have fear and anxiety, but in the actual [blockading] confrontation, I have this weirdly clear idea of what it is that you should do. A. clear feeling of, like, direct and almost absolute opposition. Although the world as a whole has all this gray, there are moments in which you have to act as if that were not the case. It is just you, following your passions and desires in a way that you really can't choose not to. There's a good feeling that comes from this intense interaction where you're finding yourself knowing exactly what you need to do. And then afterwards the emotions come back. Insurrectionary practice is, I think, like what blockades are, right? It's like we're not waiting for social change or for critical mass or whatever but instead, like, just doing it, and we're, like, actively engaging in anti-state anti-capitalist activity. If you live next to a coal plant or if you live in West Virginia and, like, the mountains are being destroyed or if your water is poisoned by a fracked gas, it's like there's no time to wait. I think in an insurrectionary practice, the concept of desire is something that we can hold on to that's a lot more concrete than, like, any of these more academic Marxist stuff about, like, proletarian revolution or whatever. It's just I have these things in my life that I know that I care about and that I have to protect.

Anonymous ends his statement on embodiment and ecological action with plans for additional organizing toward intentional communities, perhaps addressing the social aspirations noted earlier in the interview.

Anonymous: "We live in a car traveling from place to place wherever we feel. Hopefully in the future we're going to do some kind of organization that teaches people how to squat and reclaim lands. We're big into gardening and living off the grid in a sustainable way. But my heart's like, ah, but if I buy land, the government still owns it, and the government can easily just come in and be like, hell no, you can't do that and revoke it. So I'm big into reclaiming and liberating lands and just, like, occupying it. And I think after this whole struggle, I think that's what we're going to endeavor."

CONCLUSION

A phenomenological perspective privileges sensory and immediate perceptions based on human experience. This text examined the bodily sensing and somatic experiences of a small group of ecological activists who blockaded natural gas pipelines in Appalachia. These experiences were not cast as nascent passionate subjectivities or unvalidated precursors to normative scientific confirmation of the harms of natural gas infrastructure. Rather, I have proposed that normative environmental studies fail to adequately describe or address the way that personal, embodied relationships with the immediate ecosystems construct a comprehensive system of meaning that is frequently ineffable and that needs more attention. When a system of meaning or "reality" feels under immediate threat from extractive industries, direct environmental activism such as blockading can productively acknowledge and manage the somatic and emotional disorientation that individuals and communities can feel. I also propose that these systems of phenomenological meaning are specific to localities and constitute primary cultural knowledge that is frequently unacknowledged by normative environmental research, studies, or laws, let alone extractive industries that view these ecosystems as purely latent resources for profit.

Sarah Ahmed states that "moments of disorientation are vital."[36] She goes on to discuss Merleau-Ponty's theory of disorientation, wherein a disoriented physical body can collapse and in doing so falls back to becoming an object. Ahmed brings in Frantz Fanon's theory of the disorientation of Black bodies in a white world where, through the daily experiences of abject racism, the Black body can fall to being an object among objects.[37] Ahmed writes, "Disorientation can be a bodily feeling of losing one's place, and an effect of losing a place: it can be a violent feeling, a feeling that is affect by violence, or shaped by violence directed toward the body."[38] She further says, "At this moment of failure such objects point somewhere else, or they make what is 'here become strange.'" Stress can accumulate, and bodies can take the shape of such stress.[39]

A trans youth eco-activist who has experienced bodily violence at a rally and a sense of healing peace while protecting a forest where the nonnormative power balance is overtly evident and a female arboreal blockader who has studied environmental science but can't find words for her deep orientation to bird and animal relationships that move her in such a way that she finds alienation in trying to return home seem to embody such moments of queer disorientation. The accumulation of stress regarding environmental harm, political dissonance, nonnormative gender expression, and communal hopelessness due to the felt warming of the planet from climate change and an impending extractive industry invasion presses the body to make the "here" of daily life "strange," leading to collective direct action as phenomenological reorientation.

Ahmed continues to pursue and describe what Merleau-Ponty seems to feel makes something "queer." She describes this moment as when objects "become distant oblique and 'slip away.'"[40] Ahmed counters with the recuperative possibility that a queer orientation could see a retreat as an approach "in the sense that in the retreat of an object a space is cleared for a new arrival." "Queer gatherings are lines that gather—on the face, or as bodies around the table—to form new patterns and new ways of making sense."[41]

Arboreal blockading and other direct actions on the MVP are seen by those in political and industrial power as highly radical and socially disruptive actions deserving of aggressive, violent, harmful intervention and punishment. The young and old citizens affiliated with the Yellow Finch camp have overtly declared their activities as queer activism or embraced the strong presence of LGBTQIA+ youth as central to their activities. The somatic and embodied qualities described by queer, trans, nonbinary, and female activists offer a rich entry point into the personal, interior, and private experiences of contemporary direct eco-activism motivated not by patriarchal heroic oppositional bravado but by particular queer bodies and histories permeated with rich eco-phenomenological relationships with queer community and a particular Appalachian ecosystem under threat.

NOTES

1. Sarah Ahmed, *Queer Phenomenology Orientations, Objects, Others* (Durham, NC: Duke University Press, 2006), 2.
2. Ahmed, *Queer Phenomenology*, 8.
3. Ken Ward Jr., "Study Finds Increased Cancer Rates Near Coal River Mine Sites," *Charleston (WV) Gazette*, July 27, 2011, http://www.wvgazettemail.com /news/special_reports/study-finds-increased-cancer-rates-near-coal-river -mine-sites/article_c02c1580-f98c-5794-a634-e231d98d7ad3.html.
4. Maurice Merleau-Ponty, *The World of Perception* (London: Routledge, 2004), 21.
5. Catriona Mortimer-Sandilands, "Landdykes and Landscape: Reflections on Sex and Nature in Southern Oregon," *Women & Environments International Magazine*, no. 56–57 (Fall 2002): 13.
6. Cynthia Belmont, "Ecosexuals in Appalachia: Identity, Community, and Counterdiscourse in Goodbye Gauley Mountain," *ISLE: Interdisciplinary Studies in Literature and Environment* 25, no. 4 (Autumn 2018): 742–66.
7. Chris Baker Evans, "One Family's Bold Stand to Block Construction of a New Pipeline," Waging Nonviolence, June 24, 2017, https://wagingnonviolence .org/2017/06/camp-white-pine-mariner-east/.
8. Jesse Adcock, "Nutty Hangs Tough: Tree-Sitter Blocking Pipeline for 56 Days Is Being Starved by the Forest Service," *Blue Ridge Outdoors*, May 21, 2018, https://www.blueridgeoutdoors.com/go-outside/day-54-tree-sitter -blocking-pipeline-is-being-starved-by-the-forest-service/.
9. Z. Zane McNeill, ed., *Y'all Means All: The Emerging Voices Queering Appalachia* (Oakland, CA: PM Press, 2021).

10. Natalie Cox, "Mountain Valley Pipeline Files Formal Application Requesting FERC Authorization to Construct 301-Mile Interstate Natural Gas Pipeline," *Businesswire*, October 23, 2015, https://www.businesswire.com/news/home/20151023005366/en/.

11. Appalachians against Pipelines, Facebook, accessed March 1, 2020, https://www.facebook.com/appalachiansagainstpipelines.

12. Natalie Mishkin, "Mountain Valley Pipeline Cited 5th Time by State Regulators for Violations," *Charleston (WV) Gazette*, July 20, 2018, https://www.wvgazettemail.com/news/mountain-valley-pipeline-cited-5th-time-by-state-regulators-for-violations/.

13. R. J. Vogt, "Land Grab: Property Owners Fight Back against Pipeline IOUs," *Law360*, April 28, 2019, https://www.law360.com/articles/1153244/land-grab-property-owners-fight-back-against-pipeline-ious.

14. Caretta and McHenry "Pipelining," 3–4.

15. Finley-Brook, "Critical energy," 178–79.

16. Finley-Brook, "Critical energy," 179.

17. "Re-posted Announcement from Appalachians against Pipelines," Rising Tide North America, September 10, 2019, https://risingtidenorthamerica.org/2019/09/three-water-protectors-shut-down-work-at-a-mountain-valley-pipeline-site-in-west-virginia/.

18. Kyle Powys Whyte, "The Dakota Access Pipeline, Environmental Justice, and U.S. Colonialism," *Red:Ink: An International Journal of Indigenous Literature, Arts, & Humanities* 19, no. 1 (January/February 2017): 154–69.

19. Whyte, "Dakota Access Pipeline," 2.

20. Patricia M. Locke, "The Liminal World of the Northwest Coast," in *Merleau-Ponty and Environmental Philosophy: Dwelling on the Landscapes of Thought*, ed. Suzanne L. Cataldi and William S. Hamrick (Albany: State University of New York Press, 2007), 73.

21. Whyte, "Dakota Access Pipeline," 4.

22. Stephen Pearson, "'The Last Bastion of Colonialism': Appalachian Settler Colonialism and Self-Indigenization," *American Indian Culture and Research Journal* 37 (2013): 2.

23. S. R. Kostelecky, "Sharing Community Created Content in Support of Social Justice: The Dakota Access Pipeline LibGuide," *Journal of Librarianship and Scholarly Communication* 6 (2018): 2.

24. Kostelecky, "Sharing Community Created Content," 3.

25. Ahmed, *Queer Phenomenology*, 27.

26. Ahmed, *Queer Phenomenology*, 28–29.

27. Ahmed, *Queer Phenomenology*, 166–67, 176.

28. Ahmed, *Queer Phenomenology*, 40–42.

29. Ahmed, *Queer Phenomenology*, 51–63.

30. Ahmed, *Queer Phenomenology*, 158.

31. Ahmed, *Queer Phenomenology*, 167.

32. Gayle Salamon, *Assuming a Body: Transgender and Rhetorics of Materiality* (New York: Columbia University Press, 2010), 42.

33. Salamon, *Assuming a Body*, 42.

34. Rebecca L. Stotzer, "Data Sources Hinder Our Understanding of Transgender Murders," *American Journal of Public Health* 107, no. 9 (September 2017): 1362–63.

35. Salamon, *Assuming a Body*, 50.

36. Ahmed, *Queer Phenomenology*, 157.

37. Ahmed, *Queer Phenomenology*, 160.

38. Ahmed, *Queer Phenomenology*, 160.

39. Ahmed, *Queer Phenomenology*, 160.

40. Ahmed, *Queer Phenomenology*, 171.

41. Ahmed, *Queer Phenomenology*, 171.

MASCULINITIES IN THE DECLINE OF COAL

Queer Futures in
the Appalachian Coalfields

GABE SCHWARTZMAN

INTRODUCTION

In May 2009, I stood on one side of Marsh Fork Elementary School's fence in the Coal River Valley of West Virginia facing a line of people wearing orange reflective stripes. Inside the fence, we were rallying for a ban on mountaintop-removal (MTR) coal mining and for relocating the elementary school to a safe distance from a coal-processing plant. The protesters on the other side of the fence were rallying to support the coal industry, holding signs that read, "Coal Keeps the Lights On" and "Coal Miner's Daughter." Later that day, one of those coal miners' daughters would jump a police line to punch Judy Bonds, community organizer and Goldman Prize–awarded local environmental justice leader, in the face. That coun-terprotester was only the first person of many arrested that day. Tensions were high, but in the coming years, pro-coal protests and mobilizations intensified across the Appalachian coalfields, from Tennessee to West Virginia. The number of Friends of Coal specialty license plates one saw in the coalfields increased exponentially, as did yard signs reading, "End Obama's War on Coal." Politicians vied to prove they were ever more pro-coal than the others.

Today, however, with the industry riddled with bankruptcies that not even former president Donald Trump's policies could halt, it seems there is less and less coal industry to support. The industry's decline itself is not new. Shannon Bell and Richard York detail how pro-coal ideology entailed a defense of the coal industry's future despite, and, in fact, because of, the decline of the industry, with such efforts beginning as early as 2003. What has changed in the present, aside from the coal industry declining to all-time low employment and production levels,[1] is a shift in the public conversation about the future of the Appalachian coalfields. While rhetoric about coal as the economy of the future is still present in the coalfields (as seen on Virginia's Friends of Coal specialty license plate, "The Power behind America's Future"), much of the political, policy, and media conversation about the region's future has shifted to discussions of an economic transition away from coal.[2]

What, then, happens to pro-coal politics as public conversations about Appalachia's future shift from centering coal to discussing economic transition? One trend evident in pro-coal online forums has been a vocalization of grievance and nostalgia. Across rural America, scholars discuss a politics of rural resentment.[3] In the Appalachian coalfields, however, I find that grievance and nostalgia, as well as much of the discussion about an economic transition, operate through the *cultural politics* of coal mining and the family in Appalachia. Cultural politics is an analytic that "treats culture itself as a site of political struggle," paying particular attention to the relations of the material and the symbolic: people, things, and their representation. Cultural politics studies the "way that culture—including people's attitudes, opinions, beliefs and perspectives, as well as the media and arts—*shapes* society and political opinion, and gives rise to social, economic and legal realities."[4]

Scholars of Appalachian cultural politics detail how pro-coal politics were produced through the articulation of gender, race, and work.[5] Rebecca Scott discusses how support for the industry has related to ideas about masculinity—the idea of coal-mining jobs as the work of *real men*, as *real work*, and as one of the few options to really support a family—and to the workings of race and class. In a region regularly represented as a natural home to "white trash," the middle-class livelihood and position of sacrifice associated with coal mining has provided some people a position from which to evade the often racialized markings of poverty. Online grievances, nostalgia, and conversations about economic transition also operate through the articulations of race, class, and gender.[6]

As of yet, however, little of the literature on pro-coal politics and mining masculinities in Appalachia has engaged queer theory. Theories of queer time provide useful starting points to study post-coal discourses. Discourses are the social systems that produce knowledge, meaning, and social practices, all with material effect, and discourses are the basis for power relations. Language, symbols, and representation are sites from which to analyze a discursive landscape. Examining representations of the economic transition and tracing the ways people vocalize grievance and nostalgia in online pro-coal forums, I show how such discourses rely on images of a heteropatriarchal white family as the subject of economic transition and of injury.[7]

Queer theory provides a framework to understand why and how discourses of grievance and certain discourses of economic transition invoke nostalgia: as reactions to an open-ended future, one where the reproduction of the heteronormative family through the "Fordist family wage" is imperiled. Such fear of the future may be well founded. Popular public depictions of workers transitioning to new jobs that pay family wages, which allow them to support a household on one income, sit in rude disjuncture with many people's lived experiences in Appalachia. Discourses of both grievance and transition are nostalgic in the sense that they hearken back to a past of white masculine supremacy. Yet, as the nostalgic attachment I document illustrates, heteropatriarchy has an enduring purchase in part because of the sense that, in much the same way as Margaret Thatcher famously said of neoliberal austerity, "there is no alternative." Queer thought and queer community building from Appalachia present visions for a post-coal future that may counter a politics of nostalgia and may enable a rethinking of what more an economic transition can mean for the coalfields.[8]

QUEER THEORY AND QUEER TIME

Queer theory and studies of queer time provide a lens of analysis to theorize nostalgia for the family wage as a fear of the future: a fear of the inability to reproduce the heteropatriarchal family in the decline of the heteronormative family-work arrangements and in the feminization of labor.

Rather than using *queerness* as a verb in this context, scholars of queer time offer queerness as an analytic for considering the ways that temporality—the pacing, timing, and ordering of lives—is structured through gender and sexuality. As an analytic, queer time, therefore, offers a way to consider that claims about economies and economic change always relate to social arrangements of power in and through gender and sexuality.

Scholars of queer time detail temporalities that do not reproduce the patterns of the heteronormative family. As J. Jack Halberstam describes, "Queer subcultures produce alternative temporalities by allowing their participants to believe that their futures can be imagined according to logics that lie outside of the conventional forward-moving narratives of birth, marriage, reproduction, and death." Queer theories of time present critiques of these temporalities of the heteronormative family, what Lee Edelman terms "reproductive futurism." Queer time operates outside these temporalities, for some as a lack of future and for others, particularly within queer of color critique, as a radical possibility of another world. Halberstam discusses queer time as being about more than sexuality, considering it as an outcome of "strange temporalities, imaginative life schedules and eccentric economic practices." For Halberstam and other queer theorists, queering is certainly about sexuality and sex but is also defined as an outcome of temporality itself: of life scheduling and nonnormative economic activities, practices always tied up with family and gender. If we conceptualize it as such, "we detach queerness from sexual identity and come closer to understanding Foucault's comment in 'Friendship as a Way of Life' that 'homosexuality threatens people as a "way of life" rather than as a way of having sex.'"[9]

Just as the pro-coal politics that preceded the current moment demonstrated, responses to threats posed to reproductive futurism often rearticulate hegemonic masculinity and heteropatriarchy in new arrangements. During the height of pro-coal politics, in the mid-2000s and 2010s, diminishing jobs and increasing difficulty in achieving prized reproductive futures triggered a politics of resentment, nostalgia, and masculine grievance: anger at environmentalists for taking jobs, racialized resentment against a Black president, and an invocation of an imagined past of white masculine supremacy and family values. In the current moment, nostalgia once again provides heteronormative subject positions for people in the coalfields to inhabit.

SHIFTING DISCOURSES: COAL FUTURES
TO ECONOMIC TRANSITION

Before I return to questions of queer subjectivity, however, I find it useful to first explain the shifting gendered political economy of coal in Appalachia. Across the region, institutions increasingly accept the inevitability of transition when discussing coalfield communities, from media depictions to the language guiding philanthropic and governmental programs. For instance, in candidate interviews for the 2020 primary elections, West Virginia's major newspaper, the *Charleston Gazette-Mail*, asked all gubernatorial and federal candidates about their plans to diversify the regional economy in the wake of the decline in the resource-extraction economy. Even Kentucky senator Mitch McConnell, a coal enthusiast, admitted the decline of coal as he offered plans for transitioning coal workers into new employment. Perhaps even more telling, although West Virginia's coal-mine-owning governor, Jim Justice, does not use the term *transition*, his office has publicized his receipt of millions of dollars of federal aid to retrain "laid off coal workers" and get them back to work doing "something else."[10]

Outside of political rhetoric, the discourse of an economic transition has had a material effect in structuring major grant-making programs across the region. Federal and local governments, philanthropists, nonprofits, and grassroots movements have launched initiatives, funds, and projects dedicated to support an economic transition for Appalachia.[11] In the early 2010s, post-coal futures for Appalachia may have seemed like the aspirational politics of the likes of the Sierra Club's Beyond Coal campaign or the Alliance for Appalachia's efforts to secure a "just transition."[12] Yet, since 2015, the Appalachian Regional Commission (ARC)–based Partnerships for Opportunity and Workforce and Economic Revitalization (POWER) Initiative has provided federal funding to help areas affected by the decline in the coal economy diversify their economies. The POWER Initiative has deployed $250 million toward economic transition projects, with $600 million to be invested in total. Also since 2015, the Appalachian Funders Network has provided grants for projects that promise to support a just and equitable transition away from the coal economy through their Just Transition Fund. The historic social justice institution the Highlander Center operated an Appalachian Transition Fellowship, which started with its first cohort of young people in 2014. These are only several key examples of the many projects working at multiple scales that seek to build economic futures for the Appalachian region in the wake of the coal industry's perhaps final decline.[13] While some may not use the language of *economic transition* explicitly, many discussions about Appalachia's future, from politics to philanthropy, have become centered on retraining workers and starting new economies, not reviving the coal industry.[14]

RETRAINING WORKERS: REPRESENTATION AND REALITY

While coal miners and their families are readily represented in these grant documents, promotional materials, and media coverage about a transitioning economy, most of these programs have fallen short of providing pathways to jobs that pay a family wage. In fact, these representations sit at odds with an increasingly clear labor market trend in the coalfields, a labor market that has witnessed policies of neoliberalization since the 1970s.[15] These economic policies and politics have driven what feminist economic geographer Linda McDowell terms "the feminization of labor."[16]

Working in 1991 to describe "the new gender order" emerging in Britain under post-Fordism with the destruction of industrial employment that provided a family wage and the growth of service sector employment (and underemployment), McDowell wrote, "[A]ll workers were becoming women workers, whatever their gender."[17] During that period, Appalachian neoliberalization also involved a process of reordering gender roles. Since the 1980s and 1990s, employment growth in Appalachia has become increasingly limited to the service sector, overwhelmingly involving women entering the workforce, and work in general has looked more like historically gendered "women's work."[18] Coal-mining employment levels have continually fallen, and coal-industry working conditions have only worsened as the United Mine Workers of America suffered crippling defeats through the 1980s and early 1990s.[19] Today, with schools, health care, and retail making up the bulk of employment in the region, people increasingly talk of coal in the past tense (although, importantly, many mining operations are still active and still cause environmental devastation for residents).[20]

Despite the realities of labor markets in the region, many depictions of an economic transition imply that through programs, classes, or training, people could remake themselves and (importantly) still access a family wage. In many of the documents and media portrayals of economic transition programs, the barriers to success are personal: a focus on individual agency—which squarely places people's success or failure in terms of personal ability, commitment, and strength—not on systemic factors.

One instance of such representation was a former worker transition and entrepreneurship program called the Green Mining Model Business Program. The project, funded with ARC POWER Initiative funds, targeted out-of-work miners and their families for training on how to run lavender farms on former surface mines in southern West Virginia.

The program's advertisement, which aired on regional television in 2018 and spread across social media, portrays a large likely-masculine white person with a trimmed goatee in a new pickup truck driving across a surface mine, a miner's helmet on the passenger seat. The camera focuses on a family portrait taped to his dashboard: seemingly, the man in the truck, a white woman, and three white children. In a voice-over, a deep voice says, "It finally happened. I'm back here on site. . . . Running crops instead of coal. Never dreamed I'd be farming for a living. There's money in it too." A higher-pitched voice, what we might assume to be a woman's voice, comes in at the end, offering contact information as the program is "creating real opportunities for Appalachian miners and their families."[21]

Contrary to what some of the participants had come to believe when they began, the program leased surface-mined lands from coal and land companies and advocated doing the same. The training resulted in very few people becoming lavender farmers.

Another illustrative example of such representation is that of Mined Minds, a nonprofit offering free coding classes, with the intention of "turning coal miners into computer programmers." The Pennsylvania-based operation that extended into West Virginia became a regional phenomenon overnight, with dozens of news outlets and cable TV shows interviewing the providers of the coding classes, with politicians offering free space, grant funding, and publicity. The promotional materials that the nonprofit and media outlets displayed regularly depicted masculinized burly young coal miners as their target subject. For example, one slide-show from 2017 included images of likely masculine coal miners in a mine, covered in coal dust and orange-striped overalls, with the subject line "#coal2code," a hashtag that has united several software companies and training programs across the region. The nonprofit clearly touted that their program could secure substantial wages for graduates, espousing a bootstrap ethic on Twitter: "Tech bootcamps are not easy. If you aren't dedicated, passionate, & humble, you'll fail. Nobody is handed a career with a six figure salary."[22]

However, among worker retraining programs, Mined Minds is unique in that in subsequent years the classes came under legal scrutiny for fraud. They had promised internships and apprenticeships, and executives had promised employment upon completion. Few of the many attendees finished the coding boot camps, which were often taught by other recent graduates, and fewer found employment in programming. Furthermore, interviews with participants indicate that few of those taking the classes were actually miners: I found all kinds of people, most of them hoping to leave service sector employment. Like the for-profit education and credential programs that Tressie Cottom describes as "lower-ed," these tech boot camps promised middle-class jobs in a tech economy that few participants were ultimately able to find. At present, the program has been scaled back, and a class-action lawsuit is underway.[23]

In a more direct enactment of transitioning workers to new high-waged industrial jobs, a number of federal investments have also sought to create job pathways for out-of-work coal miners. The Department of Labor invested at least $20 million in grants to train dislocated workers in Appalachian coal mining since 2012. Roughly one-third of the ARC POWER Initiative's $250 million economic transition grants went to workforce development and training. While much of this funding targeted displaced coal miners, analysts with the West Virginia Center on Budget and Policy found that worker training has largely been ineffective at creating new jobs for miners. These policy analysts argue that training will not guarantee high-wage employment if those jobs simply do not exist in the region.[24]

NOSTALGIA AND GRIEVANCE

While political and policy conversations center on economic transition, people who have supported the coal industry vocalize grievance and nostalgia on online forums. Senses of injury, of aggrieved former workers and their families, and of nostalgia for the "good days of coal" flood the comment sections of pro-coal Facebook groups—the same groups where people organized pro-coal rallies and actions five or ten years prior.

In one example, a former miner posted on the national Friends of Coal Facebook page (started in West Virginia by the West Virginia Coal Association), reacting to a headline about pipeline workers who needed to find new jobs after the cancellation of the Keystone XL pipeline: "How's that working for those still left in southeastern KY . . . . didnt work out for me couldn't even find a job . . . under trump I was able to rebuild and even build a business for myself . . . four short years . . . and now I'm sure to probably lose it." Throughout the multiple Appalachian states' Friends of Coal pages, named Citizens for Coal and Count on Coal, with several hundred thousand people following each page, frequent posts air a series of grievances about the decline of coal, loss of jobs, and precarity of alternatives. Most of the posts are from likely masculine white people, as are all of those I reference here, although a significant share of feminine-presenting people post as well.[25]

In response to letters to the editors of local newspapers or news stories about fossil fuel decline and environmental policies, individuals post hundreds of comments taking aim at Democrats, "liberals," and people who believe that climate change is of more concern than fossil fuel jobs, with some at times straying into conspiracy theories about Joe Biden and Democratic leadership. One post on the national Friends of Coal page, responding to news that John Kerry had mentioned putting coal miners back to work making solar panels, retorted, "An[d] out of work politicians can learn to code," wryly referencing the rhetoric of coding classes for miners. Between comments that call President Biden a "job killer" or claim that he is "working for China," a coal miner reacting to a headline heralding the cancellation of the Keystone XL pipeline writes: "Said he was going to provide good jobs in place of those lost. They should've had that set up before they did anything. Putting the cart before the horse." An Ohio steelworker, hearkening back to better times, posted, "And from the 70's they've been promising new, better jobs for those that were lost. Back then the[y] were pushing everyone to HVAC. All we have accomplished is to shift production to areas that have no labor or environmental protections."[26]

Throughout these posts, there is a tone of nostalgia. Yet, unlike the frequent posts I documented several years ago, few express a genuine hope for the return of coal jobs. Rather, there is a sense of righteous anger and fear for a future with increasingly limited options.[27]

QUEER FUTURES AFTER COAL

Queer theory offers an analytic to consider temporality and the response to Appalachia's economic transition. Nostalgia offers unstable subject positions. Wendy Brown discusses the political rationality (the epistemological underpinnings of government) of neoliberalism (a framework to consider the gendered labor and political economic relations of the post-Fordist era) as plagued with contradictions. As a mode of governmentality, neoliberalism places the individual at the center of both success and failure, while restructuring political economies in ways that heighten wealth inequality, dismantling social welfare systems, suppressing union power, and encouraging market competition in a race to the bottom for wages and working conditions. Meanwhile, such unregulated capitalism encourages offshoring jobs. At the same time, as Melinda Cooper argues, neoliberalism's attachment to individual agency and rhetorical invocation of multiculturalism allowed many women and people of color to occupy formerly masculinized jobs and social positions. Today, however, many white men are largely doing worse than their fathers and grandfathers were before austerity and the dismantling of family wages. Under neoliberalism, as a system of rationality anchored in conservative family values (as neoliberal champion Margaret Thatcher famously declared, "there is no society," only the family), the maintenance of the middle-class hetero family is culturally exalted and at the same time increasingly unattainable for the working class. As a result, Brown argues, it seems to many that there is "no future for white men."[28]

White supremacy and masculine hegemony have only ever been maintained through political action. Other politics are possible. Melinda Cooper presents a compelling case for understanding the dismantling of the Fordist family wage as a political action against feminist, of color, and queer social movements that fought to benefit from structures of social welfare, such as high wages. Neoliberal politics, therefore, are the results of an alliance of neoliberal free market ideologues and neoconservatives focused on restoring the conservative family. Emerging from the 1970s as liberation struggles fought to include women, people of color, and queer people in the project of family wages and public goods, the neoliberal-neoconservative alliance worked to privatize those public goods—to refocus on the family. The new social order reinvented the normative family as the essential means of wealth and status distribution. The alliance that refocused on family values contradictorily eroded the ability of workers to maintain middle-class heteropatriarchal family structures in places like the Appalachian coalfields.[29]

In the erosion of those political economic supports, queer temporalities emerge, and not simply in a queer-identifying community. Rather, read through the lens of queer theory, queer temporalities might include the nonnormative eccentric economic practices resulting from the very erosion of the heteronormative family structure that was upheld through the family wage. Yet the chaos, economic instability, and poverty that accompanied neoliberalization have also constituted a rearticulation of white heteropatriarchy. Women's liberation and civil rights movements had contested the family wage as an instrument of white patriarchy, and as those wage benefits began to be extended to more people than white men through the managerial capitalism of the 1970s, the neoliberal alliance worked to destroy the family wage as a way to maintain patriarchy. In Appalachia, the fall of family wages in the decline of coal has meant increasingly dire poverty, community dissolution, and a complicated but undeniable relationship to a deadly addiction epidemic.[30]

In this context, a fear of the future can be understandable in the face of bitter and dire social and economic crisis. In this moment when it may seem there is no way out, nostalgia is an understandable reaction to the realities of the Appalachian labor market. Discursive deployments of economic transition that continue to imagine a future in the image of the fleeting Fordist family wage also demonstrate an understandable, if confining, nostalgia—an inability to imagine a different future. The radical possibility in queer time is that it provides a future for people beyond the heteropatriarchal family and the economies built around it—a future outside the confining binary of either the Fordist family or a feminized neoliberalism.

Queer time offers an analytic with which to imagine a radically more just future—a queer economic transition. Considering what a queer economic transition would entail, scholars and activists might look to those very moments that Cooper points to: when liberation movements took control of public goods. Scholars, organizers, and artists are already doing the work to envision queer post-coal futures. An emergent discourse of queer economic transition might mean considering what public services, resources, and spaces could serve all the people of the region. A queer economic transition would decenter the image of a white coal miner and his family, recognize the full breadth of the region's diversity, and consider what a transition that serves Black, Indigenous, Latinx, and Asian people would entail. A discourse of queer economic transition will require imagining how to increase the quality of life regardless of economic metrics of worth measured in work, skill, or ability. Such a discourse is emerging from queer thought and queer community in Appalachia.[31]

A QUEER APPALACHIA

There is a robust and growing body of literature theorizing queer Appalachian futurity and discussing the challenges to and vibrancy of queer rural community in Appalachia. Scholars in Appalachian studies and Black geographies have investigated questions around queer and queer of color visibility in Appalachian communities. Scholarship on rural queer community in the region, young people's decision to stay, social services, and self-organized support attest to growing conversations about building queer community in Appalachia.[32]

Furthermore, public intellectuals have focused on how rural queer networks operate in Appalachia and how the position of being both in and out of place enables a location from which to imagine and create alternative futures for the region. As writer Elizabeth Catte provocatively titled one piece, "The Future of Appalachia Is Queer." Scholars have also focused on the power of storytelling with and in queer Appalachian communities, while a forthcoming anthology of emerging queer Appalachian voices remaps the region in the full diversity and complexity of queer perspectives. Academics, artists, intellectuals, and activists are studying and building knowledge for not only an Appalachian future that would include queer communities but a future conceptualized outside a masculinized extractive industry future.[33]

However, queer futurity in Appalachia is far from the domain of academics and writers. Conceptions of queer futurity also come out of identity and community-building projects in process. From Rae Garringer's *Country Queers* podcast and oral history project to the work of Staying Together Appalachian Youth (STAY) to provide queer community for regional youth and to the chapters of Southerners on New Ground (SONG) maintaining queer community and fighting for racial and sexual justice, people are building family, community, and futures beyond normative gendered relations. Projects for building and strengthening rural queer community in the Appalachian region are strong, and from those projects visions for queer Appalachian futures arise.[34]

These projects operate in what Ada Smith, regional movement builder and community organizer, has termed "Appalachian Futurism." Smith argues that "Appalachians must . . . think about a way of working that is about possibility—using aesthetics, imagination, art, and risk as the foreground." Smith asks for young people to be given space to imagine and experiment with open-ended possibilities for their communities, their economies, and their own lives. I read Smith as implying a break with reproductive futurist imaginations of the region's futures, a break with futures that imagine the resurgence of *real men's* work being culturally and economically prized above all—that is, a break that offers a queer future for Appalachia.[35]

NOTES

1. Energy Information Agency, *Annual Energy Outlook 2019 with Projections to 2050* (Washington, DC: Office of Energy Analysis, US Department of Energy, 2019).

2. Chuck Jones, "Even Trump Can't Keep Coal Companies from Declaring Bankruptcy," *Forbes*, November 9, 2019, https://www.forbes.com/sites /chuckjones/2019/11/09/even-trump-cant-keep-coal-companies-from-declaring -bankruptcy/; Shannon E. Bell and Richard York, "Community Economic Identity: The Coal Industry and Ideology Construction in West Virginia," *Rural Sociology* 75, no. 1 (2010): 111–43; see also Philip Lewin, "'Coal Is Not Just a Job, It's a Way of Life': The Cultural Politics of Coal Production in Central Appalachia," *Social Problems* 66, no. 1 (2019): 51–68; Philip Lewin, "'I Just Keep My Mouth Shut': The Demobilization of Environmental Protest in Central Appalachia," *Social Currents* 6, no. 6 (2019): 534–52; Rebecca R. Scott, *Removing Mountains: Extracting Nature and Identity in the Appalachian Coalfields* (Minneapolis: University of Minnesota Press, 2010). For information on coal's decline, see Energy Information Agency, *Annual Energy Outlook 2019*; David Fritsch, "U.S. Coal Production Employment Has Fallen 42% since 2011," Today in Energy, US Energy Information Administration, December 11, 2019, https://www.eia.gov/todayinenergy/detail.php?id=42275. For more on Friends of Coal license plates, see "Specialty 'Coal' Plates Popular in Many Regions," *Middlesboro (KY) News*, September 8, 2017, https://www.middlesboronews .com/2017/09/08/specialty-coal-plates-popular-in-many-regions/.

3. Katherine J. Cramer, *The Politics of Resentment: Rural Consciousness in Wisconsin and the Rise of Scott Walker* (Chicago: University of Chicago Press, 2016); Jonathan M. Metzl, *Dying of Whiteness: How the Politics of Racial Resentment Is Killing America's Heartland* (New York: Basic Books, 2020); Arlie Russell

Hochschild, *Strangers in Their Own Land: Anger and Mourning on the American Right* (New York: New Press, 2018).

4. Donald S. Moore, Anand Pandian, and Jake Kosek, *Race, Nature, and the Politics of Difference* (Durham, NC: Duke University Press, 2003), 2; Steph Newell, "What Is Meant by 'Cultural Politics'?," *Cultural Politics of Dirt in Africa—1880–Present* (blog), University of Sussex, April 1, 2014, https://blogs.sussex.ac.uk/dirtpol/2014/04/01/what-is-meant-by-cultural-politics-by-prof-steph-newell/.

5. Lewin, "'Coal Is Not Just a Job,'" 58; Scott, *Removing Mountains*; Bell and York, "Community Economic Identity."

6. Scott, *Removing Mountains*; Meredith McCarroll, *Unwhite: Appalachia, Race, and Film*, South on Screen (Athens: University of Georgia Press, 2018); Rebecca R. Scott, "Appalachia and the Construction of Whiteness in the United States," *Sociology Compass* 3, no. 5 (2009): 803–10; Matt Wray, *Not Quite White: White Trash and the Boundaries of Whiteness* (Durham, NC: Duke University Press, 2006); Barbara Ellen Smith, "De-gradations of Whiteness: Appalachia and the Complexities of Race," *Journal of Appalachian Studies* 10, no. 1/2 (2004): 38–57.

7. Michel Foucault, "Orders of Discourse," *Social Science Information* 10, no. 2 (April 1, 1971): 7–30.

8. Melinda Cooper, *Family Values: Between Neoliberalism and the New Social Conservatism* (New York: Zone Books, 2017); Margaret Thatcher, "Speech to Conservative Party Conference" (Conservative Party Conference, Brighton, October 20, 1967), Margaret Thatcher Foundation, https://www.margaretthatcher.org/document/101586.

9. Judith Halberstam, "What's That Smell? Queer Temporalities and Subcultural Lives," *International Journal of Cultural Studies* 6, no. 3 (2003): 314; Lee Edelman, *No Future: Queer Theory and the Death Drive* (Durham, NC: Duke University Press, 2004); Roderick A. Ferguson, *Aberrations in Black: Toward a Queer of Color Critique* (Minneapolis: University of Minnesota Press, 2003); José Esteban Muñoz, *Cruising Utopia: The Then and There of Queer Futurity*, 10th ed. (New York: NYU Press, 2009); J. Jack Halberstam, *In a Queer Time and Place: Transgender Bodies, Subcultural Lives* (New York: NYU Press, 2005), 1; Kara Keeling, *Queer Times, Black Futures* (New York: NYU Press, 2019); Elizabeth Freeman, *Time Binds: Queer Temporalities, Queer Histories* (Durham, NC: Duke University Press, 2010); Michel Foucault, "Friendship as a Way of Life," in *Ethics: Subjectivity and Truth*, vol. 1, *The Essential Works of Foucault 1954–84*, ed. Paul Rabinow and Nikolas Rose (New York: New Press, 1997), 310; Halberstam, *In a Queer Time and Place*, 1.

10. "2020 WV Primary Candidates: Governor," *Charleston (WV) Gazette-Mail*, May 24, 2020, https://www.wvgazettemail.com/2020-wv-primary-candidates -governor/article_c12263bb-9a83-5113-9a7b-d46ef258cac5.html; Mitch McConnell and Amy McGrath, "Mitch McConnell vs. Amy McGrath Kentucky Senate Debate Transcript October 12," *Rev* (blog), October 12, 2020, https:// www.rev.com/blog/transcripts/mitch-mcconnell-vs-amy-mcgrath-kentucky -senate-debate-transcript-october-12; Jordan Damron, "Gov. Justice: U.S. Dept. of Labor Awards Additional $1 Million to West Virginia for Continuing Employment and Training Services for Laid Off Coal Miners," press release, State of West Virginia, Office of the Governor, September 26, 2019, https:// governor.wv.gov/News/press-releases/2019/Pages/Gov.-Justice-US-Dept -of-Labor-awards-additional-1-million-to-West-Virginia-for-continuing -employment-and-training.aspx.

11. "Partnerships for Opportunity and Workforce and Economic Revitalization (POWER) Initiative," Appalachian Regional Commission, 2015, accessed August 17, 2020, https://www.arc.gov/funding/power.asp; "POWER Dislocated Worker Grants: Resources for Coal Miners, Division of Coal Mine Workers' Compensation, Office of Workers' Compensation Programs," Department of Labor, 2015, https://www.dol.gov/owcp/dcmwc/powergrants.htm.

12. Brian Willis, "Sierra Club's Beyond Coal Campaign Reaches Major Milestones," Sierra Club, May 9, 2019, https://www.sierraclub.org/press-releases/2019/05 /sierra-club-s-beyond-coal-campaign-reaches-major-milestones; Lyndsay Tarus, Mary Hufford, and Betsy Taylor, "A Green New Deal for Appalachia: Economic Transition, Coal Reclamation Costs, Bottom-Up Policymaking (Part 2)," *Journal of Appalachian Studies* 23, no. 2 (2017): 151–69, https://doi .org/10.5406/jappastud.23.2.0151; Betsy Taylor et al., "Economic Transition in Central Appalachia: Knowledge/Power Mapping for Bottom-Up Policy Making," *Practicing Anthropology* 36, no. 4 (2014): 13–18.

13. Other economic transition projects include Coalfield Development's many programs, including Refresh West Virginia; Create West Virginia; the Shaping Our Appalachian Region (SOAR) Initiative based in Kentucky; the work of the Mountain Association to focus on downtown revitalization and economic transition planning through solar and energy retrofits; the work-around arts, culture, and community development divergent from fossil fuel economies at Appalshop in Whitesburg, Kentucky; and many smaller local initiatives such as experimental hemp crops at Coal River Mountain Watch in West Virginia, the Hemphill Bakery and Community Center in eastern Kentucky, and much more. These and many other instances are detailed in the forthcoming book

from University Press of Kentucky on the Appalachian transition, edited by Shauna Scott and Kathryn Engel.

14. "POWER Project Summaries by State, Awarded October 2020," Appalachian Regional Commission, 2020, https://www.arc.gov/wp-content/uploads/2020/10/POWER-Project-Summaries-by-State-Awarded-October-2020-1.pdf; "Just Transition Fund: History," Just Transition Fund, 2017, http://www.justtransitionfund.org/history; "Appalachian Transition Fellowship Program," Highlander Research and Education Center, 2017, https://static1.squarespace.com/static/522749eee4b0435937560732/t/59d285d0914e6b0cf8772723/1506969042201/AppFellows%2B2018%2BOne%2BPager.pdf.

15. Across multiple approaches, scholars agree that the term *neoliberalism* periodizes the post-Fordist era. Jaime Peck, Nik Theodore, and Neil Brenner argue in a 2010 article in *Global Networks*, "Variegated Neoliberalizations," that the term *neoliberalization* helps name the processes that achieved massive shifts in political economies and politics, shifts generally associated with the ascendancy of right-wing and liberalizing economic regimes post-1970s, iterated in various ways across the world. Neoliberalization, broadly put, comprises the variegated processes whereby privatization of public sector services has been justified through Hayekian utopian rhetoric of individualism and small government, while generally increasing spending on security, increasing prison and military spending, and gutting social safety nets. Most studies of neoliberalism periodize processes of neoliberalization as starting in the 1970s, in close connection with the rise of the right-wing governments of Ronald Reagan and Margaret Thatcher; authoritarian coups in Latin America; the Washington Consensus; structural-adjustment-based development in the former Third World; and the financialization of the United States and thus the global economy after the Volcker shock. Other scholars, such as Nancy MacLean, Wendy Brown, and Melinda Cooper, point to the alliances of the neoconservative heavily Christian Right and neoliberal "free market" ideologues, such as Milton Friedman and James Buchannan in the United States or the "ordoliberals" in Germany, as key to the rise of neoliberal governments. Most of these studies point to what Stuart Hall observed in Britain in the late 1970s: that neoliberalism was an alliance of right-wing political interests that, through a crisis of hegemony, took power as the hegemonic bloc.

16. Linda McDowell, "Life without Father and Ford: The New Gender Order of Post-Fordism," *Transactions of the Institute of British Geographers* 16, no. 4 (1991): 400; McDowell, "Reflections on Feminist Economic Geography: Talking to Ourselves?," *Environment and Planning A: Economy and Space* 48,

no. 10 (October 1, 2016): 2093–99; McDowell, Esther Rootham, and Abby Hardgrove, "The Production of Difference and Maintenance of Inequality: The Place of Young Goan Men in a Post-crisis UK Labour Market," *Gender, Work & Organization* 23, no. 2 (2016): 108–24; McDowell, "Father and Ford Revisited: Gender, Class and Employment Change in the New Millennium," *Transactions of the Institute of British Geographers* 26, no. 4 (December 2001): 448–64.

17. McDowell, "Life without Father and Ford," 400; McDowell, "Reflections on Feminist Economic Geography," 2096.

18. Bell and York, "Community Economic Identity"; Ann M. Oberhauser, "Gender and Household Economic Strategies in Rural Appalachia," *Gender, Place & Culture* 2, no. 1 (March 1995): 51–70; Sally Ward Maggard, "From Farm to Coal Camp to Back Office and McDonald's: Living in the Midst of Appalachia's Latest Transformation," *Journal of the Appalachian Studies Association* 6 (1994): 14–38; Anne Lewis, *Fast Food Women*, documentary, short (Whitesburg, KY: Appalshop Films, 1992).

19. Richard A. Brisbin, *A Strike like No Other Strike: Law and Resistance during the Pittston Coal Strike of 1989–1990* (Morgantown: West Virginia University Press, 2010); Stephen Fisher, *Fighting Back in Appalachia: Traditions of Resistance and Change* (Philadelphia: Temple University Press, 1993). The 1984–1985 Massey Strike and the 1989–1990 Pittston Strike are important in the history of neoliberal Appalachia, where several coal companies broke with the arrangements of the Bituminous Coal Operators' agreements, under the support of the post-Reagan National Labor Relations Board, and the United Mine Workers of America ultimately lost both massive strikes.

20. Matthew D. Baird et al., *Education, Employment, and Wages in the Appalachia Region: Final Report* (Santa Monica, CA: RAND, 2020), https://www.rand.org/pubs/research_reports/RR3217.html.

21. Green Mining Model Business Program, Facebook, June 27, 2017, https://mbasic.facebook.com/watch/?v=1878980752427800&_rdr&story_saved=1; Roxy Todd, "Lavender Hopes and Realities: Farming Project Doesn't Go as Planned," WV Public Radio, August 28, 2018, https://www.wvpublic.org/post/lavender-hopes-and-realities-farming-project-doesn-t-go-planned.

22. Jen Luckwaldt, "Free Program Turns Coal Miners into Computer Programmers," *PayScale* (blog), April 12, 2017, https://web.archive.org/web/20170413144534/https://www.payscale.com/career-news/2017/04/free-program-turns-coal-miners-computer-programmers; Office of US Senator Joe Manchin

of West Virginia, "Manchin Congratulates Mined Minds West Virginia Graduates," press release, January 27, 2017, https://www.manchin.senate.gov /newsroom/press-releases/manchin-congratulates-mined-minds-west-virginia -graduates; "Hillbillies Who Code: The Former Miners Out to Put Kentucky on the Tech Map," *Guardian*, 2017, https://www.theguardian.com/us -news/2017/apr/21/tech-industry-coding-kentucky-hillbillies; Mined Minds (@MinedMinds), Twitter, August 5, 2017, 5:05 p.m., https://web.archive.org /web/20171005122646if_/https://twitter.com/minedminds.

23. Tressie McMillan Cottom, *Lower Ed: The Troubling Rise of For-Profit Colleges in the New Economy* (New York: New Press, 2017), 175; Andrew Zaleski, "Broken Code," *The Postindustrial* (blog), May 12, 2019, http://postindustrial.com /featuredstories/broken-code/; Campbell Robertson, "They Were Promised Coding Jobs in Appalachia. Now They Say It Was a Fraud," *New York Times*, May 12, 2019, https://www.nytimes.com/2019/05/12/us/mined-minds-west -virginia-coding.html.

24. "POWER Dislocated Worker Grants"; "POWER Project Summaries by State"; Becca Schimmel, "Rethinking Retraining: Why Worker Training Programs Alone Won't Save Coal Country," *Ohio Valley ReSource*, October 4, 2019, https://ohiovalleyresource.org/2019/10/04/rethinking-retraining-why-worker -training-programs-alone-wont-save-coal-country/.

25. Friends of Coal, "The new administration's Energy Policy?," Facebook, January 26, 2021, https://www.facebook.com/FriendsofCoalAmerica/photos /a.297363423632587/3562469040455326.

26. Friends of Coal, "Biden 'Climate Czar' John Kerry (AKA Lurch) says coal miners should make solar panels. Sen. Ted Cruz says Kerry is 'arrogant and out of touch,'" Facebook, January 28, 2021, https://www.facebook.com/Friendsof CoalAmerica/posts/3567857229916507; Friends of Coal, "https://news .yahoo.com/biden-keystone-pipeline-action . . .," Facebook, January 28, 2021, https://www.facebook.com/FriendsofCoalAmerica/posts/3567398876629009; Friends of Coal, "So, nothing we do will make any real difference so we kill 100s of thousands of jobs? Doesn't anyone see the insanity of that?," Facebook, January 27, 2021, https://www.facebook.com/FriendsofCoalAmerica /posts/3566644483371115.

27. Gabe Schwartzman, "Where Appalachia Went Right: White Masculinities, Nature, and Pro-coal Politics in an Era of Climate Change" (undergraduate thesis, University of California, Berkeley, 2013); Friends of Coal, Facebook, January 29, 2021, https://www.facebook.com/FriendsofCoalAmerica/?ref=page_internal;

Friends of Coal—Kentucky, Facebook, January 29, 2021, https://www.facebook
.com/friendsofcoalky.

28. Wendy Brown, *In the Ruins of Neoliberalism: The Rise of Antidemocratic Politics in the West* (New York: Columbia University Press, 2019); Nancy Fraser,
"The End of Progressive Neoliberalism," *Dissent Magazine*, January 2, 2017,
https://www.dissentmagazine.org/online_articles/progressive-neoliberalism
-reactionary-populism-nancy-fraser; Thatcher, "Speech to Conservative Party
Conference"; Brown, *In the Ruins of Neoliberalism*, 180.

29. Cooper, *Family Values*, 26.

30. Karen Ho, "Corporate Nostalgia? Managerial Capitalism from a Contemporary
Perspective," in *Corporations and Citizenship*, ed. Greg Urban (Philadelphia:
University of Pennsylvania Press, 2014), 267–88.

31. Rae Garringer, "The Republic of Fabulachia: Queer Visions for a Post-coal
Appalachian Future" (master's thesis, University of North Carolina, Chapel
Hill, 2017).

32. Mary L. Gray, "'There Are No Gay People Here': Expanding the Boundaries of
Queer Youth Visibility in the Rural United States," in *Appalachia in Regional
Context: Place Matters*, ed. Dwight Billings and Anne Kingsolver (Lexington,
University Press of Kentucky, 2018), 111–30; Latoya Eaves, "Black Geographic
Possibilities: On a Queer Black South," *Southeastern Geographer* 57, no. 1
(2018): 80–95, https://doi.org/10.1353/sgo.2017.0007; Katy A. Ross, "At the
Intersection of Queer and Appalachia(n): Negotiating Identity and Social
Support" (PhD diss., Ohio University, 2019); Amy Michelle Jordan, "Those Who
Choose to Stay: Narrating the Rural Appalachian Queer Experience" (master's
thesis, University of Tennessee, 2015); Mathias J. Detamore, "Queer Appalachia:
Toward Geographies of Possibility" (PhD diss., University of Kentucky, 2010).

33. Dylan Harris, "Inside/Outside, Radically Beside," in *Electric Dirt: A Celebration of Queer Voices and Identities from Appalachia and the South*, vol. 1
(Bluefield, WV: @QueerAppalachia, 2017); Elizabeth Catte, "The Future of
Appalachia Is Queer," *Belt Magazine*, March 30, 2018, https://beltmag.com
/future-appalachia-queer/; Hillery Glasby, Sherrie Gradin, and Rachael Ryer-
son, *Storytelling in Queer Appalachia: Imagining and Writing the Unspeakable
Other* (Morgantown: West Virginia University Press, 2020); Z. Zane McNeill,
ed., *Y'all Means All: The Emerging Voices Queering Appalachia* (Oakland, CA:
PM Press, 2022); Anthony Harkins and Meredith McCarroll, eds., *Appalachian
Reckoning: A Region Responds to Hillbilly Elegy* (Morgantown: West Virginia
University Press, 2019); Darci McFarland, *Bible Belt Queers* (self-pub., 2019);
Garringer, "The Republic of Fabulachia."

34. Rae Garringer, "*Country Queers*: A Multimedia Oral History Project Documenting the Diverse Experiences of Rural and Small Town LGBTQIA Folks in the U.S.A.," *Country Queers* (blog), June 28, 2013, https://countryqueers.com/about/.

35. Ada Smith, "Appalachian Futurism," *Journal of Appalachian Studies* 22, no. 1 (2016): 75.

"I FIXED UP THE TREES TO GIVE THEM SOME NEW LIFE"

Queer Desire, Affect, and Ecology in the Work of LGBTQIA+ Appalachian Artists

Maxwell Cloe

A yard filled with trees, robotic sculptures, bushes, massive paintings of comic book characters, moss, and carefully crafted masses of industrial plastic surrounds a Lexington, Kentucky, house—doors open to visitors, human or otherwise. A woman morphs with a tree while reaching toward an alien object suspended in the sky. Performers, priests, and women dressed in elaborate costumes stage a grand marriage to the mountains themselves. These images emerge from the work of three queer Appalachian artists—the painter Dustin Hall, the sculptor Charles Williams, and the Ecosexual[1] performer and activist Beth Stephens. Through highly personal, emotional, and often erotic depictions of the natural world, these artists deconstruct and reevaluate humanity's emotional relationships to this world. Instead of relying on the separation of humanity and nature characteristic of capitalist systems, these artists instead construct relationships with nature that are highly reciprocal and interpersonal. In this way, the art of these queer Appalachians is not only "queer" in the sense that it deviates from dominant norms of gender and sexuality; it is additionally "queer" in the sense that it uses novel structures of desire to imagine a new and future-facing human relationship with the Appalachian natural world. This new future relationship to Appalachia ultimately points toward the deconstruction of settler colonial powers, both within Appalachia and beyond.

These three artists come from different racial groups, genders, time periods (Williams passed around the same time that Hall was born and the Ecosexuals were beginning their work), and artistic disciplines. At the same time, however, all three grew up in rural mining towns that have long been the site of ecological degradation and capitalist resource extraction. Moreover, all three have engaged in romantic and sexual relationships outside the heteronormative standards dominant throughout the United States. So considering these differences while also acknowledging the similarities of their queerness[2] and their roots in rural Appalachian Kentucky and West Virginia provides meaningful insight into how queer Appalachian artists use their art to explore the interrelationships among gender, sexuality, liberation, and the natural world. In doing so, these artists create a series of aesthetic blueprints that help us to reframe our relationship with the nonhuman natural world and move beyond a capitalist and colonial framework of humans and nature as separate from each other.

Dustin Hall is a painter working out of the small town of Neon, Kentucky. Neon and the neighboring town of Whitesburg are surrounded by instances of scarcely noticed environmental destruction—namely, deforestation for timber. In a 2019 interview, the artist laments this destruction, stating, "My mountain has been logged and stripped so there's nothing there but black snakes and weeds."[3] The use of the word *my* illustrates his personal relationship to his natural surroundings. Hall's lamentation highlights a significant psychological effect of capitalist resource extraction; the trees

Dustin Hall—*A Woman Alone in the Woods Sees Her Own Reflection*, Neon, Kentucky (2020), acrylic and housepaint on canvas, image courtesy of Hall (@birdsdeadbutshesnot on Instagram)

and mountains with which Hall shared a meaningful relationship have since been reduced to bland commodities in service of profit.

Indicating an understanding of the effects that resource extraction can have on the relationships between humans and non-human nature, Hall's 2020 painting *A Woman Alone in the Woods Sees Her Own Reflection* illustrates an alternate perspective on these relationships, one that avoids the sterile destruction of logging and mining. Discussing this work in particular, Hall remarks that it emerged from his own youthful experiences in the forests around Neon. This work—though widely applicable in its exploration of queerness and nature—is nevertheless incredibly specific in its Appalachian origins and Hall's personal experience with the natural world. In an October interview, Hall explains:

When I was a kid, I would go in the woods alone and just sit. A naturally fallen tree oftentimes will land halfway on the, you know, stump still in the ground so you have a natural bench and you would just sit there in the heat or like lay down and look at things. It's very dangerous in retrospect, you don't want to do that. Snakes climb a lot to eat birds so being on a tree for hours at a time in a forest is not advisable, actually, come to find out. But I would do it anyway. And so, I never really had epiphanies when I did this—until more recently when I thought about actual things. As a kid, I don't know what I was thinking about, you know? Actually, probably I was masturbating or something, you know when I was twelve. I was, like, you know, bird watching as a kid or whatever you do. So, my idea then was what I do now in the woods is go and sort of gather things and think about, you know, my myriad problems, you know there are so many. So varied, so twisted and disturbing [laughs]. And then I thought it'd be really nice to portray this figure doing that.[4]

In addition to existing as a specific expression of Hall's relationship to his Appalachian surroundings, *A Woman Alone in the Woods Sees Her Own Reflection* illustrates critical theorist Donna Haraway's concept of "natureculture." In the term's first appearance, in her 2003 *Companion Species Manifesto*, Haraway intentionally leaves the definition open, explaining that naturecultures include the joining of "flesh and signifier, bodies and words, stories and worlds."[5] Essentially, *natureculture* loosely refers to the myriad ways in which what is commonly understood as nature (plants, nonhuman animals, rocks, and water) and culture (art, politics, humans, and technology) intersect and overlap. As queer theorist David Bell elaborates, this combination of the cultural and natural worlds "reminds us that the very idea of nature itself is not natural" but rather indicates a cultural understanding of the nonhuman; the boundaries between nature and culture, with further investigation, are seemingly nonexistent.[6]

A Woman Alone in the Woods Sees Her Own Reflection contains two distinct halves. On the left, a cloaked woman reclines against a bed of leaves and cherries, her arms slightly gesturing toward the right half of the canvas. The presence of leaves, trees, and fruits positions this half of the painting as the *nature* half of *natureculture*. Opposite her is an abstract figure that Hall says is the woman "seeing a truer version of [herself] on a tree in the woods in the middle of summer."[7] Along with representing the tree in which the woman sees her "truer self," the abstract figure also contains a cross and a circular outline, reminiscent of a mirror. These signifiers of human cultural development indicate that this half of the painting is the *culture* in *natureculture*.

In the composition of both the two figures and the entire scene, Hall establishes multiple binary borders that he subsequently disrupts, particularly binaries of male/female and nature/culture. Though the title indicates that the figure on the left is a woman, the figure herself is ambiguous in both sex and gender. Her billowing, formless cloak reveals no clues as to her gender presentation. Her bald head and abstracted face similarly reinforce this uncertainty. Moreover, the figure on the right—her "truer self"—is hardly comprehensible as any known object, let alone a human with a gender. The audience must thus construct the figure's gender not through interpreting any sort of essential signifiers, as conventional understandings of gender assert, but rather through reading the title and applying the label of *woman* to both figures, an increasingly absurd act when considering the level of abstraction of the rightward figure. In this way, Hall proposes the binary category of "woman" in the title to subsequently demonstrate that such categories, constructed through language, are often unreliable for accurately describing a human and their "truer self," as they see it and as the audience sees it. This decidedly queer presentation of gender and bodies works to disentangle gender from both the audience's understanding of the woman and the woman's understanding of herself. Such an understanding of gender, not atypical in the work of queer artists and thinkers, additionally anticipates the disruption and queering of boundaries between nature and culture.

In the space left by reducing the prominence of gender in identity formation, *A Woman Alone in the Woods Sees Her Own Reflection* instead proposes the Appalachian natural world as an important category for understanding the figure's "truer self." Much as Hall sets up a binary opposition between the unambiguous gender in the title and the ambiguity of the woman, his painting sets up a binary between the human and the natural world, illustrated by the divide between the left and right figures, which, though close, never touch. Each respective side and the overall composition of the painting, however, break down this binary to suggest a relationship between human identity and the natural world that transcends commodification and extraction. The left side of the painting displays humans and nature as separate from each another, with the woman distinctly reclining on the bed of greenery. Nevertheless, the woman possesses numerous similarities to the plants, such as the formless wrinkles of her cloak and the peculiar shape of her hands mirroring the leaves that surround her—a suggestion that her long stay in the forest is slowly transforming her into one of these plants. In the figure on the right, which Hall explains embodies the tree that the woman on the left is observing, natural and human imagery combine to the point where neither is truly recognizable. This abstract version of the tree-woman is not a simple, romanticized vision of humans as a part of nature, however. The inclusion of the crude crucifix evokes the image of a small rural church, commonplace throughout Appalachia. Another important component of human identity is not just the human relationship with the natural world but the interrelationships among humans, the natural world, *and* the human institutions that shape the discourses and ideologies that help define our identities.

Hall's tapestry of human and nonhuman constructions illustrates the kind of naturecultures that appear throughout Haraway's and Bell's works; the end of the "human" and the beginning of the "natural" are not easily, and likely cannot be, discerned. As the woman reaches toward the abstract figure, her hand begins to look less like a hand and more like a pine cone or magnolia fruit, suggesting that her transformation into the human-nature-institution assemblage on the right is underway as she takes action to reach her "truer self." Thus, a human's "truer self"—a more accurate and whole representation of their identity—is one that necessarily acknowledges their intertwined relationship to the natural world and human institutions. In this way, the woman and her "truer self" embody a decidedly queer approach to the body and identity in which neither category is rigid but rather perpetually fluid and open to transformation through relationships (erotic or otherwise) with other entities in our surroundings. The anticipation of the woman's queer transformation, which has not yet happened in the painting, fills the work with the future-facing potentiality of an oncoming and novel relationship between humans and the nonhuman natural world of Appalachia. Recalling Hall's lamentation of destructive resource extraction for the sake of profit, this vision of a new Appalachia is one in which human beings interact with nature on a level of reciprocity and empathy rather than one of extraction and use, as is common in a capitalist system built on colonialism.

Where Dustin Hall's painting lays out the possibilities for new understandings of queer Appalachian naturecultures, the work of the late Kentucky artist Charles Williams embodies an exploration and execution of these possibilities. Williams was born in the small coal-mining town of Blue Diamond, Kentucky, and later moved to Lexington to work as a janitor for IBM. When not working as a janitor, Williams constructed fantastical assemblage sculptures that surrounded and often entered his house. Though he died of AIDS complications in 1999 in relative obscurity, one of his few interviews with art historian William Arnett reveals some of the ecological underpinnings of Williams's work:

> I got me this place here [in Lexington] and decided to do something with it. I have always had art on my mind and wanted to do something out front there that I hadn't heard of no other person doing. I fixed up the trees to give them some new life, some color, one idea got another idea and so on down the line, each idea kept building into another idea. I put the comic people up in the trees after that, which were the ones I remembered from my comic book drawing days, and would use a circular saw and a reciprocating saw, would draw on the plywood, paint them on, have to drill a hole in the wood with a screwdriver bit to get the saw in, then I can cut certain curves with one saw and use another saw for certain curves and vice versa. I did Superman and Batman and Captain Marvel and Mighty Mouse. Superman and Batman were all cut out of wood doors that I found.[8]

By imbuing the natural world around him with "new life," through complex assemblage sculptures, Williams uses his queer artistic vision to blend nature and culture until they are physically and conceptually inseparable. One such sculpture is an untitled piece from the 1980s consisting of a multitude of commonplace materials.[9] The sculpture is built around the slender end of a tree branch, with multiple forked twigs going in various directions. Blobs of multicolored, seemingly fluid-melted plastic surround the base and higher levels of the branch, holding it upright. Along with the branch, these puddles of paint and industrial plastic contain a few small objects, the most recognizable of which are two small painted leaves toward the front of the sculpture and a discarded bike reflector toward the rear. Such a sculpture would be familiar in both Williams's house and yard, which were filled with similar creations.

As both a discrete art piece and one of the many objects in Williams's larger built environment, the sculpture itself is quite literally an assemblage of natural and human "cultural" objects—a "natureculture"—combined in such a way that neither is the centerpiece. Certainly, the natural tree branch is an integral element to the sculpture, but the melted plastic that hangs in the branch and holds it upright is equally integral. Melted plastic and paint even cover certain sections of the branch, making it a "human" object as much as a "natural" one. The process of melting the plastic over the branch until it pooled around the base created a new object in which the human components and natural components are inseparable from one another, barring the complete destruction of the object. Moreover, the seeming equality of the found objects within the plastic—the two painted leaves and the bicycle reflector—also suggests that manufactured and natural objects are equally part of the environment that surrounds Williams, to the point where both are fair game for his artistic scavenging. Thus, Williams creates a piece combining industrial waste and natural objects that is simultaneously bright, surreal, and almost campy—capable of being read as both a critique of the pollution encroaching into the natural world and an exploration of how humans are inextricably melded to the world around them. Like the abstract, formless figure on the right of Hall's painting, then, *Untitled* depicts an object that is neither fully natural nor fully human but rather some queer combination of the two, an object that is simultaneously recognizable and alien, aesthetically repulsive and strangely enticing.

The queer boundary blurring of *Untitled* appears even more prominently in considerations of the sculpture's place in Williams's environment, which he constructed for himself in his house and yard in Lexington. Before his death, Williams's yard was filled entirely with such sculptures, including painted tree stumps shot through with pieces of metal debris, large contraptions resembling rockets and wheeled vehicles, and paintings of comic book heroes made from old doors and hung from the branches of trees—again a continuous mixture of "natural" and "cultural" elements. Williams did not just contain his art in the exterior of his house, however. As Bob Morgan, a fellow Kentucky artist who occasionally visited Williams, recounts, the inside of his house was equally filled with both art experiments and other people:

> He [Williams] was wildly sexually active and had all kinds of people visiting from all over. Now that must've been a little shocking to people who had gotten letters back and forth from Charlie and they show up at his house and it's like—it looks like—I mean, it was rough, for sure. Nothing worked the way it was supposed to work and there was piles of debris everywhere, in the house and outside the house. He had big, old fashioned refrigerators that weighed a ton and he had five of them in his house. He used them to store stuff in. Of course, they weighed a ton already. You'd open the door and all the drawers were filled with industrial refuse and jars of nuts and bolts and stuff. It looked like a refrigerator for robot people and he had five of them filled with stuff taking up one whole room. It was just the refrigerator room. So it was pretty crazy.[10]

Williams's environment was thus not simply the natural world surrounding his home. Nor was it the combination of this world and his art. Rather, Williams's artistic, natural, human, and sexual identities transcended lines of private and public, natural and domestic, to flow unceasingly in and around his home. This built environment includes his physical house, his artistic creations, "natural" entities like trees and dirt, repurposed technology, and the emotions and stories of the people who came to visit, all of which simultaneously fold into the nature and culture around him. Combining the long tradition of the Black southern yard with the queer affect and cultures of the people who appear in and around his home, Williams's artistic work takes the queer Appalachian natureculture blueprint of Hall's painting—how a queer approach to recognizing the intersection of humanity and nature can look—and begins to put that process into practice through his inextricable art and life.

This "naturalcultural" combination of care for the people, art objects, and natural elements of his environment place Williams's body of work within the loose category of the "queer garden," which queer theorist Catriona Mortimer-Sandilands describes in her edited anthology *Queer Ecologies: Sex, Nature, Politics, Desire*.[11] Discussing the literary work of gay writer Derek Jarman, Mortimer-Sandilands argues that his novel *Modern Nature*, combined with the many physical gardens that Jarman tended to during his life, create a sort of queer garden that "cultivates an ethical practice of remembering as part of a queer ecological response to loss" and other emotions tied to the natural world.[12] Nature, in this sense, is not a retreat from human problems but rather "a site for specifically *queer* acts of memory" that arose from shared trauma, such as the AIDS epidemic.[13] In the same way that Jarman used inextricable combinations of art, ecology, and queer desire to understand the affective elements of his natural and domestic spaces, so too did Williams use his house and yard to complicate lines between public and private, creating a natural-domestic space for other queer people to physically and emotionally engage with him, his art, his environment, and any memories of trauma or triumph. By filling his yard and house with transformed garbage and natural debris, the opposite of the commodifiable spectacle of capitalist nature, Williams proposes that human interrelationships with nature can facilitate more than simple escape from human problems; these relationships can consider the full range of human desire, actions, and emotions to preserve and work through these problems.

So, though distinct in their mediums and disciplines, Dustin Hall and Charles Williams—through their work—nevertheless create a space to anticipate a new ecological future in Appalachia and beyond in which human relationships to the nonhuman natural world are not constrained to impersonal, detached resource extraction but are rather open to possibilities of reciprocity, loving emotions, and the destabilization of currently rigid categories of gender and sexuality. Such an anticipation is central to much queer art making. In his book *Cruising Utopia*, performance theorist José Muñoz famously remarks that "queerness is essentially about the rejection of a here and now and an insistence on potentiality or concrete possibility for another world."[14] Per this understanding, queerness serves as a way to use desire and affect to envision and work toward a new future free from the bounds of heteronormativity and related oppressive cultural norms. Furthermore, Muñoz argues that these queer futures, while created through concrete action, can often be "glimpsed" through "the realm of the aesthetic," such as art, literature, and performance.[15] Queer aesthetics frequently contain "blueprints and schemata of a forward-dawning futurity."[16] By depicting the Appalachian people, communities, cultures, and nonhuman natural world as a constantly moving and overlapping interchange, Dustin Hall and Charles Williams reconfigure popular understandings of Appalachian queerness and ecology. These works crucially engage not only with the natural world of Appalachia but with the myriad queer emotions and structures of desire that characterize their own current and potential relationships with the natural world. Seemingly rigid categories of "humans" or "nature," "male" or "female," "private" or "public" do not appear quite as stable in these artists' lives and works. Rather, by depicting human interactions with the rest of the natural world on interpersonal, fluid, highly affective levels, Hall and Williams propose and demonstrate a new future for humans in the environment. For both Appalachian and non-Appalachian environments, this new future is distinct from a commodified cycle of unemotional sterility and the futile separation of humans and nature. Their art illustrates that human relationships with nonhuman nature, much like queer relationships between humans, often require transcending conventional binaries of gender, sexuality, and desire.

The "natural" extension of these artists' complication of boundaries is the embrace of a deep and profound love for the natural world that defies characterization by heteronormative and cisnormative standards. Explicitly representing this kind of relationship are the Ecosexuals, an artistic and identity movement championed by Appalachia-California artist Beth Stephens and her partner, Annie Sprinkle.

Ecosexuality—simultaneously an ethos, an art movement, and a sexual identity—focuses on the reorientation of human relationships to the earth to emphasize reciprocity, care, and playfulness. As Stephens and Sprinkle explain in their "Ecosex Manifesto," "the Earth is our lover. We are madly, passionately, and fiercely in love."[17] Stephens and Sprinkle manifest their relationship to nonhuman nature and each other through sex in/with rivers and forests, a physical and emotional integration with the nonhuman natural world that simultaneously evokes the cultural image of queer cruising and sex in places outside of the heterosexual nuclear household. In doing so, the Ecosexuals expand upon the predominantly artistic work of Hall and Williams to establish a natureculture union that both artistically and physically integrates queer cultures and practices.

In addition to the sexual interactions with and in the nonhuman natural world, the Ecosexuals express their queer love for natureculture through their elaborate wedding performances to facets of the natural world, such as their 2010 wedding to the Appalachian Mountains.

Stephens explained the origins of this wedding:

But really what the main thing that led up to us doing this wedding was our anti–mountaintop removal sentiments and activism and being educated about that. And, you know, wanting to have a closer relationship with that area because that is where I'm from and that's where a lot of my family still lives. I love that area so why not express our love through this wedding.[18]

In this wedding, Stephens, Sprinkle, and a host of other friends and local environmental activists gathered in Athens, Ohio. Dressed in elaborate purple costumes (many of which were also used in their previous wedding to the moon), which Stephens noted reflected the "purple haze around the Appalachian Mountains,"[19] the wedding party engaged in a ceremony that included choreographed dances, a cake shaped like the mountains, and songs celebrating the region. According to the wedding's program, this operation embodied the efforts of well over a hundred people, not to mention the countless entities living throughout the mountains that the Ecosexuals married. In this way, the Ecosexuals expand upon the social/natural/sexual intersections of Williams's work to create an artistic and sexual way of being that is wholly communal with both nonhuman and human nature.

Though Stephens and Sprinkle are recent practitioners of Ecosexuality, Indigenous anthropologists Kim TallBear and Angela Willey identify the movement as mirroring the long history of Indigenous "eco-erotics," explaining that the combination of Indigenous understandings of ecology and ecosexuality can provide a wholistic view both within and beyond "the notion of erotic relations to sex."[20] TallBear and Willey specifically cite the research of Indigenous studies' scholar Melissa Nelson, who investigates these eco-erotics in her essay "Getting Dirty."[21] Nelson explains that Indigenous eco-erotics, illustrated through countless oral traditions of people engaging in relationships with transforming humans and nonhuman natural entities, evoke an "intimate ecological encounter in which we are momentarily and simultaneously taken outside of ourselves by the beauty, or sometimes the horror, of the more-than-human natural world."[22] In this way, the explicitly queer actions of ecosexuality, alongside the noncolonial and often anticolonial praxis of Indigenous eco-erotics,[23] further develop a portrait of the new future that Hall and Williams similarly depict in their work.

An important question emerges as to whether ecosexuality engages in the cultural misappropriation of numerous Indigenous eco-erotic practices or rather exists alongside these practices without such irresponsible engagement. On one end, Stephens and Sprinkle often engage in discourse with Indigenous scholars on the similarities between ecosexuality and various eco-erotic practices. Kim TallBear, for example, writes in her 2012 article "What's in Ecosexuality for an Indigenous Scholar of 'Nature'?" that ecosexuality exists in conversation with "indigenous and feminist critiques [of] colonial and chauvinistically scientist approaches to articulating and studying" nature. TallBear also warns, however, against "the appropriation of Native American knowledges and motifs to the ecosexual ceremonial and artistic repertoire," indicating that less aware practitioners of ecosexuality have the potential to enact real harm and theft against numerous Indigenous practices. TallBear is not a voice for all Indigenous people, but she nevertheless provides a vital perspective and engagement with the movement that suggests that a similarly balanced consideration of ecosexuality alongside (and constantly deferring to) Indigenous eco-erotics can be not just respectful but actively helpful for building solidarity and novel considerations of natureculture throughout Appalachia.

The queer ecological future present in the work of Hall, Williams, the Ecosexuals, and practitioners of Indigenous eco-erotics necessitates the decolonization of Appalachia and the United States at large. Alex Wilson (Opaskwayak Cree Nation) writes, "European newcomers … brought with them their commitment (rooted in their own cultures, spirituality and ways of being) to heteropatriarchy and gender binaries. They saw the acceptance of gender and sexual diversity that prevailed in our lands as sinful and threatening."[24] In a very different, though often intersecting, manner, non-Indigenous queer people also face violence and marginalization in the name of gender binaries and sexual norms. So to use queerness "to see and feel beyond the quagmire of the present"[25] and construct a new future free from ecological destruction and systemic violence, we must upend and decenter rigid systems of heteronormativity and cisnormativity and, more importantly, the imperialist frameworks that uphold them. Through a queer, decolonial lens, the work of Hall, Williams, and the Ecosexuals present a future free from not just cisheteronormativity but the deeper foundations of America's settler colonial structure. It is necessary to note two qualifications. First, art and discourse alone will not bring about decolonization. As sociologists Eve Tuck and K. Wayne Yang famously remarked, "Decolonization is not a metaphor," and it "must involve the repatriation of land."[26] As such, art and discourse are only useful insofar as they work to shift the ideologies of the colony and propose novel understandings of what society *could* look like. Second, Hall and Williams do not explicitly engage with anticolonial thought as the Ecosexuals and scholars of Indigenous eco-erotics do. Nevertheless, without decolonization, the queer ecological futures imagined in their art are impossible, as colonial understandings of gender, sexuality, and the environment will likely reemerge in equally oppressive forms. Therefore, the work of decolonial Indigenous scholars is not only helpful for understanding what this queer Appalachian future will look like; it is inescapably necessary.

One must also consider that the decolonization of Appalachia would render the concepts of "Appalachia" and "queerness" as less useful. The region currently known as "Appalachia" is partly a political fabrication put together by the Appalachian Regional Commission in 1965 to decide which counties and states received certain financial development opportunities, an action that excluded many places culturally and historically regarded as Appalachia. This fabrication exists on the violently colonized land of multiple Indigenous nations, the borders of which are not always constrained strictly to the mountains. So decolonization in Appalachia through the repatriation of the land to these Indigenous Nations may render the term Appalachia—an already slippery signifier—as even less conclusive or helpful. Similarly, *queer* or *LGBTQIA+* as identities and descriptions of groups exist largely as a response to and subversion of heterosexual and cisgender norms, many of which have been imposed (at least in the United States) through the process of settler colonialism. If the decolonization of the land is combined with the decolonization of social structures and these norms are decentered, then umbrella terms such as *queer* and *LGBTQIA+* may not contain the same political utility that they currently possess. From the work of these artists and scholars, then, we can conclude that a crucial aspect of reconsidering our relationships to queer Appalachian natureculture is not just engaging with the plants, animals, and minerals around us but also our languages, signifiers, and structures of colonial power and ownership.

The complex abstraction of Hall's and Williams's art and the radical openness of eco-erotic practices like those of Beth Stephens, Annie Sprinkle, and the numerous Indigenous networks that Nelson describes often pose a dilemma to their audiences. "What am I to do," someone may ask, "with these paintings or these sculptures or these people having sex in the woods? Am *I* supposed to have sex in the woods? What good do all of these works of art do in the face of a global climate catastrophe?" I'm reminded of the quote (often attributed to Kurt Vonnegut) that argues that the entire force of anti–Vietnam War art amounted to a custard pie dropped from a low ladder. At the same time, however, I'm reminded of Toni Cade

Bambara's declaration that "as a cultural worker who belongs to an oppressed people [her] job is to make revolution irresistible."[27] The intimacy, desire, affect, sex, ecology, and embodiment that appear throughout the work of these queer Appalachians make specific references to Appalachian ecologies and queerness, but their application extends far beyond the mountains. As Nelson remarks, in reference to the Indigenous eco-erotic systems she discusses, "Sex is a symbol for intimate, visceral, embodied kinship relations with other species and with natural phenomenon."[28] The naturalcultural world, the queer and decolonial revolution against ecological destruction, and the fate of both are all to be rendered irresistible: our collective beloved. And just as we so often risk everything to protect our beloved, so too must we put our bodies and our futures on the line to work toward a new ecological horizon.

NOTES

1. Ecosexuality is an art movement, ideological ethos, and sexuality that centers erotic engagement with the "natural" world. It has roots in queer cruising culture and Indigenous practices of "eco-erotics." I go into further detail about the complex definitions and origins of ecosexuality later in this essay.

2. It is important to note that Charles Williams's gender and sexual identity were never publicly disclosed. Though he was often a patron at gay bars throughout Lexington, it is possible that his sex with other men was strictly financial in motivation. As such, the label of *queer* or *LGBTQIA+* may not be accurate. Nevertheless, as I later discuss, his art and his influence on those around him certainly reflect a deviation from standards of heteronormativity and cisnormativity that, at the very least, gesture toward queerness.

3. Dustin Hall, interview by Maxwell Cloe, June 12, 2019, transcript, oral history, Monroe Summer Research Project, College of William and Mary, Williamsburg, VA.

4. Dustin Hall, interview by Maxwell Cloe, October 15, 2020, transcript, ecology oral history, College of William and Mary, Williamsburg, VA.

5. Donna Haraway, *The Companion Species Manifesto: Dogs, People, and Significant Otherness* (Chicago: Prickly Paradigm, 2003), 20.

6. David Bell, "Queernaturecultures," in *Queer Ecologies: Sex, Nature, Politics, Desire*, ed. Catriona Mortimer-Sandilands and Bruce Erickson (Bloomington: Indiana University Press, 2010), 143.

7. Bell, "Queernaturecultures," 143.

8. Charles Williams, interviews by and correspondence to William Arnett, 1995, transcript, Lexington, KY.

9. Because of Charles Williams's passing and his lack of remaining kin, it is not possible to receive any kind of permissions to reproduce his work in a publication. I direct the reader to the Souls Grown Deep Foundation, an organization dedicated to preserving the art of Black artists from the South. On the foundation's website, Charles Williams's body of work, including all of the pieces I discuss in this chapter, are visible.

10. Bob Morgan, interview by Maxwell Cloe, October 1, 2020, transcript, ecology oral history, College of William and Mary, Williamsburg, VA.

11. Catriona Mortimer-Sandilands and Bruce Erickson, eds., *Queer Ecologies: Sex, Nature, Politics, Desire* (Bloomington: Indiana University Press, 2010), 351.

12. Mortimer-Sandilands and Erickson, *Queer Ecologies*, 352.

13. Mortimer-Sandilands and Erickson, *Queer Ecologies*.

14. José Muñoz, *Cruising Utopia: The Then and There of Queer Futurity* (New York: New York University Press, 2009), 1.

15. Muñoz, *Cruising Utopia*, 1.

16. Muñoz, *Cruising Utopia*, 1.

17. Beth Stephens and Annie Sprinkle, "Ecosex Manifesto," 2005.

18. Beth Stephens, interview by Maxwell Cloe, 2020, transcript, oral history, College of William and Mary, Williamsburg, VA.

19. Stephens, interview.

20. Kim TallBear and Angela Willey "Introduction: Critical Relationality; Queer, Indigenous, and Multispecies Belonging beyond Settler Sex & Nature," *Imaginations* 10, no. 1 (2019): 6.

21. Melissa Nelson, "Getting Dirty," in *Critically Sovereign: Indigenous Gender, Sexuality, and Feminist Studies*, ed. Joanne Barker (Durham, NC: Duke University Press, 2017), 229–60.

22. Melissa Nelson, *Getting Dirty: The Eco-eroticism of Women in Indigenous Oral Literatures* (Durham, NC: Duke University Press, 2017), 230.

23. This Indigenous perspective could be applied even more explicitly to Appalachian lives and cultures through the centering of voices of Indigenous groups throughout the region. Looking to the intellectual and political leadership of the Cherokee, Seneca, Shawnee, and dozens of other recognized and unrecognized

Indigenous Nations throughout Appalachia will be a necessary component of liberation for all Appalachian people.

24. Alex Wilson, "Our Coming In Stories: Cree Identity, Body Soveignty and Gender Self-Determination," *Journal of Global Indigeniety* 1, no. 1 (2015): 1–5, 2.

25. Muñoz, *Cruising Utopia*, 1.

26. Eve Tuck and K. Wayne Yang, "Decolonization Is Not a Metaphor," *Decolonization: Indigeneity, Education & Society* 1, no. 1 (2012): 1–40, 7.

27. Toni Cade Bambara and Thabiti Lewis, "An Interview with Toni Cade Bambara: Kay Bonetti," in *Conversations with Toni Cade Bambara*, ed. Thabiti Lewis (Jackson: University Press of Mississippi, 2012), 35.

28. Nelson, "Getting Dirty," 252.

CONTRIBUTORS

Tijah Bumgarner is filmmaker, scholar, and professor. She teaches narrative and documentary video production at Marshall University. Since writing and directing her first feature film, *Meadow Bridge*, in 2017, she has co-made the feature documentary film *Picture Proof* (2023); cowritten and directed the pilot episode of *Her Hope Haven* (2021); and codirected the short documentary *Patchwork* (2022). As a doctoral candidate at Ohio University, in her dissertation she explores how extraction in Appalachia is narrativized. In both scholarship and practice, Bumgarner seeks to disrupt stereotypes that conform to a single defining narrative of the region.

Maxwell Cloe is scholar of queer Appalachian art and archives. They operate *The Wildcrafting Our Queerness Project*, a digital exhibition of queer Appalachian art, oral history, and theory. They are an instructor of community studies at the College of William & Mary.

Jessica Cory teaches at Appalachian State University and is a PhD candidate specializing in Native American, African American, and environmental literature at the University of North Carolina, Greensboro. She is the editor of *Mountains Piled upon Mountains: Appalachian Nature Writing in the Anthropocene* (WVU Press, 2019) and the coeditor (with Laura Wright) of *Appalachian Ecocriticism and the Paradox of Place* (UGA Press, 2023). Her creative and scholarly writings have been published in the *North Carolina Literary Review*, *North Dakota Quarterly*, *Northern Appalachia Review*, and other fine publications. Originally from southeastern Ohio, she currently lives in Sylva, North Carolina.

MJ Eckhouse was a beloved and passionate member of the Ohio community who continually found ways to fight for his progressive values. In his too-short days, he made a far larger impact than many people do in a more generous lifetime. He and his husband, Lis Regula, were vital in passing inclusive nondiscrimination protections in Kent, where he found love and activism during his time at Kent State University. He graduated with a bachelor's degree in political science in May

2018 and quickly put those skills to work, first as Campaign Manager for the 2018 Democratic candidate for Portage County auditor, then as Outreach Coordinator for CANAPI in Akron, and most lately as Communications Coordinator for the Ohio Environmental Council. His career path throughout his time at Kent State and after graduation was focused on political communications, public outreach, and advocacy. After a Lake Erie beach wedding in July 2019, his husband and he moved from Kent to Columbus as a compromise in their respective career paths. Nearly equaling his passion for progressive causes was his passion for music. During high school, he performed with the Glassmen Drum Corps, where he played trumpet and coronet, and with many high school bands as well. His college career began at Ohio Wesleyan University as a music education major but was set aside temporarily while life happened. Throughout his life, he found pleasure in playing a variety of instruments, including guitar and, most recently, drums. He also wrote prose and songs, including many for Lis.

Stephanie Foote is the Jackson and Nichols Professor of English at West Virginia University, where she researches and teaches American literature and culture from the nineteenth century to the present with a particular focus on environmental issues. Foote is the author of two single-author books, *The Parvenu's Plot: Gender, Class, and Culture in the Age of Realism* (2014) and *Regional Fictions: Culture and Identity in Nineteenth-Century American Literature* (2001). In 2006, she edited and contributed original afterword for *We Walk Alone* and *We, Too, Must Love*, Ann Aldrich's 1955 and 1958 sociological accounts of lesbian life in the United States. She coedited (with Elizabeth Mazzolini) *Histories of the Dustheap: Waste, Material Cultures, Social Justice* (2012), and in 2022 she and Jeffrey Jerome Cohen edited *The Cambridge Companion to the Environmental Humanities*. She is the coeditor and cofounder of *Resilience: A Journal of the Environmental Humanities*, which is available on ProjectMuse and JSTOR. She is currently working on a book about garbage and waste. She has published more than twenty articles and book chapters in journals such as *PMLA, Signs, American Literary History*, and *American Literature*, and her work has been funded by the Carnegie Foundation, the Mellon Foundation, the National Endowment for the Humanities, and the National Humanities Center.

Kandice Grossman is postdoctoral research fellow in sociology at the University of Missouri, Columbia. Her research focuses on race, class, and gender; relationships with place; and coalition politics in environmental justice activism. Kandice Grossman is the author of "TigerSwan at Standing Rock: Ethics of Private Military Use against an Environmental-Justice Movement," in *Case Studies in the Environment*, and coauthor (with Kathleen Fitzgerald) of *Sociology of Sexualities*, 2nd edition, published with Sage, among other publications.

Rebecca-Eli M. Long is a PhD candidate in anthropology and gerontology at Purdue University. They have a master's degree in Appalachian Studies from Appalachian State University, and they coedited *Engaging Appalachia: A Guidebook for Building Capacity and Sustainability*. Rebecca-Eli works across geographic and disciplinary contexts to find creative ways of disrupting ableism. As an ethnographic knitter, Rebecca-Eli crafts new forms of knowledge that contribute to disability justice. Learn more about their work at https://www.rebecca-eli.com.

Zane McNeill is independent scholar-activist from West Virginia who has published edited collections with PM Press, Routledge, and Lantern Publishing and Media.

Aaron Padgett is a PhD candidate at the University of Missouri, Columbia. His upbringing was situated in the limestone bedrock and rolling hills of Kentucky's Eastern Pennyrile region. He is broadly interested in decoloniality, critical geographies, and cultural and environmental sociology. His academic work centers Indigenous histories, narratives, and experiences of global migration processes. At an applied level, he is engaged in the field of refugee resettlement.

Chet Pancake is award-winning transmasculine filmmaker, video, new media, and sound artist. He has exhibited at national and international venues such as the Museum of Modern Art, Wexner Center for the Arts, Royal Ontario Museum, Murray Art Museum Albury (Australia), Mexican Film Institute, and Shanghai Conservatory of Music (PRC). Pancake's narrative and experimental documentary work has been screened at over 150 venues nationally and internationally, as well as licensed for broadcast (entirely or as excerpts) in the United States and the United Kingdom on the Sundance TV Channel, PBS, Channel 13 WNET, Free Speech TV, and Together TV. His films are nationally and internationally distributed by Frameline, Bullfrog Films, Canadian Filmmakers Distribution Centre, and Mostra Films Dones Barcelona, Spain, and are held in permanent collections in over seventy-five university and museum archives nationally and internationally, with a recent acquisition by Archive BORA in South Korea. Recent festival awards include Best Picture from QFest Houston and the Boundary Breaker Award at the Buffalo International Film Festival. Pancake is Interim Chair and Associate Professor in the Film and Media Arts Program at Temple University. He received his master of fine arts at the School of the Art Institute of Chicago in 2012, winning the MFA Studio Art's highest honor, the Edes Fellowship. Pancake is a recent Leeway Transformation Award winner.

Lis Regula is lecturer in the biology department at the University of Dayton. In his professional role, Lis is an out trans man teaching biology and anatomy in an accurate and inclusive manner to future health-care professionals. In his free time, Lis serves on the board of Planned Parenthood Advocates of Ohio, League of Women Voters of Ohio, Ohioans for Sustainable Change, and Highland Youth Garden. He also works to facilitate peer support groups, serves on his synagogue's men's Chevra Kadisha Committee, and does what he can to organize advocacy efforts around progressive policies in Ohio. His dissertation research was primarily ecology oriented and has transitioned into his current human focus as a response to the need for more inclusive medical training and job market forces. Lis has enjoyed his life at the intersections in many ways—an ecologist teaching human anatomy, a single dad to a teen daughter, a Jewish man teaching at a Catholic college, as a few examples. Living in the Central Hilltop neighborhood of Columbus has helped his Ohio country boy heart get used to the big city he now calls home with his little girl, their cat, and the memory of his husband, MJ Eckhouse.

Baker A. Rogers (they/she) is associate professor of sociology and the master of social science program director at Georgia Southern University. Their research focuses on inequality, specifically examining the intersections of gender, sexuality, and religion in the US South, specifically in rural areas. Rogers is an award-winning scholar of gender and sexuality. Recently, they were awarded the Mid-South Sociological Association Lyman Book Award for *King of Hearts* (2022); the Sociologists for Women in Society–South Early Career Gender Scholar Award (2020); and the College of Behavioral and Social Sciences Award of Distinction for Research (2019). Their work relevant to this project includes their books *Trans Men in the South: Becoming Men* (Lexington Books); *King of Hearts: Drag Kings in the American South* (Rutgers University Press); and *Advances in Trans Studies: Moving toward Gender Expansion and Trans Hope* (Emerald Publishing), as well as journal articles published in *Men and Masculinities*, *Gender & Society*, and *Qualitative Sociology*.

Gabe Schwartzman is assistant professor in the department of geography and sustainability at the University of Tennessee. He studies the cultural politics and political economy of fossil fuel transition, most recently focusing on the collapse of the coal industry in the Appalachian region. His work has been published in various journals including the Journal of Peasant Studies, Journal of Political Ecology, and Journal of Appalachian Studies.

Rebecca R. Scott is associate professor of sociology at the University of Missouri, Columbia, where she teaches classes on environmental justice, gender, and social theory. She is the author of *Removing Mountains: Extracting Nature and Identity from the Appalachian Coalfields* (University of Minnesota Press, 2010).

APPALACHIAN FUTURES
Black, Native, and Queer Voices

SERIES EDITORS: Annette Saunooke Clapsaddle, Davis Shoulders, and Crystal Wilkinson

This book series gives voice to Black, Native, Latinx, Asian, Queer, and other nonwhite or ignored identities within the Appalachian region.

No Son of Mine: A Memoir
Jonathan Corcoran

Tar Hollow Trans: Essays
Stacy Jane Grover

Deviant Hollers: Queering Appalachian Ecologies for a Sustainable Future
Edited by Zane McNeill and Rebecca Scott

Appalachian Ghost: A Photographic Reimagining of the Hawk's Nest Tunnel Disaster
Raymond Thompson Jr.